SARTRE'S RADICALISM AND
OAKESHOTT'S CONSERVATISM

Sartre's Radicalism and Oakeshott's Conservatism

The Duplicity of Freedom

Anthony Farr
Visiting Lecturer
Department of Politics and Modern History
London Guildhall University

First published in Great Britain 1998 by
MACMILLAN PRESS LTD
Houndmills, Basingstoke, Hampshire RG21 6XS and London
Companies and representatives throughout the world

A catalogue record for this book is available from the British Library.

ISBN 0–333–68449–4

First published in the United States of America 1998 by
ST. MARTIN'S PRESS, INC.,
Scholarly and Reference Division,
175 Fifth Avenue, New York, N.Y. 10010

ISBN 0–312–21288–7

Library of Congress Cataloging-in-Publication Data
Farr, Anthony, 1956–
Sartre's radicalism and Oakeshott's conservatism : the duplicity
of freedom / Anthony Farr.
p.   cm.
Includes bibliographical references and index.
ISBN 0–312–21288–7 (cloth)
1. Sartre, Jean Paul, 1905–   —Political and social views.
2. Oakeshott, Michael Joseph, 1901–   —Contributions in political
science.   3. Political science—Philosophy.   I. Title.
JC261.S372F37 1998
320'.01—DC21
97–41047
CIP

© Anthony Farr 1998

This book is printed on paper suitable for recycling and made from fully managed and sustained forest sources.

10   9   8   7   6   5   4   3   2   1
07 06 05 04 03 02 01 00 99 98

Printed in Great Britain by
The Ipswich Book Company Ltd
Ipswich, Suffolk

Contents

Acknowledgements

Primary thanks are due to Dr Robert Orr, the supervisor of my research work at the London School of Economics: not only did he suggest the topic but through nearly five years of gentle prompting and genial responses he helped me find my way. Thanks must also go to the Economic and Social Research Council for their assistance and to my mother who gave me her kind support through the final penurious months of writing.

I should also like to take this opportunity to recognize Margaret Finnegan and the late Professor Elie Kedourie for their role in developing and encouraging my interest in political philosophy. I must also recognize the loving help given by my partner Kim Nielsen throughout this time; his encouragement and admonitions made the difference between completion and abandonment. I would also like to acknowledge the assistance of Marc Gander and Callum Wright of the University of Westminster and that of Roderick Cotton.

Material from Michael Oakeshott's *On Human Conduct* (1974) is reproduced by kind permission of Oxford University Press and from Oakeshott's *Experience and its Modes* (1933) by permission of Cambridge University Press. Thanks are also due to Methuen & Co. for permission to reproduce material in copyright from Michael Oakeshott's *Rationalism in Politics* (1964) and from *Being and Nothingness* (1959) by Jean-Paul Sartre translated by Hazel Barnes.

List of Abbreviations

For full bibliographical details, see Bibliography

AR	*Appearance and Reality* (Bradley)
BN	*Being and Nothingness* (Sartre)
BT	*Being and Time* (Heidegger)
CA	*The Concept of Anxiety* (Kierkegaard)
CDR	*Critique of Dialectical Reason*, Volume 1 (Sartre)
CP	*The Claims of Politics* (Oakeshott)
CPR	*Critique of Pure Reason* (Kant)
CUP	*Concluding Unscientific Postscript* (Kierkegaard)
EM	*Experience and its Modes* (Oakeshott)
FT	*Fear and Trembling* (Kierkegaard)
IN	*The Idea of Nature* (Collingwood)
LH	*Letter on Humanism* (Heidegger)
LHP	*Introduction to the Lectures on the History of Philosophy* (Hegel)
M	*Meditations on First Philosophy* (Descartes)
MRD	*The Masses and Representative Democracy* (Oakeshott)
MSW	*Karl Marx: Selected Writings* (David McLellan)
OHC	*On Human Conduct* (Oakeshott)
PF	*Philosophical Fragments* (Kierkegaard)
PH	*The Philosophy of History* (Hegel)
PFM	*Prolegomena to Any Future Metaphysics* (Kant)
PI	*The Psychology of the Imagination* (Sartre)
PM	*Paris Manuscripts* (Marx)
PR	*Philosophy of Right* (Hegel)
RP	*Rationalism in Politics and Other Essays* (Oakeshott)
SD	*The Sickness Unto Death* (Kierkegaard)
SM	*Search for a Method* (Sartre)
TE	*The Transcendence of the Ego* (Sartre)
WD	*War Diaries* (Sartre)
WM	*What Is Metaphysics?* (Heidegger)

Introduction: The Idea of Freedom

The 'freedom' dealt with in this work is political freedom, an equivocal aspect of a contrived relationship. It represents an aspect of our humanity we value and wish to attain, sustain or reinforce. It is a term we use to articulate our aspirations, to measure our achievements and to identify the difficulties or inadequacies of our situation.

Freedom is of interest because it gives emotional considerations an intellectual specification. It is a concept which crosses the boundary of academic and everyday politics and gives ordinary discourse a resonance of importance. Significantly, it is a term used with equal enthusiasm by the political Left and Right.

Here we seek an academic understanding of the term, an insight into its employment in the arguments of the Left and the Right, through the work of two of the most impressive modern representatives of radical and conservative thought. This, I believe, will offer an insight into the preoccupations of both 'wings' of intellectual political thought. And, while the disputes which mark this distinction will not, of course, be settled by this account, it is to be hoped that both parties will more clearly understand their opponent's doctrine and their own presuppositions.

FREEDOM IN COMPLETE ABSTRACTION

Any concept reduced to its definition becomes awkward. Freedom is no exception, indeed, it is something of a prime example. For 'freedom' considered outside of specific applications becomes pretentious and overbearing.

Freedom is the state of being free. To be free means not to be bound. It means not to have our capacities taken away. It means not to be tied, gagged, incarcerated, or restricted nor to be deceived, deluded, or doped.

What fulfils these conditions is a matter of debate, and that debate concerns what it is to be human, what it is to be fully alive,

1

whole and complete. In our culture the issue of freedom has become associated with the problem of self-control and of self-realization. At the heart of this lies the concept of the 'self'. Freedom and the nature of the human person are inseparably linked issues and much discussion of the problem of freedom must necessarily take place in the process of clarifying the concept of self.

In everyday life the antonym of freedom is constraint. There are as many types of freedom as there are forms of restriction hence one must specify what type of bondage is concerned before one may speak clearly of freedom. Ordinarily freedom is set in opposition to a manifest, even physical, deprivation; slavery or confinement come to mind. What state is considered to be free will depend upon what is felt to be a constraint.

The idea of freedom is a central part of the inheritance of our civilization. It stands as the image of our uniqueness, a vision of the character of man as a species and as a person. Freedom details and husbands our creative powers. Like most concepts it is both descriptive and normative, used both to explain and to recommend. It seeks a notion of our power over destiny, an awareness as to how we might intervene in our fate.

'Freedom', then, denotes our place in the order of things. However, we must be careful to denote what we mean by 'our' and to what we refer when we speak of an 'order'. The 'our' may sometimes refer to mankind viewed as a whole, as a species, or it may refer to a certain section or part of mankind, a race, nation or people but it most commonly it is used to speak of the human agent, the individual person.

Each of these 'subjects' is confronted by a different category of constrains or limitations upon their self command. From the point of view of man, the species, self-determination is constrained by whatever power God or nature have reserved for themselves – facts which may or may not be available to us. From the point of view of the nation, self-determination is limited by the designs and abilities of our enemies and competitors but it is also conditioned by our own abilities and state of development, products of the endeavour or indolence of our forebears. Finally, from the point of view of the individual agent, self-determination is constrained by our subjection to the will of others; the limitations placed upon our capacity to realize our ambitions by the law, and by moral opprobrium or by the economic power of others. Abstracted from the complex of its use the idea of freedom is ambiguous, vague and contradictory.

THE USE OF FREEDOM AS AN ABSTRACTION

Implicit in this work is a criticism of the ordinary, 'liberal', notion of freedom; the tradition which holds personal liberty to be a primary value but which fails to explore the dynamics which control the concept of personhood. It operates at an uncritical, naturalistic level of understanding and lacks any awareness of the relation between social order and the notion of the self.

Its mundane outlook sees freedom as literally not being bound or hampered, it accepts the chosen ambition of the individual as a *fait accompli* and asks only what actually counts as an obstruction. As the designs of man, his expectations of life, are boundless what he may perceive as a constraint is also limitless.

The burden of what might be called 'Continental Thought' is that the pattern of human relations and institutions is the model and prototype of the intellect, that is to say, the social and political order is viewed as the paradigm and archetype of consciousness itself. From this is may be deduced that the collective order is primary and the 'person' is derivative. The concentration upon the mere abstraction of the self and maximizing 'personal liberty' is, in this view, not without cost in terms of the general resource – the ground of our individuality.

The naturalism of liberal thought has given it a licence which finds its most extreme expression in the libertarians' privatization of the law; the view which uses an abstract notion of the individual to deny the legitimacy of any authority not voluntarily conceded. In its concern for liberty, liberalism does not pass beyond articulating the currently fashionable notion of the proper expressive sphere of the agent. Its preoccupation with authority, with the relationship between citizen and law-maker, signals its belief that social order is largely natural and that law merely minimizes contingent inconveniences. Its reliance on an innate order underpins its failure to acknowledge the 'artificiality' of human order and of our intellect. The danger of this way of thinking is not its indulgence or its permissiveness – for that, surely, is its charm – the problem is that it harbours its own enemies. Its shallow understanding of the relation between social order and personal psychology leads it to a carelessness which endangers the order it treasures.

The order of a community does not merely concern the permissibility of various actions; it is the ground and stuff of reason, of understanding, of thought itself. Liberalism fails to recognize that the self and its notion of freedom are products of organization. It fails to be troubled by the provenance, ancestry and pedigree of the ideas of which it is composed. As soon as we recognize the individual as a secondary form, a product of contrived activities and engagements, we become embroiled in the matter of the significance of competing forms of order. The notion that the person or self is a construct which 'liberty' may corrode is an issue upon which liberalism is silent.

THE TRADITIONS OF FREEDOM

Intellectual history has given us a number of discourses or traditions which have employed and developed the notion of freedom. It is possible to distinguish three of primary importance: the theological, the scientific and the historical.

They represent an evolving debate, an evolution in our understanding of what it is to be human. Its origins were and, to a considerable extent are, in religious thought. These views were transformed by the scientific interpretation of the world and then were transformed again by that understanding of ourselves which pictured mankind as the product of 'education', the outcome of an historical accumulation of knowledge. Each preoccupation has its own view of how man differs from the patterns he perceives around him and of how he might be free.

The scientific view – dominated by a picture of the world as controlled or ordered by causal laws, saw man as that which was not caused, that which stood beyond or outside the causal matrix. Much of the contemporary debate is still obsessed with this argument because the causal image of reality remains dominant. In this scheme man's being free is his independence from the causal matrix, man is essentially and naturally something other than a thing. The notion of what this 'something else' might be has, unsurprisingly, been dominated by prevalent religious, spiritual and occult notions. But this paradigm has given us an idea of man as above, beyond or other than the general pattern of this world, as 'spirit', distinct from matter in essence, free *a priori*. Man is viewed as a stranger in a foreign land, thus the scientific world view gave scope for an extension to and an exaggeration of the religious notion of man. The vision of freedom which has emerged from this is rooted in notions of autonomy and responsibility. Man is seen as an author of events, events which are the manifestation of some sort of hidden nature, an inner character or the pure cause of ourselves absolutely without pattern or outward determination.

The preoccupation with science was followed, in the history of thought, by a world view dominated by the idea of history, more specifically, by the relationship of the past and the present, the dependence of our comprehension upon inherited or acquired talents. This understanding of the world arose within the preoccupation of intellectuals with the nature of culture, learning and education, with the distinctions found between nations and peoples rather than the distinction between man and things.

It draws us away from the obsession of causality and offers us an image of the human mind as constructed from the resource of our inheritance, a notion that 'mind' has been made by man through the trial of the generation and passed to us in our habits, our education and our cultivation. It accepts as a matter of course that man is free *a priori* from the causal world because it views causality as only one of our techniques of understanding experience. However, the issue of freedom arises for adherents of this 'historical' school with renewed vigour for, if the human intellect is a product of the collective way of life, it appears to raise the prospect of our re-making ourselves to our own command.

ROMANTICISM

There is a sub-plot to this story, and that is the Romantic idea of man as adventurer, inspired by natural or innate desires to toil to make life vivid, heroic and full. Much of the stress which has come to be placed upon the notion of human freedom owes something to this outlook on life. For the Romantic Movement required men to take hold of life, to hunger for life. It emphasized the natural completeness of life and, as a corollary, viewed all constraint as mendacious, capricious and expendable. It, poetically, pictured life as a quest and thereby gave value to the struggle to overcome those forces, natural and human, which disturb the inner unity, the forces which pervert our self-possession, our wholeness. In this Romantic tradition freedom was to become the emblem of what is truly human in a de-humanized world and to stand as a critique of contemporary man.

In the Romantic vision 'freedom' points to a millennial age, to attributes we believe ourselves to have but have been prevented from attaining by the malice of others or by inadequate, inefficient or perverse institutional arrangements. It pictures contemporary life as enervating and polluting and presents an image of purity, a fullness of life, available and attainable through the termination of this disturbing and deluding order. It has fuelled our eagerness to designate blame for life's disappointments and fed our inclination to find conspiracy in every misfortune.

The Romantics and their allies have berated man for his willingness to succumb, to behave as though he were at the mercy of causal forces, or the passive product of his inheritance. They have revived that religious tendency which saw man's self-creation as an essential part of his dignity and his honour. The Romantic tradition indicts man for the poverty of his demands upon himself. The ideal of freedom, has been used to inspire man to be more vigorous, more authentic and to throw off the dulling influence of habit and convention.

SARTRE AND OAKESHOTT

The two writers brought together as the subject of this work issue from what is broadly the same movement of modern thought, namely, German Idealism. The fact that they are in so many respects antithetical makes simultaneous treatment all the more instructive. They are, arguably, the senior representatives of, respectively, radical and conservative political thought in the twentieth century. Both employ the concept of freedom as a key to their view of the world.

Sartre stands with the Left – absorbing a great deal from the Romantic tradition – he believes much that we inherit and learn is nonsense, rubbish which clear thinking can exorcise. He views freedom as the clearest principle of humanity. A 'principle' not in the sense of a rule or maxim but a fact from which we can logically deduce our capacities and powers. Freedom is real. It is the one aspect of our being not contrived by the understanding. It is known intuitively, completely untainted by convention and abuse. It is the key to our true being and the measure of our way of life. Sartre uses freedom to remind men that they are uncaused, that they are bound only to the habits that they endorse and that only self-delusion permits slavishness to custom or morality.

Sartre uses the 'fact' of our not being bound to argue two rather different cases:

The first is a critique of our indolence, our laziness, our propensity to view ourselves as formed by forces beyond us, as though we were thing-like, as though conventions actually produced us without our involvement. This mystification Sartre seeks to remove by a dramatic and impressive presentation of man as self-originating.

However, Sartre, an instinctively political thinker, came to view social conventions and institutions as the real source of mystification; to insist that individual delinquency, the drift into thing-like-ness, is ultimately traceable to the perversity of social institutions, i.e. the classic 'Left Wing' position.

In Sartre's work the idea of freedom is used to diagnose the 'disorder' which encumbers and deludes mankind – the mystification which deprives him of his absolute self-possession. For the Right neither introspection nor intellectual exertion can provide the sort of immaculate insight that Sartre and the Left use as a critique of contemporary society. For the Right the inherited order is the source of our sense of right, justice and truth. Freedom, far from being a natural and innate capacity against which such values may be judged, is a form of skilfulness. It is the agility and dexterity of the individual in the employment of such resources and institutions as are available for the attainment of their ambitions and projects. In this view, freedom has no nature; it is an aspect of the achievement of the culture. As such the quality of freedom is dependent upon and derivative of the wider cultural resource and is vulnerable to its neglect and mismanagement. Oakeshott stands with the tradition of the Right in being more concerned with the erosion of order than with its reform. In his work liberty is seen as no less threatened by the excesses of intellectuals than by the ambitions of despots or priests.

He is cautious of political change – appreciative of established institutions. He is hostile to the practice of basing reform upon abstract ideas and wary of the qualification of intellectuals to recommend. He holds freedom to be an accomplishment, in the first instance, of the culture and, by derivation, of the individual. Freedom in Oakeshott's thought is a form of wealth, a richness obtained by experience. His work concerns the conservation and preservation of the collective resource, i.e. of what man learns.

We will see that in the work of both Sartre and Oakeshott the idea of freedom develops in close association with their major interest – the role of the intellectual. For Sartre, the intellectual has a seminal didactic role, he is the possessor of a fundamental insight into the truth of life. For Oakeshott, such an outlook exemplifies the arrogance of the intellectual, an unguarded faith in abstract ideas which has been destructive and pernicious.

Sartre, and the Left, are impressed by the perversity of our ordinary inheritance of custom and habit, they seek to purify it by a critique rooted in 'reason'. Oakeshott, and the Right, are impressed by the brilliance of our inheritance and seek to defend this against impoverishment from abstract critiques.

Freedom is important to Sartre and Oakeshott because both thinkers hold the intellect to be a product of our own adventure, they are interesting because they share the dilemma of deciding whether the richness of human life rests more heavily upon the development of the collective structures or upon the resolve of the particular individual.

* * *

My own interest in these issues evolved, somewhat paradoxically, from my enthusiasm for the work of Sigmund Freud. I wanted to obtain a clearer understanding of the unconscious. Sartre and Oakeshott concerned me because they both, in their differing ways, dismiss the idea of the unconscious – they both reject as occult the view that we have a determination outside of our awareness. I wanted to understand why I do not share their views.

THE ANTECEDENCE

However, we begin our story with neither Sartre nor Oakeshott but with those who established the terms of their debate. Writers who not only introduce the ideas and arguments which were to figure in the latter writers' work but established the virtues and the mood in which they must be understood.

We start with the emergence of the idea of 'reason', the struggle to understand ourselves in a world perceived to be governed by universal laws. This produced a way of thinking that was to transform our understanding of the state, the law and ourselves. The self we know, the social order we dwell in and the order that we wish to bring about carry with them the inheritance of this style of viewing the world.

The notion that a certain style of 'clear thinking' could reveal the truth, unchanging and universal, was a view which migrated from religious practice and belief. But the pious scholars who began this search for 'reason' unwittingly served to overthrow the Church of their Faith and prepared the instruments for less cautious characters. For their quest to find God's unchanging truth gave their progeny, the intellectuals, the mantle of a new priesthood.

Before we can understand our thirst for freedom and our notion of self-hood we should know something of this past.

1
Nature and Mind

Our notion of ourselves, of our being and, hence, of freedom has many sources; religious, literary and cultural but to our age the most influential has been the intellectual view, that proffered by and supported in the arguments of the philosophers. Why intellectuals have moved into the place of priests and the significance of this priesthood will form a significant sub-plot of this work. In the last four centuries the intellectuals have taken on at least some of the role of the medieval clergy and our way of thinking about ourselves includes within it a reverence for 'reason' a reverence which was formerly reserved for the divine.

The origin of this respect lies deep within the assumptions of European culture specifically that Christianity granted reason the possibility of knowing the divine, a possibility which drew us into thinking of our mental capacities as quite distinct from any other capacity we might enjoy. Indeed, the age of this reverence for reason began not with the decline of faith but in a period of robust defence in the face of tremendous change. In terms of religious belief, that change centred upon the notion of personal salvation, an awareness of an individual destiny and a sense of unique and particular worth. The isolation and self-questioning that Protestantism generated and required was itself exaggerated and embellished when our understanding of the natural world was altered by changing beliefs about the workings of nature. To understand the rise of the intellectual's view of man, his self and his freedom, we must begin with the shift in our understanding of the natural world.

Modern thought can be said to have its origin in the revision of the understanding of the physical world which began in the seventeenth century. This pictured physical nature as categorically distinct from the nature of man. In viewing the world as governed by universal laws of causality it found man peculiar and exceptional. This simple understanding of the world served to exaggerate the element of man that was distinct – his capacity to calculate, and this became the emblem of his identity. At the same stroke the natural world became better understood and more alien and remote from the being of man. The separation of world and man; the categorical division of these two abstractions, is one of the seminal moves in the history of modern thought. For subsequent thinkers, understanding the relation of these elements of man and his environment became the abiding challenge. It is in the attempt to give a coherent account of this duality that the idea of human freedom as we currently understand the term grew.

It has become an axiom that: 'Modern philosophy begins with doubt' and 'doubt begins with Descartes'. What actually begins with Descartes is a concern to demonstrate that we are capable of certainty, that each individual may, on the authority of their own reflective self analysis, achieve unquestioned assurance that we do know what we ordinarily believe to be true.

Descartes' doubt was borne of an intensified sense of uncertainty, itself a by-product of the newly acquired skilful and methodical way of dealing with the natural world, coupled with the style of self-examination that Lutheran faith had required. The rise of epistemology illustrates a relationship which, it can be argued, approaches a general principle in the history of thought, namely, that alterations in the idea of mind follow upon changes in the understanding of nature. The classic presentation of this argument is to be found in Collingwood's *The Idea of Nature*. Collingwood argues that nature is invariably the primary ground upon which ideas of mind are established.

The new physics of Descartes' time challenged an understanding of the natural order which, with degrees of variation, had persisted from the times of the early Greeks. Retrospectively we can describe this cosmology as anthropocentric. The natural order was viewed as purposeful, nature had life and intelligence and everything that moved itself, every type of plant, bird and animal was a particular vital individual (IN 9). There was no felt need to seek a system or a series of integrated relationships. Each object was understood in terms of its own activities and there was little incentive to look for general underlying laws. Instead interest centred upon classification and categorization, the accumulation of detail. Each object, plant, and creature was complete in itself, to know it was to recognize its peculiarity, its own 'nature'; it possessed its essence as a vital whole, as a drive or life effort, this being its unique purpose in the order of the universe. Nature was, for the Ancients and for the Schoolmen, radically diverse – a collection of individuals each demanding to be understood in their isolated context.

In contrast, the age that begins with Copernicus, the modern age, is characterized by the view of the world governed by uniformity and compliance with general laws. The background to this new movement rested in the Christian conviction that man dwelt in a purposeful universe. This generated an attentive and diligent attitude toward nature, one that actively sought a theme or signs of harmony or co-ordination. However, it was the rise in the successful design and operation of machines which appears to be the seminal model for the new view of the world. The machine demonstrated that objects, distinct but incomprehensible in themselves, could be understood in their total relation, working together for some specific end. Once the construction and use of machines became widely understood, 'it was an easy step to the proposition: as a clockmaker or millwright is to a clock or mill, so is God to Nature' (IN 9). The natural world was no longer viewed as intelligent but was, rather, a series of shapes, governed by geometry and arithmetic. The motions of the stars, plants and the oceans appeared to illustrate a law, universal, uniform and soulless, a law of divine origin accessible to man because he shares the divine intelligence. Man seemed closer to God and the natural world seemed less so. Mind became divorced from nature, set over against it as something alien, without equivalent or like in the world. Mind was distinct not just from the rest of Creation but also from that aspect of man which belonged to nature; his body.

The most complete formulation of this new relationship between man and the natural order is to be found in the work of Galileo:

> Philosophy is written in that vast book which stands ever open before our eyes, I mean the universe; but it cannot be read until we have learnt the language and become familiar with the characters in which it is written. It is written in mathematical language, and the letters are triangles, circles and other geometrical figures. (IN 102)

Collingwood responds, 'The meaning is clear: the truth of nature consists in mathematical facts; what is real and intelligible in nature is that which is measurable and quantitative' (ibid.). When this quantitative methodology was associated with the innovations of seventeenth century physics, i.e. with the idea of inanimate, universal laws applicable to the entire cosmos, a new world view was created one that was to receive its original coherent, that is, philosophical presentation in the work of Descartes.

Descartes is the outstanding thinker of this period because, in contrast to the optimism of physicists such as Copernicus and Galileo he is troubled and uneasy in the changed intellectual environment. When compared with the methodical rigour of science, the old axioms of philosophy appeared shallow and unsatisfactory. At the beginning of the *Meditations* he tells us.

Some years ago I was struck by the large number of falsehoods which I had accepted as true in my childhood, and by the highly doubtful nature of the whole edifice which I had subsequently based on them. I realized that it was necessary, once in the course of my life, to demolish everything completely and start again right from the foundations if I wanted to establish anything at all in the sciences that was stable and likely to last. (M 12)

It is perhaps a paradox that the precision of the 'language written in the universe' disclosed the unsatisfactory nature of our notion of truth and drove Descartes to a radical and methodical scepticism, one which would open a gulf between the mechanical world of matter and the logical world of mind.

Descartes' explicit project sought a complete account of the world which would secure the existence of God and the immortality of the soul, and would trounce, once and for all, the arguments of atheists. Descartes' method was reminiscent of confessional self-examination but the standard of rigour used in this examination was taken from the attitude of inquisition employed by physicists. The dictum 'Modern Philosophy begins with doubt' reveals his concern, the search for apodictic, timeless and certain, knowledge amidst the flux of experience.

In the Dedicatory Letter at the beginning of the *Meditations* Descartes declares 'the existence of God is capable of proof by natural reason, and also that the inference from Holy Scripture is that the knowledge of God is easier to acquire than the knowledge we have of many created things.... Everything that may be known of God can be demonstrated by reasoning which has no other source but our own mind' (M 3). Here 'own mind' means the mind of an individual, anyone. And he goes on to say that his model for correct reasoning is 'the proofs of geometry' and that his arguments 'require a mind which is completely free from preconceived opinions and which can easily detach itself from involvement with the senses'. That is, propositional logic will ensure that a mind emptied of its habit and caprice will arrive at a natural, innate and universal self-assurance.

Descartes speculates that normal consciousness might be entirely false; one may be mad, be dreaming, or dwell in a world governed by a malicious deceiver. These doubts are set along more mundane error: that we are aware of having been deceived in particular observations, that material things lack continuity and are transformed by contingent events.

Descartes develops his case along two main paths; the first is the argument of innate self-certainty and the second is the argument from the good will of God. If we turn to the immediate consciousness we see that there is a level at which one is unable to doubt. Thus there appears to be a natural limit upon what one might reasonably bring into question, for were one to doubt the entirety of experience then the very capacity which permits questioning, the ability to distinguish the real from the false, would be undermined. Were I to claim that I was deluded all of the time I would lose the right to make any claim at all including the claim that I was deluded at all, therefore, amongst my thoughts there must be a standard which establishes veracity. Most famously, if I were to attempt to deny my own existence I would by my very act falsify the proposition. Descartes assertion that to think is to assure being gave us the 'cogito' the principle of the universal, self-certain mind. However, conceptual self-certainty could only assure knowledge of the world if a link could be made between the conceptual and the perceptual worlds.

For while the assurance of conceptual truth 'seems to derive simply from my own nature' those ideas which are derived from outside concern him (M 26). Material things are so vulnerable to change, even to dramatic change, e.g. wax melting in the heat, that Descartes holds that it is the mind which maintains the identity of a thing, its continuity through change.

> I know that even bodies are not strictly perceived by the senses or the faculty of imagination but by the intellect alone, and that

this perception derives not from their being touched or seen but from their being understood. (M 22)

Descartes' confidence in the actuality of the material world rests on his faith, his rational belief in the existence of an omni-beneficent Creator. God is the ultimate guarantee of the true correspondence of mind and the corporeal world. The existence of the beneficent God assures us of the veracity of our sensual experience, i.e. that we can be sure that we were not so created that the true world would differ vastly from our experience of it:

I recognize that it is impossible that God should ever deceive me. For in every case of trickery or deception some imperfection is to be found; and although the ability to deceive appears to be an indication of cleverness or power, the will to deceive is undoubtedly evidence of malice or weakness, and so cannot apply to God. (M 37)

From the fact that 'God is not a deceiver' we can be assured our senses do communicate the true state of the world. However, while we are not deceived, we are often mistaken, for error enters our perceptual judgements despite the good will of God by our lack of diligence and by our inadequate and inattentive attitude to experience.

Descartes' thought follows faithfully the Christian tradition seeing the will as the obstacle to truth; disorder enters the Cartesian world through man alone. However, for Descartes the world itself is not fallen but stands before us as a potential truth veiled only by our sinfulness; the material world is dubious only as a consequence of our indiscipline, our sensuousness our indulgence.

Descartes' originality lies in his conviction that each individual holds for himself the parameter of truth. Indeed the ultimate key to Descartes' philosophy is to be found in its belief that each mind has the capacity to attain certain knowledge, non-contingent, ahistorical and atemporal. It was Descartes' assumption that each particular mind is fully self-possessed; that the individual alone in his room could subject the entirety of thought to examination without further reference. For he views the mind's adventures and activities as self-procured and, hence, thoroughly clear and accessible to self-investigation. The mind is transparent the immediate source of itself and is, therefore, the most searching critic of its own experience.

Descartes, then, viewed the world as composed of two radically distinct substances – the immediate conceptual and the mediated perceptual, the former being self-possessed and self-governing and the latter being a realm of material cause. A world of faith and certainty and a mechanical world known to us by the sensorial transmission of ideas, ideas which may be well or poorly incorporated into our mental scheme.

Such incorporation is enacted via quantification. Cartesian discipline leads inexorably to the mathematicization of the notion of reality, and the veracity of our experience of the external world comes to stand or fall by the test of measurement. Our other form of experiencing the external world, the more sensually indulgent or qualitative, must be set aside and disregarded. Legitimate mental procedure was modelled upon mathematics and geometry. This indicated that only the quantifiable part of sensual experience is acceptable. That aspect of mind which was not quantitative became awkward, second rate, a world of caprice and a part of man's Fallen Nature. Not only did Descartes' work authenticate the division of mind and matter, it also served to undermine the legitimacy of intuition, designating only a specific aspect of mind as 'rational'.

Descartes' philosophy retained and exaggerated the separation of mind and body implicit in the work of the physics. Our freedom and certainty were won at a heavy price. The strictures of Calvinism were raised into the precepts of reason.

The gulf between the world of mind and matter posed the problem which was to dominate the philosophy of this period. While interaction of the two realms is a primary fact of consciousness, the dualism seemed to critics and followers alike a flaw which a system of certainty should be able to resolve.

Those who follow Descartes, usually listed as either Empiricists or Rationalists, attempted to overcome this divide. In each case they attempted to preserve the independence of mind from cause, some by giving the material world an incipient form of spirituality, others by portraying God as present in the substance or the transfer of material ideas into the realm of intelligibility. The various techniques of reduction are of interest to historians of philosophy because of the ingenuity displayed and the conceptual preparation they offered for the solution that was to eventually arise. It was Immanuel Kant who made what today may seem a most obvious response; one, however, which in his day was presented and received as philosophy's Copernican Revolution. Very briefly, it was Kant's genius to point out that the division between matter and thought was an understood difference, not a distinction imposed on thought by a foreign, material realm, but a distinction achieved by thought in order to understand a part of its world, a world that innately and radically belongs to mind.

With Kant's work, the Critical Philosophy, we finally reach an explicit attempt to harmonize the competing claims of human self-determination and the laws of physics. Reconciliation between the world of freedom and that of causal determination had been the tacit project of philosophy for the preceding two centuries. Kant's work is an attempt to show that human freedom, religious faith and morality are as sure and certain as the rules of the natural order. The essence of Kant's thought is that the rules by which we come to understand natural events cannot themselves be subjected to doubt – that doubt has, as it were, a natural limit which is implicit in our very capacity to experience and to question. We can be confident that what has been conventionally considered to be our understanding of nature is true and well founded and we can be quite sure that neither the permanence of substance nor the causality of events are merely based upon habitual expectation. In short, Kant holds that the rules upon which knowledge of nature is based are part of our way of knowing. The principles precede even the most primitive of experience, sensation.

The philosophy is referred to as 'Transcendental' because Kant argues that we must accept that there are principles which, while they may not be capable of proof themselves, must be the case because they are the ground of actually possessing the experience we know we have. Thus 'transcendental' should not be confused with 'transcendent' which means beyond.

> The word "transcendental" ... does not signify something passing beyond all experience but something that indeed precedes it a priori, but that is intended simply to make knowledge of experience possible. If these conceptions overstep experience, their employment is termed 'transcendent'. (PFM fn 122)

Thus the 'Transcendental Self' is not something belonging to another world but is the foundation of the known world. While space and time are the ground of sensation, causality is the basis of our identification of 'things' and events, and freedom is the basis of morality. Because transcendental concepts belong to us, they cannot be explained in terms of the understanding, they are simply manifest. Thus in order to know of their existence we must look to their manifestation. Kant's argument proceeds; we have sensation, hence space and time are real; we dwell in a world of events therefore causality is necessarily true; we know man to be responsible for his deeds, therefore, we know him to be free *a priori*.

The argument can be summarized quite briefly. The world as we know it is formed around principles of experience and understanding which the mind imposes upon the world. These are necessary and universal, they are the ground of ordinary experience. Thus, the Empiricists are wrong to think sensuous experience is the source of the principles of experience. Experience is the product of the application of innate and necessary rules.

The world of experience, the world we make the effort to understand, is composed of judgements. What we see in natural events is how things appear to stand towards each other, not things in themselves. Kant makes his primary distinction between knowledge of appearances or phenomena and knowledge of things in themselves or noumena. Basically, scientific method deals with phenomenal facts, and metaphysics deals with noumenal facts. Confusion ensues when this distinction is ignored or blurred.

Kant was to demonstrate that neither duration nor extent could be coherently considered as learnable, they must be principles inherent in the mind's way of knowing the world. We cannot learn of space from examples of various relations of position, nor can we learn of time from the different temporal relations. In both cases the whole must precede the part; the division and metrication of the world is an exercise performed within the context of these 'forms' or foundational elements.

Kant says 'we never can imagine or make a representation to ourselves of the non-existence of space, though we may easily enough think that no objects are found in it. It must, therefore, be considered as the condition of the possibility of phenomena, and by no means as a determination dependent upon them' (CPR 44). Space is, then, the form of all phenomena of the external sense, it is the condition of material experience.

Likewise, time, as the ground of simultaneousness and of succession, must precede all our experience. It is plain that all phenomena must exist in time, i.e. possess duration as well as extension, but time unlike space underpins our capacity to experience *tout court*. Space and time are, then, the formal conditions through which experience is possible, 'they instruct us respecting experience, and not by means of it'. (CPR 49)

Kant holds that the lapse or flux of time represents the immediate quality of spirit, it belongs to man as his vital quality, his mode of being. Moreover it is the source of his sense of being other than the world. For the material world resists the mind's flight, the world presents the quality of permanence. The mutual dependence of flux and permanence is the ground of experience. Kant thereby re-characterizes the mind/matter distinction of Descartes, for mind relies upon matter to know itself, to differentiate itself, to be manifest, and matter has no form separate from mind. The classical epistemological problem of two substances is therefore resolved; mind and matter are radically involved in shaping each other. Judgement issues from a mind preoccupied by the material world and the diversity belongs to a physical world unified in experience.

The other grave difficulty indicated in the work of Kant's predecessors was the difficulty of guaranteeing the rules which our understanding of the world assumes, namely the law of causality. Hume had argued that there were truths of mind, tautologies such as are found in mathematics and geometry and there are truths of fact which are found by experience, but that the truths of experience have no necessity or universality. Kant counter-argued that the method of the physical sciences could be rooted in truths that were more than empirical, facts which were founded upon the way we experience events. Just as space and time must be *a priori* forms of sensuous experience, so cause must be the *a priori* principle of our understanding. So we might say that causality precedes the recognition of an event or experience. To look for the way we learn causality is to have overlooked the point that nothing could exist within the frame of the understanding were it not couched in terms of cause. The very act of identification of an event presupposes such a relation.

While causality is the principle or the condition of our understanding a physical event, this process does not grant or donate particular character to the event or specify its exact nature, this identity is a product of our judgements. It was Kant's great contribution to the history of thought that all events are identifications, that nothing is known without judgement. It is this aspect of his thought which earns it the name of 'idealism'. The achievement of Kant's idealism is that it explains how such a mind-dependent world still permitted philosophical certainty and assurance of the universality of experience. Critical Idealism holds that we can, by a full appreciation of our faculties, disclose that both certainty and doubt are rooted in experience.

In this manner even the basic elements of judgement – quantity, quality, and relation – are ultimately traced to the modalities of time – the primary form of human awareness – so that even the fundamental articles of the mind's capacity to judge are not learned from the bodies of the extensive world but are, rather, the condition of our having an awareness of an 'external' world.

Kant's major achievement was to show that certainty lies in the very ground of experience, something present plain and evident, something that can only be disturbed or destroyed by false reasoning. It is the misapplication of the principles we use to order our experience, the use of those principles in abstraction, which he believes has brought metaphysics into disrepute. Indeed it is helpful to recall that it is actually metaphysics rather than the empirical sciences which he is trying to salvage. Kant makes it plain that his real concern is to deal with the traditional issues of metaphysics, that is, God, immortality and freedom. However, the issue which concerns us rests with his attempt to distinguish the order of nature from the order of human freedom.

The point of following Kant in all these details is to understand how he solves the problem of there being freedom in a world of causal determination. Kant's world is dualistic, but his dualism is rooted in the distinction between what is known by sensual experience and what is known by intellectual intuition. Knowledge of the world of objects is merely phenomenal. We know only what can be absorbed into consciousness via the categories of the understanding. We cannot know the essence of these things. But in regard to matters of pure intelligence, we may know them completely and transparently for we are in spontaneous unity with them. It is to this latter relation, the noumenal, we shall now turn.

* * *

Kant argues that our knowledge of freedom is not related to phenomena, it is part of the system of pure reason. The world of sense contains merely appearances, which are not things-in-themselves; but this limitation does not prevent reason from leading us to the objective boundary of experience, namely, to something which is not itself an object of experience but is the ground of all experience. While the transcendental ideas lie outside experience, they none-the-less, as the ground of all possible experience, are available to our reason and it is by examining the nature of experience that reason might speculatively deduce the nature of the noumenon.

Kant holds that introspection reveals nothing of any worth. We find only chaos, an endless flux. We can designate a character to ourselves only by referring to the actual arrangement of the world attributed to our deeds, beyond this there is no content for the self. In the internal intuition, I am conscious not of how I appear to myself or of how I am in myself, but only that I am. Direct introspection reveals nothing but 'an empty space'. We must examine the world in order to deduce the powers which reason possesses which accounts for this world. Therefore, Kant tells us, our knowledge of ourselves must necessarily be in the manner of an object, that is, phenomenal.

We understand ourselves from the character manifested in the phenomenal world. Kant insists that the question of whether man possesses 'free will' must be answered by reference to the character of his practical life, the way man appears in the phenomenal world.

A will, which can be determined independently of sensuous impulses, consequently by motives presented by reason alone, is called a free will (*arbritrium liberum*); and everything which is connected with this free will, either as principle or consequence, is termed *practical*. The existence of practical freedom can be proved from experience alone. (CPR 455)

Experience discloses to us that our world has two species of cause; 'natural', that contained within causal chain and available to the laws of physics and 'spontaneous', that which is the outcome of the human will. The brilliance of Kant's work lies in its appreciation that the problem of freedom is inseparable from the actual existence of the practical world; indeed, they are one and the same phenomenon. This argument follows the pattern of the 'Critical Philosophy' in viewing the human faculty as prior to and the ground of the world we encounter. The practical world is constructed upon our capacity for freedom and freedom is that phenomenon which disturbs and challenges the natural world.

The fact that we have the power to affect our situation, to avoid what we fear will be hurtful or do what is desirous, and also the capacity to direct oneself to the good, to what we approve and away from what we disapprove, is the proof of free will. He explains that practical freedom 'presupposes that, although a certain thing has not happened, it ought to have happened, and that, consequently, its phenomenal cause was not so powerful and determinative as to exclude the causality of our will – a causality capable of producing effects independently of and even in opposition to the power of natural causes, and capable, consequently, of spontaneously originating a series of events. Hence for 'practical world' we can read 'moral world', that is, the introduction of the principle of reason into the natural world. This freedom in the practical sphere is all that genuinely concerns us, metaphysical freedom has no real practical significance.

Kant is straightforward in declaring that 'experience demonstrates to us the existence of practical freedom as one of the causes which exist in nature, that is, it shows the causal power to reason in the determination of the will'. The world, therefore, demonstrates an 'alternative' type of causality, the source of which is ourselves. This is the order of reason, the orderliness to which humanity aspires and the principle of which is found in the unity of purpose of our deeds. The goal of reason is consistency, and it is the manifestation of such regularity, the moral laws, that is the proof of human freedom. The goal of the moral law is only a goal because we must operate in the realm of phenomena. Hence 'reason can have only a regulative and not a constitutive influence', i.e. what we intend and what we achieve will often diverge. The will is manifested in the empirical world in an oblique fashion, rarely exactly intended, but the point is, man is an original source of events, things happen because of him. Kant recognizes that there may well be an outstanding problem, that 'the ideal of Transcendental freedom, requires that reason should be independent of all sensuous determinate causes; and thus it seems to be in opposition to the law of nature and to all possible experience. It therefore remains a problem for the human mind' (CPR 456). However, he thinks that we should not deliberately invent a metaphysical difficulty for it is a fact that we have to accept natural causality on trust of our experience.

How such a faculty [as spontaneous origination] is possible, is not a necessary inquiry; for in the case of natural causality itself, we are obliged to content ourselves with the *a priori* knowledge that such a causality must be presupposed, although we are incapable of comprehending how the being of one thing is possible through the being of another, but must for this information look entirely to experience. (CPR 273)

Our knowledge of natural causality is actually no stronger than that of free causality, it is simply manifest in our experience of the world. Kantian dualism ultimately rests upon our ordinary appreciation that the world is available to our determination, that amidst mechanical cause are events originating with ourselves. In distinguishing such a world, the practical world, we also distinguish our self-hood; the practical world and human agency mutually define each other. And while this is one of the crucial and defining aspects of any idealist philosophy in Kant's system it acts as a bridge to his moral thought, for the self we come to know is a self made by us, it is phenomenal, but man as both noumena and phenomena dwells in two orders, and action is both the expression of and the realization of this strange otherness, the human principle. Kant expresses this principle as reason. It is the capacity to give ordered expression to ourselves to shape our humanity according to universal principles and bring reason into the world.[1] Actual immediate spontaneity would not be recognizable. It would be senseless and shapeless, it would be only nonsense. It is the task of reason to bring our free acts under the rubric of universal and unchanging laws, to give substance to our freedom and to grant it meaning.

Reason in the form of the primary judgements or 'categories' – quantity, quality, duration, etc. – is the regulative aspect of thought. It gives experience universal form, hence gives us understanding in the realm of action, that is, the practical sphere. We are not confronted with the task of recognizing what is real but, rather, what ought to be. It is in this sphere that reason offers direction. The phenomenalization or expression of freedom, if it is to make sense, must itself be subject to universal and unchanging laws, that is, the agent must strive to manifest a singularity or unity of intent. Mere capriciousness, that is, the aimless manifestation of freedom, denies the principle of freedom itself, the principle that we can give substance to our reason.

From this requirement Kant produces his famous 'categorical imperative' which demands that one conforms to a notional universal law when designing an action. That is to act so that the maxim upon which one's action is based may be used as a universal law. One is obliged to adopt those 'policies of life' which, were they to be generally employed, would sustain the intelligibility of human action, the possibility of human happiness. Kant appears to believe that this formal requirement is itself enough to produce an order amongst mankind, that reason alone will ensure we acknowledge the other's right to life, to possessions, need for truthfulness, etc. for the violation of any of these will entail that one countenances one's own destruction or the ruination of the circumstances required for self expression. It is, then, in the normal sense, our duty. We are obliged in the name of moral law to set aside not only capriciousness, that is, the absence of judgement, but also our 'sense of justice', our compassion and our affection for customs, traditions and the like as well as our tremulous adherence to dogma and codes of convention. Kant's moral freedom is a very stringent master indeed. (CRR 29)

> By having a will free of sensuous impulses man transfers himself in thought into an order of things entirely different from that of his desires …. This better person he believes himself to be when he transfers himself to the standpoint of a member of the intelligible world, to which he is involuntarily forced by the idea of freedom, i.e. of being independent of determination by the causes of the world of sense. (GMM 454)

This association of law and freedom owes much to Rousseau and can be taken to be the emblem of the idealists' attitude to freedom, namely, that freedom is an attainment; imposing discipline on the chaotic nature we find in and about us.

Kant and Descartes share a context of concern. Put briefly, it is that of the 'new physics' of the seventeenth and eighteenth centuries. They were both simultaneously impressed and horrified by the spectre of a mechanistic world, impressed because they shared its love of order and completeness and horrified because it seemed to leave little room for the human element, to undermine the importance of judgement. They share an idea of freedom because they share a view of the world. Despite all the indications to the contrary they both begin with an idea of what freedom is and then establish a philosophy to maintain their view. That presupposed view of freedom was that man was not part of the chain of causality but commanded himself as a particular person awaiting the judgement of his Creator. Descartes' simple substance set man apart from nature, asserted that he was in command of his world and took the laws of physics as a guide to the ultimate rigour of Creation, a regularity which we could share if we applied ourselves diligently to the task. Kant overcame the vicious problem of two substances by acknowledging that man must be the ground of the natural world because he possessed it as his experience. But Kant shares the view of the epistemologists that there belongs to man a different species of cause. For Kant, this power disclosed man himself, it was his identity, the manifestation over which he had total and immediate command. The innate and universal categories which give pattern and meaning to the events of nature also provide the rule by which our own free conduct should be performed.

Kant alienated man from the totality of his sensual experience, and reinvigorated the mastery of the intellect over the sensual realm. Both Descartes and Kant reveal freedom to be the source of discipline and self-control and both disclose preoccupations which are ascetic and distrustful of sensuality.

These events in the history of thought were, of course, not entirely self-propelled. Religious reform and economic change were both potent elements which served to fuel and enhance the intellectual changes. However, it was the idea of a universal man, a being with inviolable possession of an innate and universal pattern of mind which had the most important impact upon the notion of freedom. Freedom came to be viewed as being a species of causality distinct from that found in nature, a universal quality which distinguishes man from all the rest of Creation. The rise of science entailed a vision of the world but also a notion of the mind – an idea of what it was to think.

The notion that calculation rested upon a skill quite separate from our sentiments, feelings and devotions colours a whole genre of intellectual effort, and still does so. Indeed, it remains the backbone of liberal thought. Man was not only equipped with a universal resource, the intellect, he was uniform even in his diversity, for the real diversity of man was his particularity. Man was universal in his resource and atomic in his performance. This world view designated a special performance which it called Reason. This, in fact, was a peculiar form of mesmerism rooted in a range of intellectual disciplines; mathematics, geometry and formal logic. It designated a received sort of behaviour as civilized, and specified a proper practice of thinking. It owed much to Scholastic disputation but was most surely indebted to the religious meditation by which isolated contemplators abstract themselves from their deeds, and feign to judge them as though they were the deeds of another. This new propriety specified what it was to command the intellect. It viewed freedom as mastery of this type of command which it valued, because it was different from the laws that it believed to pervade the rest of nature, and in that same vision proclaimed man to be self-controlled.

2

The Past and the Self

Kant's great achievement was to recognize that the problem of dualism arose from the exaggeration implicit in the accepted conceptions of mind and world. Mind, having been defined as other than the natural world, could not then have its contact with the world explained. For Kant the mind constitutes reality; the world is an attainment of mind. Kant was succeeded by thinkers who extended and elaborated the mind's role in the construction of reality. In their work the mind was not just the medium in which the external world appeared it was the substance of experience itself. In short, human experience was identified as a dynamic network or system of judgements, as a 'phenomenology'. In such a system the faculties and capacities of the mind are not innate or natural but are made to be; they are an historical achievement. The intellect is a product of culture; it is, itself, an artefact of civilization.

The recognition that intellect was a set of acquired skills was itself sustained by the emerging view that human history had been a learning process, a progression, in which ability and civility had grown and developed. The most impressive account of such a process was presented in the work of J. G. von Herder.[1] Herder had argued that the central element of human thought and expression was man's language. Language is not only the resource we use to express and understand ourselves, but is also the repository of the common wisdom and outlook of a people. He saw the values and ways of a people as evolving organically in response to environmental factors; moral systems were not only relative to the culture but to the age. The understanding of any text or artefact was, therefore, to be related to the context of its creation and required a 'sympathetic' knowledge of the society and the period. Herder's abiding contribution to German thought was the image of the nation as a living being, almost a person, a spirit, and a corresponding faith in history as a dynamic force, a collective adolescence.

Because of the emphasis he placed upon creative expression, Herder is often portrayed as one of the fathers of Romanticism but his view stood in marked contradiction to that of his fellow Romantic J. J. Rousseau. Where Herder saw advance and sophistication, Rousseau saw degeneration. While Romanticism is one of the more difficult passages in Western thought to characterize, mostly because its attributes dove-tail into other interests and obsessions of that age, nonetheless its emblems are its hostility to sophistication, to the artificialities of courtly life, to the pieties of orthodox religion and to the nervous conformity of reformed religion, more generally to the dishonestly and rigidity of public life. Its enthusiasms were youth, intuition and courage. Generally, it sought an inner truth and a more thorough-going self-determination, in this sense, it has been seen as a fuller working of the principles of Protestantism. It found inspiration in nature and in retreat from association and corollary of the trust in intuition was a distrust and distaste of cultured society, for its mannerisms and conventions, its indulgence and dishonesty. The Romantics looked to the ordinary folk and found rustic charm and frankness. They looked to the young and saw spontaneity and hope.

In the work of Rousseau, Romanticism is expressed as an affection for man untainted by society, a belief in his inner goodness and brilliance, an abiding trust in his natural sentiments. It is constantly framed within the context of the isolated individual finding within himself an intuitive sense of purpose, an innate idea of life, one which is provoked by the challenges of this world, brought into sharpest relief by meditation upon the beauty and strength of nature. Rousseau ultimately offers an ambiguous view of social order which is acknowledged as being both the source of our corruption but also, after radical reform, of being the source of a new vitality. Social relations are then both the problem and a solution and, hence, bear the burden of the contempt for the established order and the promise of a new age. He sees mankind as stunted by bad habits and shallow self-appreciation, but capable or renewal and rebirth through a more thorough-going honesty. Most importantly Rousseau's political philosophy gave social change a moral dimension that was to permanently alter the nature of political thinking.

Whether protagonists sided with Rousseau or Herder, whether they saw civilization as progress or degeneration the debates they initiated generated the most dramatic shift in intellectual outlook since the rise of the physical sciences. For, however acrimonious the disagreements about the nature of human history the issue itself began a new chapter in Western thought, one in which we still dwell, dominated by the problem of the relationship between the past and the present.

The philosopher who came to dominate the post-Kantian period was primarily a philosopher of history G. W. F. Hegel.[2] Hegel's thought self-consciously and deliberately contained and developed the themes of the time; the vision of history as a learning process and an understanding of social order as both the product of our acquired skills and the source of the capacities we refer to as intelligence. Hegel's thought incorporates the enthusiasm of the Romantics and the discipline of the Kantians: a recognition of the significance of social change and respect for the inherited order.

Hegel's philosophy is the philosophy of the whole; the term 'mind' or 'spirit' [*Geist*] is used to characterize this whole. Hegel is an Idealist because he holds the material world to be an aspect of *mind's* understanding. By this he does not mean that things are imaginary, rather, all manifest events and objects only have significance, i.e. meaning, in relation to other events and objects and that these relations are judgements. When he says that 'mind is only what it does' he offers a clue to the paradoxical nature of this Idealism for, far from asserting that reality is merely mental, Hegel asserts that the intellect's capacities are made by the way we deal with the world.

An implicit difficulty for any philosophy which holds all experience to be phenomenal is that it requires some non-phenomenal element, that is, a solid foundation that is not purely a product of experience, in order to justify its contention that experience is phenomenal. Any system that is entirely phenomenal would collapse into mere assertion and open itself to the attack that it cannot supply a reasoned justification of itself. Hegel's great achievement is to provide a structure that both explains how human experience is entirely phenomenal and is able to offer a justification of itself.

This structure is the key to Hegel's thought, its underlying principle or 'logic', it is the truth that stands behind the appearance of the world, the universal set of rules which govern human comprehension. In short, for Hegel human experience is entirely phenomenal, a system of judgement, but behind this show lie forces that are unchangingly and unvarying true. This structure explains what thought is, it is the pattern which governs equally each individual mind and the consciousness of humankind. The same structure will explain the experience of each person and human history. This underlying structure also explains the trend of progress which Hegel detects beneath the contingencies of history.

In Hegel's thought the true meaning of any individual event lies in knowing its position in the whole scheme of things but the governing logic dictates the order in which matters must be treated. The need to place things in their 'logical' order explains the thematic and sometimes obscure treatment of topics in Hegel's work. However, it must be recognized that this logical order – sometimes referred to as the dialectic – is crucial to revealing both the logic of human progress and the everyday operations of human intelligence.

The systematic treatment of matters is referred to by Hegel 'scientific' as 'philosophical' and, most notably, as Reason [*Vernunft*]. In Hegel's work Reason, that is, thought that is aware of the underlying principles of the dynamic at work, is contrasted with the Understanding [*Verstand*]. Understanding is ordinary, analytic thinking, thinking which seeks comprehension by reference to definitions or essences. This, in Hegel's view, is fine for everyday life where we need to make distinctions in order to make choices but it is flawed as a means of obtaining the truth. Thinking at the level of the 'understanding' fails to recognize that the intellect is an achievement, a resource which enriches itself. It is not simply that knowledge is accumulated by human endeavour – the mind is changed in its actual active substance; its structural capacities are created by the culture. Philosophy traces the history of this self-development and reveals the principles which lie at its heart.

The key to Hegel's thought lies in Spinoza's concept of substance. Hegel stands squarely in the tradition that the concern of philosophy is the truth and that in order to know what is true we need something unchanging and unquestionable, i.e. that which is certain. Spinoza was the first to glimpse that the certainty for which philosophy yearned could only be one thing: the totality. Understanding what this totality is and how the distinctions within what we call experience occur is the task to which Hegel sets himself.

Hegel begins with what is absolutely certain and that is an unstructured totality, something utterly complete and without character. This totality is not something that can be thought about, rather, it is that frame in which consciousness occurs. We have an ordinary awareness of ourselves and a material world over against us. Hegel does not begin with this 'natural self' but moves towards it from an inclusive ground – a state of mind in which the ordinary operative distinctions are suspended in order for us to explore how the distinctions come into being. Each of Hegel's readers must, if they are to proceed with his work, find this level of consciousness in which we surrender all distinctions – including that distinction modern consciousness finds hardest to renounce; the distinction between our own existence and the existence of things and events. We live in an age where the sense of self is so developed that it is hard to attain that consciousness which disregards the distinction of self and world. Once each of Hegel's readers accepts that the sense of self-possession we give to thought is one of the qualities attained by civilization then he or she will have surrendered the prejudice which separates ordinary thought from Hegel's philosophy.

The contemplative state reached by setting aside the ownership of thought brings us close to the total, the universal *mind*; the impersonal, formless whole which is objective *mind*, the *mind* which is the one true substance the abiding potential upon which civilization has been built and humanity constructed.

Next, we must attempt to understand the dynamics of Hegel's structure; that aspect of *mind* which – through its yearning to be – has brought increasing sophistication and ability into existence and made history a progressive process.

Spinoza characterized substance as 'that which is the cause of itself', likewise, Hegel's conception of *mind* is that it needs nothing from outside itself, it is utterly self-sustaining and self-possessed. Yet Hegel argues that there is a weakness in this self-possession, for *mind* is not 'being'. It has no stuff or matter in which to 'actualize' itself. *Mind* is other than *being* and must pass beyond itself into this alien stuff if it is to make itself 'real'. Thus there is a paradox in *mind*, its principle of self-possession is sustained only at the price of a total withdrawal from being. In order to *be* it must surrender its autonomy and enter a world that is capricious and chaotic and abide by alien rules.

So, *mind* is, in the first instance, pure self-possession or pure freedom. However, this freedom is merely the power to escape being. *Mind* as totally self-possessed *is* 'nothing'. In order to give itself actual existence, *mind* must venture into *being*, into the stuff of existence, and must allow itself to be governed by the rules of *being*. By learning these rules, or as it is in practice, by acquiring these skills *mind* actualizes its potential. In Hegel's terms; that which is indeterminate becomes determinate, the implicit becomes explicit.

This 'becoming' takes the form of an elaborate performance or set of performances, the creation of a series of structures, patterns, habits and practices which form the intelligence. It is a way of dealing with the world which creates and develops our conceptions of 'reality' and 'reason'.

For Hegel, freedom is the theme of human progress because history is the growing sophistication of *mind*, its ever increasing ability at being in the world. *Mind* learns how to *be* and in so doing makes the world its home. This is manifest in the way it orders its activity, by the way it deals with the contingent problems of the body, others and the material world. This order is our freedom; our power to be. For Hegel, freedom is the story of *mind* taking possession of being, i.e. taking control of the world. Where there was randomness and chaos – what Hegel calls indeterminacy – there will be order, or determinate being. Freedom is, therefore, in the first instant a discipline it is an attainment, a set of observations, dispositions and recognitions which are acquired and accumulated. This discipline is the basis of human order of human power what Hegel calls 'right' [*das Recht*]. The aspect of *mind* which Hegel identifies as the source of this discipline is determination, that is the human will. Will, is *mind* entering being. The *Philosophy of Right*[3] is Hegel's account of the manifestation of will, of how *mind* comes into being and makes itself at home in this world.

Will is the aspect of *mind* which seeks to manifest the self-possession and self-control *mind* has as its inner potential. The freedom found in man's inner self-possession yearns to be made real, to be given actual effective being. This is manifest in human order, in organization, in property, in commerce, law and justice and in the formation of relationships such as the family. Under all these phenomena lies the human will. Order and reason are produced as *mind* becomes familiar with the requirements of *being* and acquires the ability to be for itself in this world.

The first part of the *Philosophy of Right* is an account of how *mind* makes its first faltering steps into the material world. *Mind* immediate and complete is powerless. In order to take hold of the world, it must act and, in doing so, it enters the capricious world of being. The sole vehicle for this realization is the human body. Each person is an instance of *mind's* realization; therefore, in the first instant, *mind's* manifestation is atomized. An act must always be the act of some particular individual and *mind's* disclosure to the world is chaotic. Fragmentation is the primary fact of *mind's* actualization, overcoming this initial confusion is the function of 'right'.

In this world deeds manifest the *mind* but the world has no way of sustaining such efforts. Each act enters this freakish and uncertain world, a world without rhyme or reason; what *mind's* determination – the will – achieves in one act it may erase in another. At this simple level of 'right', *mind* struggles for personhood, the capacity to make and do, to lay claim to its world. This is achieved by making a province for action; this region must include the immediate person, the body, and an area or zone of operation, that is, some sort of rudimentary property.

In order that any achievement will be sustained, it is necessary for the individual to obtain the acquiescence of others. This agreement to mutually recognize such zones of personhood Hegel refers to as 'contract'. This mutual agreement, however, is itself vulnerable to capricious action as such 'contract' may be flouted with impunity. If personhood and human agency are to obtain any grip upon the world, and if *mind* is to take the first steps towards actualizing itself, there must be a judgement that is not merely in one person but commands the relations between persons. That is, before we can realize any stable sense of being there must be a determination of *mind* – a will – which is able to enforce its decisions and maintain a rudimentary order.

Hegel portrays such an agency as the first stage of civilization, for, in order to deal with this external judge, the individual *mind* must be systematic, no longer just a series of deeds but a real will, a determination that has an awareness that it is a unitary agency with something to achieve and something to loose. At this level, the level of the subject of judgement, the person becomes a self-conscious will and we move to the next level of 'right' which Hegel calls 'Moral Right'. This is the level where the person turns inward, striving to be consistent and thematic, aiming to be the 'subject' the objective world conceives it to be. In order to live up to the demands of agency it internalizes the order which maintains the possibility of its realization in the objective world. The person toils to realize the full ramifications of the determination to give itself being; it resolves to live by those rules which make the realization of human determination a possibility or, in other words, to do what is good. At this stage human order is enriched by the notions of purpose, responsibility and duty.

The individual becomes a champion of the self. Each takes it upon themselves to act for the principle of self-hood, to sustain those rules which facilitate the realization of the will. Each uses their agency in the interest of the will or of *self*-determination. They strive to maintain, in themselves and in others, the disciplines which enhance the coherence of the sense of self-hood, that is, the ownership of determination. It is a pattern of regulation which respects the will as a force which has a right of its own, not this or that will but willfulness itself. The individual strives to create a world where human determination can flourish. They become an agent of will. This is, quite literally, a self-discipline – the imposition of rules which sustain self-hood. This discipline is 'morality', the sense that capriciousness in oneself or others weakens mankind's hold upon the world and 'offends' us personally.

Each acts for the self; with an awareness that the self is a universal form. This corresponds with Kant's categorical imperative, that is, with the principle of the universalizability of each particular deed or belief. In Kant's work such universalizability was viewed as the substance of moral action, however, for Hegel it only outlines a principle, it lacks the actuality which permits the individual to make appropriate moral judgements, in short, it lacks 'content'. Hegel points out that such maxims as are produced by this rule, e.g. "honour your debts" do not tell you either what actually fulfils an instant of the case i.e. when a debt has been incurred, nor does it inform the agent of the subtleties and nuances whereby other rules or maxims may take precedence. These observations lead to the real innovation of Hegel's political system the level referred to as 'Ethical Life' [*Sittlichkeit*].

The first section of the *Philosophy of Right* revealed will 'in-itself' determined to take hold of the world, to act. The second section disclosed will 'for-itself', the individual will governed by the principle of will's realization. The first sphere was active but unprincipled the second was principled but lacked any concrete orientation, it recognized its obligation to be guided by the principle of the whole but as isolated could locate no real act. In the third sphere, that of 'Ethical Life', the will is 'in and for-itself', *mind* strives to take hold of the world in a ordered way one that gives substance to its self-realization and makes freedom real.

The title of this sphere in German is *Sittlichkeit*, that is, judgement guided by custom or habit, more accurately for Hegel's purpose, it is conduct formed by institutional practices, organization and arrangements. For Hegel the intellect is phenomenal, i.e. it is acquired; *mind* has no natural, innate and active content. What is actually acquired are the ways, customs, habits and institutions of a people. The intellect is a set of patterns or structures whose origin is the pattern of life, a culture. To be rational is to use the patterns of thought one learns and these are specific, topical and local. It is the burden of his argument that 'custom is the law appropriate to free men'.

'Ethical Life' evolves through three stages. The first is the *family* where right is nurtured, where the individual is treated largely without reference to his individuality but as someone who is one of us, where belonging is unconditional. The second is the free market or *civil society* where individuality finds expression and all worth and value is earned through toil and adaptation. The third element is the *state* where right and individuality are drawn into mutually beneficial co-ordination and we find ourselves at home in the world, being the person we wish to be and valued in our own right.

The family is for Hegel the starting point as it is the place of generation, both in the biological and spiritual sense. It provides us with sustenance and affection but most significantly it is the place of education. Here we procure all that is basic to human life, obedience, loyalty, responsibility. We appropriate it from the ways of our folk, through emulation, instruction and via the myths and customs that guide our people. While it gives us intelligence, the disciplined ability to live, it is a restricted arena for the expression of this intelligence. The individual seeks a role in the world. Education into the customary ways is the ground of ethical life but it creates needs which the *family* is unable to fulfil. For it develops in the individual a self-awareness which it can not satisfy. For the developed character, the strong personality, the youth who wants to lead his own life the *family* is a bind and must be left in order that the individual may make his own way in life.

Such individuals are able to express themselves in the market place, to freely offer the talents, skills and abilities they have mastered and in return seek satisfaction of the various needs, desires and whims which belong to them as individuals. But such a system is based upon exchange, contract and enforceability and this requires a system of law which contractors themselves are unable to provide. Administration of the necessary regulatory functions of civil society can only be performed by a body that has inherent authority, a power which is final. This final authority is, for Hegel, the state, it is the actualization of *mind* itself.

For Hegel, the state actually completes what the family attempted; it is the ethical home which permits and includes the particularity of individual expression. Hegel took from Rousseau the idea that social order is prior to personal identity. Moreover, because the individual's intellect and self-awareness is a product of the social order, the individual is an abstraction while the collective order is the concrete. From this observation both Rousseau and Hegel justify the power of the state and the legitimacy of law.[4] The right of the state lies in the fact that within its regulation lies a deeper freedom for each and every individual. If law were merely a particular will set against other wills its right would be redundant but this is not the case, law sets free by creating the conditions where all can pursue their own well-being.

Hegel's view of the state has been influential and controversial. His grandiose and politically dangerous remark that 'the state is absolutely rational inasmuch as it is the actuality of the substantial will... [it is] the *mind* of a nation [*Volkgeist*] the divine, knowing and willing itself' when read in conjunction with his view that 'since the state is *mind* objectified it is only as one of its members that the individual himself has objectivity, genuine individuality and an ethical life' (PR 156) seems to reveal a totalitarian contempt for individuality. Hegel attempts to clarify his view by saying 'in considering freedom, the starting point must not be individuality for the essence of self-consciousness is externally realized as a self-subsistent power in which single individuals are only moments', i.e. freedom must be a discipline. The individual in turning inward, to their 'subjective' desires, may discover all manner of wants but the social order is the keeper of right, it must defend itself for only by its preservation is civilized existence possible, is individuality possible.

Hegel recognizes the right of the individual. Individuality is the primary source of will, thus 'the state is actual only when its members have a feeling of their own worth' (PR 281) and 'subjectivity must attain its full development [for] only then can the state be said to be genuinely organized' PR 280) a point which is made even more clearly when he writes:

> The principle of modern states has prodigious strength and depth because it allows the principle of subjectivity to progress to its culmination in the extreme of self-subsistent personal particularity.
>
> (PR 161)

Indeed, Hegel goes on to remark that:

> The essence of the modern state is that the universal be bound up with the complete freedom of its particular members and with private well-being .... The state is actual only when its members have a feeling of their own self-hood ... [it] is the one and only prerequisite of the attainment of the particular ends and welfare.
>
> (PR 280)

There is no question that creating the legal framework which would permit each to find his own true self is difficult and delicate, indeed, this is what makes it the highest achievement, but the state is the 'divine will' only insofar as it creates the conditions where *mind* in all its infinite variety is able to flourish. Each actual state is a product of particular forces and circumstances and its laws reflect the life of its own people their traditions, religion and moral convictions. Actual states may well fail to reflect the riches of these elements; they may use brute force to impose the design of some particular will and abuse the custom and morality of their people Therefore, in interpreting Hegel we must recall that it is not just any state which is the 'march of God in the world' rather it is one that incorporates the riches of its historical achievements.

Again, it is important to recognize that for Hegel not every notion that enters the head of each subject is worthy of realization; each individual may harbour any number of scheme and projects, but only those ambitions which the contemporary order is capable of sustaining will succeed. Many of our ideas are mere whims and fancies which have no place in the becoming of *mind*; and they cannot be incorporated within the structure of our community and cannot sustain them. In some instances, this unsustainablity will be realized in the hostility of the state. This opposition may be felt as one will set against the individual's self determination, but this is only an appearance and the truth is that the state and its laws stands to judge what should be achieved, and the basis of this right is its understanding of itself, an understanding constructed and composed of its historically achieved structure. The attempt to alter law – to change a people's view – is the work of history, the labour of generations. This struggle to work change into the world is toilsome and bloody; indeed Hegel famously remark that history was the slaughter bench upon which 'the happiness of peoples, the wisdom of states and the virtues of individuals has been sacrificed'. But reason has no other resource than its historical attainment. It cannot leap out of its fashions and ways. We must use the resource of intelligence we actually have.

It is the thesis of 'Ethical Life' that the institutions, customs and habits of a folk are the ground of a people's liberty because they are the source of the structure of *mind*. They are the concrete attainment of *mind* and the origin of the intellect. The labour of human determination is to produce order, the order in which man can *be* more comfortably and more vividly. Each within the chaos of his self-awareness might find many urges which do not find favour with his people or with the law. The struggle of history is the struggle to find what novelty contemporary order can sustain and what it cannot. For Hegel, there are no short cuts; history is made by people willing to be bold and be ready to face the often terrible consequences of failure. It is a genuine tragedy that those who are most valuable to *mind's* becoming will in their own time face the greatest conflict and only rarely will they live to see their innovation prosper and human life enriched.

History is the final judge of the rationality of our efforts. History is the emancipation of *mind*, its growing real freedom or the actualization of its potential. The enrichment of the structures allow an ever increasing diversity of expression to be sustained. The accomplishment of each new generation is made within the established ways of their ancestors, nothing is ever totally new – it is always the enrichment of existing structures. We do not have the ability to foresee which ambitions will and which will not find a home in the theatre of reality, only time can tell. It is only possible to explain the struggles and disruption of each age once it has made it mark and passed on, once new ways of life and new institutions have their place in the world and are part of reason. Only then can we perceive and understand. Understanding extends from the real, the merely ideal has no place before it is realized in practice and the structure of our reason is reformed. It is this fact that draws Hegel to make his most famous remark:

> The teaching of the concept, which is also history's inescapable lesson, is that it is only when actuality is mature that the ideal first appears over against the real and that the ideal apprehends this same real world in its substance and builds it up for itself into the shape of an intellectual realm. When philosophy paints its grey in grey, then has a shape of life grown old. By philosophy's grey in grey it cannot be rejuvenated but only understood. The owl of Minerva spreads its wings only with the falling of the dusk.
>
> (PR 13)

The philosophy of human order, of justice, morality and social order is the study of will – human determination – being brought into being, it is the study of something attained and still in process, it understands the achievement as all that now exists. It has no insight into what must be, no prophetic notion of how the spirit will next emancipate itself, for philosophy is dependent upon the concepts we have and these are products of mind's attainment so far. To believe that philosophy can advise or direct is to believe it has access to patterns which are not yet formed. This misconceives the nature of *mind's* becoming and the nature of reason as the product of this becoming.

There is no doubt that freedom, the emancipation of the *mind* into the world through toil, is the key to Hegel's political thought. Hegel is Rousseauean in that freedom is viewed as a discipline, it is a learned pattern of self-control. Mere freedom; capriciousness, is a form of bondage, it weakens the possibilities of life. Life's potential is developed through organization. The determination of *mind* to *be*, manifest in the 'will', is realized in social order, it creates and recreates the structures and patterns of the intellect of a people, the resource they know as their intelligence. For Hegel the power of understanding is a product of the wealth and effectiveness of actual organization.

But Hegel's work provoked a fierce debate as to the exact source of man's inspiration. Depending on how his work was read, history seemed to be either 'mind' intruding through a series of accidents or the glorification of social convention; to most neither seemed particularly desirable. Hegel's account appeared to rob man of his genius, the individual appeared to be an outcome of processes over which he had no true command. This passivity struck many as an offence to the dignity of mankind. The most remarkable of these critics was the Danish thinker Søren Kierkegaard.[5]

In his most extended philosophical tract the *Concluding Unscientific Postscript*[6] he argues for a re-examination of the eighteenth century theologian G. E. Lessing's[7] view of religious faith. Particularly, that Hegel and those who had understood religious belief as merely one aspect of the education of mankind had missed the subtlety of Lessing's work. Kierkegaard thought that Lessing had correctly argued that God's revelation as disclosed in the Scripture was, for us, inevitably phenomenal, but the vital element is the 'for us'. For men God was the impossible, the unrealistic, the divine for which they had to reach out beyond the appearance of this world. When Lessing said that individual facts of history, i.e. the resurrection of Christ, could not serve as proofs of the eternal, he did not mean that revealed religion was redundant, rather that the historical fact could only become evidence of God by an act of faith. For Kierkegaard, God could only enter our world through our determination – no fact, no structure, no church or state, no priesthood and no custom or practice could relieve the individual of the act of conviction. To follow God's will, Kierkegaard argued, was to act without ulterior motive, without justification; it was an absolute leap.

Kierkegaard's antipathy to Hegel rests upon the pivotal value Hegel gave to worldly achievement. As we have outlined, in Hegel's thought *mind* enters the world through action and organization. The world becomes the repository of human achievement and the vessel of his intelligence. For Kierkegaard, such entities as social order, the institutions and practices are genuinely phenomenal, phenomenal in the derogatory sense of a show, a mere display which distracts from the real truth. For real truth is found within our soul – the personal and intuitive sense of self, the determination which lies beyond the indulgence of compliance, conformity and weakness. Kierkegaard writes in order to rescue that aspect of ourselves which is not phenomenal but rather is eternal and essentially ours and which if it is to be true to itself must resist mere absorption into the ordinary compromises of social convenience.

In a sense Kierkegaard took the romantic notion of man to its apogee, giving priority to the struggle for personal authenticity, viewing the mundane issues of life as sterile and trivial. The ultimate romantic image of the mission or quest undertaken in the face of titanic hostility, an endurance, a challenge and an odyssey come to life in Kierkegaard's work. He shares with Rousseau a deep personal distrust of organization and merely conventional or habitual behaviour. Kierkegaard holds it to be utterly wrong to look to the world, to custom, convention and law as a moral guide. He describes such a belief as 'mimetic', that is, he identifies it as a theory whereby proper judgement is acquired environmentally, copied and emulated from those around us. Such mimicry is for Hegel the basis of our self-discipline, the disciplines which provide us with the referential system in which we can identify and develop ourselves. For Kierkegaard mimicry could achieve nothing but anonymity; the worst possible fate. We must strive for the passionate inwardness that would make us worthy before God. This earnestness Kierkegaard refers to as 'pathos'. His commitment to the 'pathetic' truth, to the veracity of intuitive and personal inspiration, confirms his loyalty to the Romantic Movement.

The point of his work is to lift men out of lives of mere emulation towards the most passionate being, this he called a 'pathetic–mimetic dialectic'; a personal striving for truth within the constrains of this world, a search for the eternal amidst the transient. Kierkegaard defines the highest truth available to an existing individual as an irresolvable subjectivity, as 'an objective uncertainty held fast in an appropriation-process of the most passionate inwardness' (CUP 182). This is not a dialectic of world progress it is the ordeal which gives the person fully and completely to themselves. It is a surrender to inspired judgement.

Kierkegaard returns to a much more traditional, more theological, model of philosophy which sees the world as flux, as inessential, as merely contingent. For 'precisely by coming into existence, everything that comes into existence demonstrates that it is not necessary, for the only thing that cannot come into existence is the necessary, because the necessary is' (PF 74). What is really true can neither pass into nor pass from existence. It, as true, must be stable, timeless and unyielding. It is indifferent to the fortuitousness of life. It is transcendent not immanent.

It follows that for Kierkegaard history holds no innate power of right or truth, for what is true or good is essentially so and its nature as past or as future is irrelevant. What matters is our lives. The past can possess right, value or truth only by our designation. Our understanding of history is no more and no less a choice than the present. Were history – the mere outturn of events – to be favoured as the embodiment of truth in place of personal determination, then responsibility would vanish.

> Freedom would then be in dire straits, something to laugh about
> and to weep over, since it would bear responsibility for what did
> not belong to it, would bring forth what necessity would devour,
> and freedom itself would be an illusion.
>
> (PF 78)

Those who are willing to accept Hegel's understanding of history, that the world embodies mind's becoming, embrace personal impotency. They allow themselves to believe that they are an outcome of alien processes. Such an understanding excludes true becoming, the act of will. 'It is ... impossible for an Hegelian to understand himself by means of his philosophy, for his philosophy helps him to understand only that which is past and finished, and a living person is surely not dead'. (CUP 272)

The Hegelian notion of objective truth, subordinating the particular to the whole, is abhorrent to Kierkegaard, for it pretends that the eternal needs to take hold of the world and in so doing pretends that we need look no further than the world for our inspiration. The real truth must be found in men's lives, for as spirits we are of this world and not of this world, we are finite and infinite, we are the point of contact, the point of crisis. Hegel's philosophy had been pernicious inasmuch as it deludes us into believing that we extract our identity from the phenomenal world. It is 'the doctrine of the superiority of the generation over the individual'. (SD 151)

Kierkegaard considered Hegel's system to be a symptom of a wider malady of his times, a willingness to abandon oneself to the crowd and subjugate oneself to some objective notion of right and good, the desire loosens one's grip on the one thing that truly matters, one's own life. The denial of the eternal, the transcendent possibility, would turn men into phenomena, externally defined, obedient to the conventions of their country, to lives of mere habit, the denial of life. Equally, the radical, 'Left Hegelian', view that reorganization of the world could free man from the abuse of other men, from exploitation, was not shared by Kierkegaard. The actual world was merely the stage upon which the real struggle for life was to be played out, the quest for true inwardness. To be drawn into the matters of the world was to be diverted from the real concern of life, namely, how to live in the presence of God. It was against this tendency that Kierkegaard wrote.

Kierkegaard's method is basically theological. What is generally held to be 'reason' is in fact nothing but pride or arrogance, to be true to the spirit required something more than reason, it required faith, courage and a willingness to take on the role of outcast. It is the very unreasonableness of our ambitions which isolates us, it is the very difficulty of the Christian legend which is the road to passionate inwardness. It is its lack of rationality which commands that we believe what we cannot know which draws us into earnestness. If belief were simply a matter of conforming to the pronouncements of the established church, then belief would not be belief. We would merely have to accept that it was the proper authority and comply, however, such easy complicity is as far from faith as one could get. One must choose utterly for the eternal, this 'leap' is absurd in the sense that the choice has no rational grounds, it stands alone and incapable of justification.

At the centre of Kierkegaard's thought is the Christian notion of 'transformation', the belief that the world we know is merely a show which will one day be washed away and totally replaced but our deeds are eternal, they are an utter declaration of our being. Each act or decision is a monumental moment of transformation, we declare ourselves before eternity. This declaration has no guide or 'context', it is ours alone. This moment of choice must be seen for what it is, the most terrible thing, an endurance, a trial. Man is not, as Hegel had argued, the gradual and evolving outcome of a synthesis of finite and infinite, rather, he is the troubled point of contact. Man is the possible in the world, that is he is the infinite which has finitude as a possibility. This paradox of abandoning infinitude in order to *be* and yet at the same time needing infinitude to give real value to life lies at the core of Kierkegaard's 'system'.

Kierkegaard's 'dialectic' develops the conflict of being and eternity, finite and infinite, possibility and actuality. This conflict is realized in man's despair, which for Kierkegaard retains its conventional theological meaning of losing all hope, of having lost faith in the power of salvation, of abandoning the eternal for the finite. However, for Kierkegaard, despair has a curiously ambivalent value. For one must despair of worldly achievement in order to abandon the values one has lazily acquired.

Another way of pursuing the dialectic is through the concept of sin. Sin is finitude, a turning away from the eternal towards the merely earthly. It is a denial of the absolute, but this must be understood as a structural part of the spirit's actualization. What Kierkegaard refers to as the ethical view, that is the attitude based on conscience and duty is overwhelmed by the need to find the true particularity, to give witness to that true self, a notion close to the Christian idea of the soul. He tells us that 'only with Christianity does eternity become essential' to man. The problem with the Ethical Life, the outlook advocated by Hegel, was that it led man into the dishonesty of seeking himself in the opinions of others, it encouraged turning the least important into the most important. For Kierkegaard this was a pretence one could sustain only by a deadening of the true sense of life, that one could have no content that one did not grant to oneself. The recognition that earthliness or finitude originate with one's own will. Men are the creation of themselves, our mode of being; indeed, the mode of being of this world is one of self-finitization.

While Kierkegaard is a great admirer of the achievement of Socrates even his innovation of conscience was formed in innocence of the religious truth. Despite his bold challenge to conventional values, his world and ours are separated by the most enormous gulf in that his age lacked the loneliness of guilt, that is, the sense of being the true origin of finitude. The Greeks lacked the awesome realization, belonging to the Christian age, that the past, the accumulated wisdom of earlier generations, cannot bind men save by their consent. The truth is not something fixed and given but made and sustained by commitment, it is always simply an assertion of the individual, unique, specific and without reason, that is, it is *absurd*.

Even in the Christian epoch, most people confront the infinite only when fate compels them to do so, when things in everyday life go badly, when routine and habit abandon us, when failure, rejection or grief are thrust upon us. For Kierkegaard the common attitudes to life which seek to quell outbreaks of such 'disorientation' are misplaced. Such evasiveness is worse than the anguish it seeks to flee and represents an attempt to avoid the sense of the uttermost. Here despair comes into life as a illness, a sickness of hiding from oneself which can lead to a cycle of self-deceit a growing impermeability. It is a disease which takes upon itself all the evasive stratagems of an addictive illness; the attempt to lose oneself in the crowd, the pretence of conventionality and conformity, a diverting pastime, or the retreat into daydreams and fantasy. These symptoms belong to the type of personality Kierkegaard refers to as the self which dwells in inauthentic despair. This 'normally alienated' individual is so lost that a momentary vision of his truth, utter inwardness, fills him with unease and even terror. At this point either madness or faith will develop.

Kierkegaard argues that it is to this inauthenticity that Hegel's theory of the *Sittlichkeit* has made its appeal, for it seeks to legitimize the objectivity of value. Hegel has given intellectual respectability to those who wish to numb their anguish. The notion of 'objective becoming' has offered yet another ploy to those who seek to live inauthentically, to define themselves through the lives of others.

However we are concerned with Kierkegaard's positive philosophy, that is, his view of true or authentic being, that being which achieves the spiritual level and pursues its own most passionate inwardness. Epistemologically, Kierkegaard is close to Hume in believing in a world that is at root accidental, transient, and where contingent knowledge is constructed solely from our experience. However, whereas Hume had considered that his philosophy made religion appear ridiculous, Kierkegaard believes that only within such an epistemology does religion makes sense, for the essence of faith is that it must have no ground but our consent. It must rest utterly upon our self moved willingness to believe. Its demands are beyond conceptual reasoning and require a commitment which is absurd in any expressible terms. The requirement of faith isolates; it makes the individual take upon himself his life, pursue that path which is distinctly his. Faith is the way of knowing which liberates the individual from the bonds of this world, of convention, of mimicry, of passivity and hollow fatalism.

As for a definition of faith, Kierkegaard says we must understand it as that state that is without despair, that rests utterly in possibility, i.e. hope and prayer.

> The formula for that state in which there is no despair at all: in relating itself to itself and in wanting to be itself, the self is grounded transparently in the power which established it. Which formula in turn ... is the definition of faith.
>
> (SD 165)

This capacity is always more than mere knowledge. It is a venture which places one's established life, habits and recognitions in peril. It is a choice, which rests entirely with the individual. It is the affirmation of one's spirit, a deed unique and specific, lacking the consolation of fitting in with conventional logic or morality. It is not an act but a 'making', a poetic moment without portent, inaccessible to speculative reasoning. It is a yearning which only total commitment to an inexpressible infinite can bring to pass.

Kierkegaard argues that the ethical level, the type of morality advocated in Hegel's *Sittlichkeit*, ought to be understood as rooted in retrospection, an attempt to comprehend oneself by seeing oneself as an outcome, as the work of former generations. Kierkegaard describes this conception as 'ethnical' meaning that by giving accent to this point of view we subjugate our particularity to the culture. Kierkegaard tells us that for the religious outlook, the Christian view, the reverse is the case, one has to 'do the truth' (R 189) and this requires that one has to return to one's true insta-bility; a return he termed 'repetition'. His task is to give eternity its true force and to pursue inwardness or freedom in earnest. Repetition is the demand that we return to ourselves as the true continuity, that we set aside all that is alien and turn to what is ours throughout the flux of life; it is our salvation and it asserts what is eternally true. It is the earnestness of existence (R 133). 'In the individual repetition appears as a task for freedom, in which the question becomes that of saving one's personality from being volatized and, so to speak, a pawn to events.' (R 315)

Repetition is Kierkegaard's conception of the true passion, of the transcendental demand that we rescue what is truly ours amidst 'the fractions of the world'. It is the task of philosophy to give right to this passion, to humiliate the forces that would subdue it with 'consol-ation'. In the realm of freedom, the Hegelian system has done harm which Kierkegaard is attempting to correct, for by placing the development of 'mind' in the objective or collective sphere, that is, by giving history the task of actualization of spirit, Hegel's philoso-phy made the transcendent appear redundant and superfluous, it distracts us and ties us to an ethnic identity. The spiritual level embodies the awareness that 'eternity is the true repetition'. (R 133)

> Repetition is a movement via the transcendent in which each moment is separated from the former by a chasm. The subject has, objectively, the uncertainty; but it is this which precisely increases the tension of that infinite person which constitutes his inward-ness. The truth is precisely the venture which chooses an objective uncertainty with the passion of the infinite.
>
> (CUP 182)

What the spiritual has introduced into life can be characterized in a number of ways, *nothing, possibility, anxiety, freedom* or *eternity*. This saves man from the phenomenal, from the everyday world of events and cares and makes him the care of himself. One charges oneself with the struggle for the upmost degree of subjectivity for that, for Kierkegaard, is truth. One must set out on the path of a constant striving. In this venture the only way society or 'culture' may help is 'by making the difficulties greater' (CUP 536), to accentuate despair. The paradox of the sickness is that one ought to feel unwell. For Kierkegaard, the point of his work was to inspire a hunger for being, to make demands of life, or rather to take up life's demand that we should require of ourselves our ownmost existence.

The state of innocence lost in the Fall was our oneness with the world. Adam found nothing. Nothing is the phenomenal manifestation of our not being amidst the finite but being the origin of finitude. Knowledge of nothing is anxiety. Anxiety is the infinite possibility understood. The grace that Adam lost was the grace of innocence to live with anxiety latent in our being. 'Anxiety is freedom's actuality as the possibility of possibility' (CA 42). It is our true self-recognition. In a much quoted passage he says that 'Anxiety may be compared with dizziness. He whose eye happens to look down into the yawning abyss becomes dizzy' (CA 61). For to look or not to look are always equally possible; in order to look one must look and in order not to look one must desist from looking. Once the sense of freedom has arrived, unfreedom, the finite, the habits of conventional behaviour all become the work of freedom; they are re-established in the context of choice. At this stage, men find life weighed with guilt; responsibility before God – the absolute pure possibility.

This responsibility is spirit's true earnestness, its recognition of itself as the origin of itself. At this point the spirit has found its highest state; an openness to being which contrasts with that self which views itself as given, the product of alien forces; social, genetic, fateful. With earnestness, Kierkegaard reaches his ultimate concept. In a note he remarks, 'inwardness is earnestness ... when inwardness is missing, the spirit is finitized – inwardness is the eternal' (CA 208). Anxiety consumes all finite ends; it is the root to inwardness and to the truly earnest life (CA 155), anxiety is an education in infinitude. Anxiety is the actualization of our most categorical condition; it is freedom.

The issue raised by the conflict between Hegel and Kierkegaard is essential to our understanding of freedom. For we are presented with the alternative of viewing freedom as our immediate possession, as something we must find beyond the appearance of the world, or as our mediated possession, as something only enjoyed insofar as we master this world of appearances. Kierkegaard's 'spirit' is essentially Kant's noumenon, which is to say that Kant's noumenon is essentially the Christian idea of a human spirit, as a real divine creation set into a fallen world of illusions and error. The phenomenal idea of freedom, that is, the image of freedom as the skill of our attaining what we set ourselves to achieve is, then, a very radical critique of the tradition we have inherited, and it is this phenomenal notion of freedom which has been so influential in the thought of the last two centuries. But Kierkegaard's work reveals a very important issue which this view of the world must confront, namely, 'amidst the conventions of reason, who am I?'

Sartre

3
The Condition of Consciousness

No interpretation can do justice to such a fruitful thinker as Jean-Paul Sartre.[1] However, the assertion that an understanding of human freedom is the key to Sartre's thought has much to commend it, indeed, an exploration of his idea of freedom entails an extensive treatment of his work.

Sartre was an intellectual very much in the French tradition of the great author with its attendant obligation to raise the prospect of humanity. This was a responsibility for which he was well equipped and well disposed; he never doubted that he had a role to play in the education of mankind, in its deliverance from ignorance and oppression. His vitality, range of interests and verbosity were legendary. During his life-time he attained a stature which was and will probably remain without equal and which will almost certainly be difficult for later generations and for the non-Frenchman to comprehend. For thirty years he effectively held state office of Moral Critic.

Sartre's work is a unique corpus, a record of his own interests and orientations, and an assembly of influences. In trying to understand Sartre's thought there is good reason to pay regard to these influences largely because it was something of a character trait of his to align himself with movements and schools.

Generally he was taught in the Cartesian tradition and was greatly impressed by that philosopher's search for certain knowledge. The consequent importance of propositional logic and the association of truth with validity are perhaps rather quaint aspects of thought which colour his work. In Sartre's early work we find an aspiring writer with views about the nature of mind, combined with a philosopher unafraid to devote very considerable attention to what are sometimes rather irksome and archaic technical problems. The result is a rather schizoid output composed of, on the one hand deeply personal documents including a novel and some short stories and, on the other, a number of technical works, contributions to a genre of philosophy with all its associated idiosyncrasies, obscure quarrels and disputes.

* * *

Objects ought not to touch, since they are not alive. You use them you put them back in their place, you live amongst them: they are useful, nothing more. But they touch me, it's unbearable. I am afraid of entering into contact with them, just as if they were living animals.

(N 22)

The attitude attributed to Roquentin in *Nausea*[2] discloses the dominant preoccupation of Sartre's thought; the paradox that the real material world is both the very stuff of our lives and a repulsive alien other. It is beyond us, outside our immediate self-possession, yet totally captivating. It is, at once, a frightening turmoil and our home. Sartre displays an almost Lutheran awareness that man is the sole source of sense and order in a chaotic world and yet tragically frail and vulnerable, that the veneer of stability is precariously thin.

The 'nausea' to which the book alludes is the realization of our inescapable dependence upon a capricious world, that this is to be the substance of our lives. It is the recognition of a dependence which violates our innate sense of self-possession.

Sartre as a young man was in the habit of explaining his ideas in terms of the concept of *contingency*. By this he meant to indicate that the world was without reason or pattern and that this nonsense had to be accepted as the content of men's lives. *Nausea* reveals the philosophy, or rather, the view of the world, which Sartre held at the time he discovered Husserl's[3] thought, now generally referred to as Phenomenology.[4] It was an outlook he felt Phenomenology would help him to explore, develop and articulate, the significant point being that for Sartre. Phenomenology was employed to express an already developed view of the world, i.e. one characterized by contingency. The initial problem in Sartre's work therefore relates to the compatibility of Husserl's method and Sartre's philosophy.

Sartre was introduced to the thought of Husserl in the early thirties and his enthusiasm lasted to the beginning of World War II and his period of intense study of Heidegger. He believed

Phenomenology, in its quest to take things as they appeared, could make philosophy out of everyday objects and events. It seemed to offer Sartre an intellectual framework through which his own type of realism could be developed. (IT 46)

Phenomenology like all schools of thought has its obsessions, its technical vocabulary and esoteric disputes. With Brentano, Phenomenology had begun as part of the late nineteenth century reaction to Idealism and systematic philosophy. Brentano was an empiricist of the Lockean school and believed that consciousness was composed of a content other than itself. That is, consciousness is always directed at an object. As a psychologist Brentano's problem was to understand the object of a consciousness preoccupied with belief, emotion, imagination and hallucination. He called these pseudo-objects 'intentional', meaning they were a world reconstructed by mood or correlative of states of mind. While Brentano's thought was experimental and produced no finished system or dogma he established a method which placed mood and attitude at the core of its realism.

Husserl returned to the dominant tradition of European thought, that of Descartes and Kant, by seeking that which is necessarily true. Husserl was a mathematician and his ambition was to construct a philosophy which would resist the slide into scepticism and complacency. He believed that ordinary thought was peppered with unacknowledged assumptions and presuppositions, and that philosophy tended to accept rather than demolish this mysticism. He held consciousness to possess an essential structure which is necessary and universal and which it is the job of philosophy to disclose and defend.

Husserl offers an attack upon Hegel's system and logic, one which appealed to his generation's understanding of Hegel. In short, he was hostile to the idea that thought is radically artificial, i.e. created by man, a set of conventional practices, relative to place and time. Even though most thought might be composed of beliefs or opinions it was quite wrong for philosophy simply to accept that this must be the case. It was the duty of philosophy to find the universal structures that lay behind human cognition, to create a science of philosophy. Like Descartes, Husserl believed that reflection upon consciousness would reveal intellectual processes which were incontrovertible. What is sought are essential structures which all people everywhere use to order experience. In this sense it is a search for categories in the Kantian meaning of the term.

Like Descartes' thought Phenomenology is presented as a method, a way of proceeding with as few presupposition as could be conceived. It is the scrupulous examination of consciousness in order to discern the necessary and universal truths of experience. Husserl's method consisted of a 'reduction' which sought to concentrate attention on the way things revealed themselves. No distinction can be made between what is perceived and the perception of it. Perception is the essences of consciousness. We must learn to avoid prefacing reflection by declaring that some thing or event belongs to reality or imagination or emotion. That is, we must suspend or 'bracket' the existential judgement. This move is referred to as the *epoché*. Instead we are encouraged to describe the character set before consciousness and use only this description as the foundation of our examination of experience. This gives us the meaning of the motto of Phenomenology 'to the things themselves'.

Phenomenology appealed to Sartre because it accepts the diversity of the world and aims to confront the opulence of experience without dulling or blunting it. Phenomenology aims to capture the flux of immediate consciousness by postponing questions of the origin of data or the nature of mind. By this means Phenomenologists hold we can reach an impersonal base, a universal 'consciousness'. Such a consciousness was to dominate Sartre's thought. Husserl's philosophy is difficult. His style of writing and the manner in which his ideas developed make any summary rather problematic. Our principal concern is what Sartre understood Phenomenology to be and this itself is an esoteric reading of an obscure philosophy. Nor should it be assumed that Sartre's re-working of the ideas of Phenomenology can be assembled to form a single coherent vision. There is no definitive Sartrean understanding of Phenomenology, the books and essays which are in this style do not present a consistent doctrine or method but show developments of an interest, experiments in which Sartre used what he had learned from Husserl mixed with other influences, such as, Bergson, Nietzsche and Heidegger, in an attempt to articulate his own abiding interests.

Sartre and Husserl are united in holding a view of consciousness as pure and self-given, as possessing a structure which, because it is produced by consciousness itself, was permanent and unchanging. Both also maintain that all consciousness is consciousness of something other than itself. To think of consciousness separate from the series of appearances which manifest its being is to construct something where there is nothing, for consciousness is known only by its content.

Sartre says, in his first published work, 'For consciousness, to exist is to be conscious of its existence. It appears as pure spontaneity, confronting a world of things which is sheer inertness'.[5] Sartre pictures consciousness as pure motion, 'a bursting [éclatement] towards the world' and says that 'there is nothing in it but movement of fleeing itself, a sliding beyond itself', and 'to be is to fly out into the world, to spring from the nothingness of the world and of consciousness in order suddenly to burst out as consciousness-in-the-world' (I 5). For Sartre 'consciousness has no "inside". It is just this being beyond itself, this absolute flight, this refusal to be a substance which makes it a consciousness' (ibid.). In these remarks we see the first intimations of Sartre's notion of consciousness as nothingness.

The actual structure of the world beyond us, the substance which consciousness adopts as its content, is necessarily a mystery. There should be no attempt, the Phenomenologists believe, to think of essence as dwelling in the thing itself. 'Consciousness and the world are given in one stroke: essentially external to consciousness, the world is nevertheless essentially relative to consciousness' (ibid.). For Husserl and his followers, and in this respect Sartre can be counted as one of his followers, consciousness is constituted in the intentional act.

> Imagine for a moment a connected series of bursts which tear us out of ourselves, which do not even allow to an 'ourselves' the leisure of composing ourselves behind them, but which instead throw us beyond them into the dry dust of the world, on to the plain earth, amidst things. Imagine us thus rejected and abandoned by our own natures in an indifferent, hostile, and restive world – you will then have grasped the profound meaning of the discovery which Husserl expresses in his famous phrase. 'All consciousness is consciousness of something'.
>
> (I 5)

In what amounts to a reversal of historical usage reality is 'transcendent', that is, beyond consciousness. Consciousness was the ground of experience but not the content. This ground is referred to by Sartre as the 'Transcendental Field'. Indeed as all reality is transcendent so consciousness is itself nothing.

Sartre's early essays are concerned with the operation of mind, with emotions, imagination and perception. In each of these matters his enthusiasm is for the material world as the sole existing thing. Sartre sees the imaginary aspect of experience as being intentionality working against the real. By turning to the imaginary, it is almost as if we abuse the situation in which we find ourselves. This hostility to the imagination was to be a key to Sartre's ideas on art and literature and to his notion of the committed artist. In order to understand this hostility we must return to the intellectual root of Sartre's thought, to the *cogito*.

The spontaneity of the *cogito* is the one principle Sartre was to hold unswervingly throughout his life. In *The Psychology of the Imagination* Sartre offers the first outline of his notion of mind as emptiness. This emptiness is a variation upon the *cogito* and is the most significant innovation of Sartre's entire philosophy. The technical question of how nothing could be the inspired source of intentional acts was to dominate his early work, an issue which remained unsettled until *Being and Nothingness*.[6]

In these essays Sartre tended to emphasize the significance to everyday life of the Phenomenological attitude. His desire for a general popular awareness of the theory of intentionality rests on two beliefs; firstly that Phenomenology has significance not just to psychology, but it also has therapeutic potential for psychiatry. Secondly, the political belief that a disciplined attitude to the imagination is a prerequisite for full being, that used without the strictures of Phenomenology the imagination is capable of being debilitating and alienating, that Phenomenology can emancipate men from the dulling mythologies which Nietzsche had so vividly traced.

The Transcendence of the Ego[7] is a manifesto for Sartre's thought it presents, in foetal form, his central interests and preoccupations. These include:

1. the essential clarity and transparency of consciousness
2. the generation of consciousness from 'nothing'
3. the impersonality of consciousness's underlying spontaneity
4. the synthetic nature of the self or *ego*.

As a manifesto it proclaims that the activity of intellectual criticism is not an indulgent peculiarity belonging to a certain character type but is central to the life of man, to civilization, and history, giving man an insight into the original impersonal level of awareness, and a new sense of possibility.

The Transcendence of the Ego attempts to confront the problems of Husserl's conception of a 'transcendent personality'. For Sartre, personality is developed as a product of the anxiety and frailty of being. It is for the sake of sanity that we conjure out of the chaos of the flux a theme, a self, a synthetic principle of unity. For Sartre, Phenomenology is not an idle curiosity for intellectuals but is the key to a fresh vitality an understanding of man's hold on life, cleansed of its isolation and fear, a really human, social and communal awareness. Husserl, by adopting an innate personality, something like Christian soul, has betrayed the purifying strength of Phenomenology, he has surrendered the vision of objective being that Phenomenology, in its original form, had held as its promise.

> For centuries we have not felt in philosophy so realistic a current. The Phenomenologists have plunged man back into the world; they have given full measure to man's agonies and sufferings, and also to his rebellions. Unfortunately, as long as the I remains a structure of absolute consciousness, one will still be able to reproach Phenomenology for being an escapist doctrine, for again pulling a part of man out of the world and, in that way, turning our attention from the real problems.
>
> (TE 105)

This discloses not merely the argument of *The Transcendence of the Ego* but the burden of Sartre's philosophy.

Kant's notion that reality is constituted by mind is obviously at the heart of Phenomenology and the central principle of Sartre's work. For the Phenomenologists the material world is transcendent. It is beyond us in the sense that it is utterly unlike consciousness, it is dead and solid. Consciousness is the power of transcendence, it is alive, it remains beyond the material. Indeed the issue which Sartre addresses in *The Transcendence of the Ego* is Kantian, in that Kant's work left open the matter of whether the transcendental subject was a universal ground for which human particularity was phenomenal or whether it was necessarily and essentially particular, a soul or a self, that is to say, real in the metaphysical sense. It is this 'reality' of the self which Sartre is disputing with Husserl. Indeed, in Sartre's eyes the emancipating power of Phenomenology rests upon the destruction of just such an innate self.

> A pure consciousness is absolute quite simply because it is con-
> sciousness of itself. It is all lightness, all translucence .... All the
> results of Phenomenology begin to crumble if the I is not by the
> same title as the world, a relative existent; that is to say, an object
> for consciousness.
>
> (TE 42)

Sartre's primary argument against Husserl, is that such a residual
substantive self would be an opacity in the heart of consciousness.
Giving consciousness innate quality, he argued, deprived it of the
agility it required to explain awareness.

Sartre argues that it is consciousness, not the self, the substantive
particular human character, which is transcendental. Consciousness
surpasses all content. It is utter spontaneity – this instantaneous-
ness gives Phenomenology its basic rule that no distinction is possible between appearance and being (TE 63). Consciousness is the
source of unity and the source of our sense of isolation.

> [T]he type of existence of consciousness is to be consciousness of
> itself. And consciousness is aware of itself in so far as it is con-
> sciousness of a transcendent object. All is therefore clear and
> lucid in consciousness: the object with its characteristic opacity is
> before consciousness, but consciousness is purely and simply
> consciousness of being consciousness of that object.
>
> (TE 40)

Consciousness, according to this view, unifies because it is merely
the endless escape of consciousness from any content it might
adopt. For Phenomenology all consciousness is 'consciousness of...',
that is, it is intentional. To give the self an innate being deprived
consciousness of being. For the same reason, consciousness is the
foundation of individuality for only consciousness is capable of limiting itself. The sense of isolation which each consciousness wit-
nesses is not an expression of some substantive transcendental
particularity but a product of the utter inwardness of consciousness.

Sartre goes on to define the ego as 'the spontaneous, transcendent unification of our states and our actions' (TE 76). This
unification is enacted with the paradoxical objective of knowing its
own freedom, of being aware of what it is not. The synthetic ego is,
therefore, an intentional construct of consciousness created in the
effort of preserving its own spontaneity.

Consciousness gives itself identity, a purposeful character and the ability to recognize itself as a force within the temporal flux, that is, a sense of continuity, by projecting its own creative power onto a pretended transcendent object. However, consciousness is only aware of itself as a self, never as pure spontaneity, as to know pure spontaneity is to know no identity at all. Hence, 'everything happens as though the ego were of consciousness, with only this particular and essential difference: that the ego is opaque to consciousness' (TE 85). This inability to think itself without projecting itself into a self is what Sartre calls the intimacy of the self. Whenever consciousness is turned upon itself it finds a self, an illusory transcendent point of origin.

The self therefore, always an inadequate realization of consciousness, represents something alien, and is recognized as degraded, as being not consciousness. Immediate consciousness is then left with the realization that it is other than the world, that it is incapable of objectification. Consciousness feels itself to be unabsorbed by the world, as 'a pure form of being, anterior to all being'; as pure vitality finding itself as an endless potentiality.

These remarks compose the foundation of Sartre's philosophy; an individuality constructed by determination, without an essential character, nature or destiny. As the *ego* is an ideal unity abstracted from the actual material world, synthesized from performance, its possessor has no superior access to its own nature. We all are solely a being in the world. The Sartrean *self* is essentially 'objective' and public. The tantalizing but deceptive intimacy of the 'me' creates the mirage of the *self* as a permanent point of origin, a personal nature, whereas in fact the *self* can be known only as things are known; as a series of relations. Hence Sartre's dictum that consciousness has no privileged relation to its *self*.

Perhaps of even more significance in the development of Sartre's thought is the notion of duality that Phenomenology suggested to him. Sartre moulded Phenomenology into a metaphysics and used it to portray a radical schism in nature; two types of being. He grants consciousness an awareness of its unique status distinct from and yet entirely dependent upon an alien material world.

[Consciousness], purified of all its egological structure, recovers its primary transparency. In a sense, it is nothing, since all physical, psycho-physical, and psychic objects, all truths, all values are outside of it …. But this nothing is all since it is consciousness of all these objects.

(TE 93)

This recognition of the original transparency of consciousness represents the 'doctrine' of *The Transcendence of the Ego*. As the self is not the owner of consciousness but the object of consciousness, consciousness itself is impersonal. The purifying reflection delivers men from isolation and egotism to an absolute, essential and impersonal consciousness.

We may therefore formulate our thesis: transcendental consciousness is an impersonal spontaneity. It determines its existence at each instant, without our being able to conceive anything before it. Thus each instant of our conscious life reveals to us a creation ex nihilo. Not a new arrangement but a new existence.

(TE 99)

This reveals the core of Sartre's early thought, the exhilaration and anxiety of spontaneous self-creation from nothing, the awareness of nothingness. Phenomenology becomes a way of dealing with the 'anxiety which is imposed on us and which we cannot avoid' (TE 103). This existential Phenomenology is to be the foundation of a psychology of the original project and an account of human relations based upon the reality of personality. It will also be the beginning of a campaign to acknowledge the possibility of comprehensive self-creation, making known to a wider public the fact of the ubiquitous nature of consciousness. Sartre's Phenomenology will be a vital and potent political force.

It has always seemed to me that a working hypothesis as fruitful as historical materialism never needed for a foundation the absurdity which is metaphysical materialism. In fact, it is not necessary that the object precede the subject for spiritual pseudo-values to vanish and for ethics to find its basis in reality. It is enough that the me be contemporaneous with the World, and that the subject–object duality, which is purely logical, definitively disappears from the philosophical preoccupations …. No more is needed in the way of a philosophical foundation for an ethics and a politics which are absolutely positive.

(TE 106)

The Transcendence of the Ego proffers a manifesto for the Phenomenological reduction. The ultimate equality of mankind is no longer dependent upon some historical or sociological analysis, but is inherent in our psychological constitution. For if the self is synthetic, an ideal construct of our encounters, then men have immediate access to their original homogeneity and absolute access to one another. Sartre believes himself to have developed a theory of the radical commonality of mankind.

But for this to be a forceful political philosophy it had to be more than a theory, and Sartre's argument is that his Phenomenology merely gives a coherent account of what is true for ordinary people in everyday life. His is not an analysis of what life might be but a description of the actual structure of our being. Once it is commonly recognized that the self is not essential to our being, the purifying reflection will become the key to a fresh humanism.

> Reduction seems capable of being performed only at the end of lengthy study. It appears, then, as a knowledgeable operation, which confers on it a sort of gratuitousness. On the other hand, if a simple act of reflection suffices in order for conscious spontaneity to tear itself abruptly away from the I and be given as independent, then the epoché is no longer an intellectual method, it is an anxiety which is imposed on us and which we cannot avoid, it is both a pure event of transcendental origin and an ever possible accident of our daily life. (TE 103)

This is Sartre's contribution to the theory of Phenomenology. The whole population dwells within reflective reach of a demystified understanding of consciousness and, hence, of its humanity, a clarity which holds the possibility of a totally frank self-disclosure.

Phenomenology not only takes us to the things themselves but takes us to the essential universal man, stripped of all his accidental or situational conditions. Phenomenology for Sartre reveals the mythology of the 'natural self', that it is a construction, the response to a pervasive fear for which the reductive exercise can be an emancipation, a cure.

For Sartre, the key element of Husserl's Phenomenology is the view that consciousness is intentional; it is always of something other than itself. This rests upon acceptance of the traditional presumption that what we refer to as consciousness is a simple substance, that consciousness is self given, self-originated and spontaneous. Sartre declares that 'as consciousness makes itself, it is never anything but what it appears to be ... consciousness is itself the fact, the signification, and the thing signified (E 46). This transparency of consciousness – self-evident recognition of its own activities – lies at the root of Sartre's rationalism; there is a world and there is human activity and that is all. Again it should be emphasized that it is the return to a pre-Hegelian *cogito* which distinguishes the Phenomenology of Husserl and Sartre from *The Phenomenology of Spirit*. In summary, by grounding his thought on the Cartesian doctrine of the simple substance, Sartre has developed a theory of the radical commonality of mankind.

* * *

The Transcendence of the Ego initiated a decline in Sartre's enthusiasm for Husserl. The problem of the discrete ego was associated with an issue which was to draw Sartre away from Husserl – the issue of the inter-relation of minds.

> Gradually without my fully realizing it, the difficulties were piling up and a deeper and deeper gulf was separating me from Husserl. I reverted to seeking a realist solution. In particular, although I had numerous ideas concerning the knowledge of others, I could take them only if I had solidly assured myself that two distinct consciousnesses did indeed perceive the same world.
>
> (WO 184)

It was the problem of 'others' that was to lead from the Phenomenology of *The Transcendence of the Ego* to the ontology of *Being and Nothingness*. He says, 'It was to escape this Husserlian impasse [of solipsism] that I turned towards Heidegger' (ibid.). But his qualms were not limited to this problem for Sartre also sought a philosophy of his time, reflecting the turmoil of Spain and the violence of Hitlerism, a philosophy 'that was not just a contemplation but a wisdom, a heroism, a holiness', indeed he now wanted a 'pathetic' philosophy (WD 185). It was at this time that an essay by Heidegger, 'What is Metaphysics?', was translated into French.

Sartre had read Heidegger in an apparently rather cursory fashion during his months in Berlin. There is no doubt that at that time he found Husserl the more impressive writer. In his journals of 1940 he recalls that:

Husserl had gripped me. I saw everything through the perspect-
ives of his philosophy – which was in any case more accessible to
me, thanks to its semblance of Cartesianism …. I did begin
Heidegger and read fifty pages of him, but the difficulty of the
vocabulary put me off.

(WD 185)

But Corbin's translation of Heidegger's 1928 inaugural lecture
was a turning point in Sartre's intellectual development; the
moment he began to use *nothingness* as the central concept of his
thought. The idea of nothingness [*le Néant*], a correlate of the transparency of consciousness and of the *cogito*, was to come to dominate Sartre's thought. Sartrean ontology was to declare that the
world is and consciousness is not. 'The world exists for consciousness insofar as it is concretely and singularly what the world
is not' (WD 182). The key to Sartre's work is that transparency,
nothingness and freedom mutually define one another.

Before we move on to the ontology of *Being and Nothingness* it
might be helpful to look at the thesis of *What is Metaphysics?* and try to
isolate what Sartre learned from Heidegger's essay. We have Sartre's
own testament that reading Corbin's translation marked a turning
point and was the root of his own central idea of the dynamic unfolding of the *Néant*. Indeed it is probably not too strong to claim that his
war-time reading of *Sein und Zeit* was to be entirely coloured by the
formulations developed from *What is Metaphysics?* It ought to be
emphasized that the strangeness of Heidegger's thought means that
all readings are an effort of interpretation in a particularly direct
sense, and we should not pretend that there is any 'solid' ground
behind the interpretations, i.e. an orthodoxy. Hence we should keep
in mind the very real difficulty of the essay and the problem of what
Heidegger understood by the idea of Nothing [*Nichts*].

Heidegger's philosophy seeks to make a new beginning in a way
that is almost diametrically opposite to the 'new beginning' of
Husserl. Heidegger believed that philosophy ought to cast the
scientific attitude aside. Science has perverted our relation to the
world, to one another and to ourselves. The task of philosophy is to
free mankind from this hideous creed not to emulate it. Heidegger
insists we must not confuse 'exactness' with 'strictness', that is, we
must not conflate the mania for quantification found in the scientific
attitude with the intensity of philosophy. Heidegger's quest for a
new beginning takes us back to the pre-Socratics, to a time before

philosophy had acquired the mannerisms of the Academy. These affectations are extremely difficult to isolate because our whole culture is built upon them, they are implicit in our language. Indeed, Heidegger's main task is to rescue language so that it can once again take hold of the world with a simple frankness.

The problem for Heidegger is how to turn to the world without using the tainted resources of the intellect, he attempts a number of ways to do this all of which have at their centre the idea of Being [*Sein*]. Being cannot be expressed but is the foundation of our life, of our being-here [*Da-sein*]. Heidegger believes that the pre-Socratic thinkers' wonder of our ability to question being marks the origin of our awareness of being distinct from what is. Heidegger holds language to be intimately connected with this peculiarity, for it marks a 'primordial' turning to being, but again, one which has become strained. However, great poetry has the capacity to renew language's original lust for Being, it restores something of its original sense of awe. In the poetry of Hesse, Rilke, Trekl and, most notably, in that of Hölderlin, wonder returns to language and speech takes on its power to reveal. Another way of turning to Being is to face death without the amelioration and blandishments of conventional religion or 'science'. We will return to this later.

Heidegger opens his inaugural lecture with a critical description of science. He thereby furthers the attitude, first voiced by Rousseau in his *Discourses*, that what has been perceived as progress has in fact been decadence, a departure from the rich fullness of life. His argument is involved; science has fostered a certain outlook, a way of attending to the world or to 'Being'. It allows the 'object' first and last word. Its order is one of submission to 'what-is' and rejection of all else, it excludes and what it excludes cannot be specified, quantified or measured, hence, for science, it is nothing. Here Heidegger makes one of the most controversial moves in twentieth century thought, for he asks; 'What about this Nothing?' (WM 358). Science has encouraged man to view himself as a thing among things. This attitude has been a vital part of what Heidegger sees as the brutalization of mankind. We might say that he has become unthinking except that the opposite is true – he has become all too 'thinking', and has utterly immersed himself in his impoverished activity of world-taking.

However, what is not clear is quite why turning to 'nothing' should be a way out of this cycle of impoverishment. Indeed it remains unclear just as what exactly he means by *nothing*. The aim of *What is Metaphysics?* is to take man beyond things to 'an attunement which takes possession of the essential man so that he may come to experience Being in Nothing' (WM 386), to experience that 'marvel of marvels: that what-is is'. It is to enrich contemplation. Heidegger argues that science, while adopting an attitude of superior indifference, abandons *nothing* as that which 'is not'. But what is this 'not'? What gives us the right to dismiss all negation as pure emptiness, an abstract imaginary category 'existing' only in 'mental' exercise? This negligence engendered the Cartesian division of the world into stuff and ideas, a realm of things and a realm of 'mind' or 'spirit', the dualism which Heidegger considered the source of our perversity.

For Heidegger all negation, all questioning, owes its existence to the primal *nothing*. We cannot expect reason to lead us to *nothing* for reason employs the logic of negativity and negativity is an aspect of *nothing*, one of its showings. *Nothing* must be 'given in advance' (WM 362). On the same page Heidegger goes on to say:

Where shall we find Nothing? In order to find something must we not know beforehand that it is there? Indeed we must! First and foremost we can only look if we have presupposed the presence of a thing to be looked for. But here the thing we are looking for is Nothing. Is there after all a seeking without pre-supposition, a seeking complimented by a pure finding?

It is 'when we are not absorbed in things or our own selves' that a 'wholeness' comes over us. It is at this point that the influence of Kierkegaard is most apparent, for the mood which reveals this wholeness is dread [Angst] (WM 368).

All things, and we with them, sink into a surf of indifference. But not in the sense that everything simply disappears; rather, in the very act of drawing away from us everything turns towards us. This withdrawal of what-is-in-totality, which then crowds round us in dread, this is what oppresses us. There is nothing to hold on to. The only thing that remains and overwhelms us whilst what-is slips away, in the 'nothing'.
Dread reveals Nothing.

(WM 366)

As with Kierkegaard's 'sickness' we fight the realization of dread, we seek diversion and occupation which will draw us into the what-is and away from the eerie, empty silence of Nothing.

> Only in the clear night of dread's Nothingness is what-is as such revealed in all its original overtness: that it 'is' and is not Nothing. This verbal appendix 'and not Nothing' is, however, not an a posteriori explanation but an a priori which alone makes possible any revelation of what-is, the essence of Nothing as original nihilation lies in this: that it alone brings Da-sein face to face with what-is as such.
>
> (WM 369)

This states more clearly than any other part of the essay that *nothing* 'is'. But the exact relationship between 'what-is', *nothing* and *Dasein* is very hard to pin down, for Heidegger *Dasein* must make its being, but equally it must employ *nothing*. It is by 'projecting into *nothing*' that *Dasein* goes beyond the totality of what-is, that is, it achieves transcendence. This transcendence is the 'essential basis' of its relation to what-is. Hence 'Nothing is that which makes the revelation of what-is as such possible for our human existence'.

Herein lies the germ of Sartre's adaptation of Heidegger's argument, of effectively dispensing with *Dasein*, the notional point of being-here, and replacing it with 'nothingness', a sort of spirit, a Cartesian simple substance which is pure nihilation. It has been argued that this is exactly what Heidegger sought to avoid, an atomized determination, because he believed that this idea was itself deeply infected with the ethos of what-is. The notion of 'my nothingness' would have been a nonsense to Heidegger but for Sartre 'nothingness' is a personal possession, and this reduction of Heidegger's notion made Sartre's *nothing* both more accessible and less challenging than the almost impenetrable ideas of Heidegger.

Heidegger's view of nothing is that of a path to enrichment, what might elsewhere be called a spiritual view. It is a call to courage in the face of an overwhelming propaganda of material reason. 'Courage knows, in the abyss of terror, the all-but untrodden region of Being' (WM 386). *Nothing*, experienced as the anxiety of uncertainty, guides us towards a renewed wonder at Being which brings the prospect of a reassessment of the ground of all phenomena. He makes his call to thinkers and to metaphysicians, 'to experience in *nothing* the vastness of that which gives every being the warrant to be. (WM 385) *Nothing* is human possibility, it restores what is ours from the mystification of habitual judgement, from science.

By the time of the composition of the *War Journals* Sartre recognized Nothingness to be the key idea of his work. But for Sartre 'nothingness' [*le Néant*] was not the path to Being [*L'être*] but the being of transcendence. For Heidegger *nothing* stood on the far side of being and could draw men more reverently towards being but Sartre's 'nothingness' [*le Néant*] is a personal possession, an individual experience. It is a negative awareness that one is not 'this' or 'that' but is the determination which is the source of experience. Each individual was the source of the power which governs their particular experience. The substance of consciousness is always a 'choice'. He thereby returns to the natural individual which Heidegger considered a product of brutalization.

Against this Sartre characterized 'being' as extension, reviving one of the elements of Descartes' dualism. Indeed Sartre's dualism, the two forms of being characterized as the 'in-itself' and the 'for-itself', rests on the Cartesian notion of the world as extension known by mind, the simple substance. In Notebook Eleven of his journal he writes:

> It is the being of consciousness not to be extension. In other words, the not is an existential characteristic. This will be understood at once if the following two judgements are compared: extension is not consciousness, and consciousness is not extended.
>
> (WD 176)

For consciousness to escape from the extension which surrounds it, it must not only be not extension it must also be *nothing*, it must be 'by not being what it is' (WD 179). Sartre begins by accepting the very notion that Heidegger had set out to dispel, namely, that being is manifest and simple. Whereas for Heidegger, being was something inherited, a disposition to be troubled in a certain way. For Sartre, being is what is.

> Consciousness – which is separated from the world by nothing – is transcendence. The in-itself vests consciousness in order to be surpassed by it in Nothingness .... Consciousness in its for-itself, transcends the world towards itself. It is vested by the in-itself precisely insofar as it is numbed by Nothingness.
>
> (ibid.)

Heidegger believed in 'the Nothingness which retains the world in it' while Sartre believed 'in the Nothingness which consciousness itself is'. Sartre says that 'the world exists for consciousness only insofar as it is concretely and singularly what consciousness is not'. The relationship between the Nothingness at the centre of consciousness and the dark massif of being is to become the kernel of Sartre's philosophy. '[The] for-itself lacks the world because, for the for-itself, the world is the concrete totality of the in-itself that it is not'. (WD 232)

This illustrates that Sartre's idea of consciousness is rooted in a hybrid of Heidegger's 'nothing' and a Husserlian intentionality, of consciousness as consciousness of something – this 'something' being the world as in-itself. And this, as we have seen, is a dualism which emulates Descartes' juxtaposition of extended matter and consciousness. Despite all these obvious influences Sartre's thought is quite distinct and original. Consciousness, the phenomenal world, is a certain grasping of the in-itself by the for-itself, this relation is never one-sided for the for-itself wishes to be free, that is, 'for-itself' but wants to possess the substance of the world which gives it its sense of freedom and without which it is *nothing*.

> That which the for-itself is to itself is a lack: precisely, lack of the totality of which it is the negation – or world. The in-itself is present in face of it as that which is not; and the for-itself precisely *is nothing* – nothing in itself but a total translucidity that is also degradation of the in-itself.
>
> (WD 233)

Consciousness is nothingness lit by being, or being inhabited by nothingness. Nothingness does not give life to being, there are many forms of being, some of them 'living', but nothingness is that detachment of man which is the opportunity for reflection, for that divorce or lack which is the source of value and meaning. Consciousness demonstrates that the for-itself desires to be what it lacks, the in-itself, without itself becoming dead. Consciousness issues from the dependence of nothingness upon being; consciousness is consciousness of something, and consciousness itself is nothing but a total translucidity. The first expression is Husserl's and the second is Sartre's development of the *cogito* – nothingness is the demystified simple substance.

For Sartre nothingness is our innermost cause of being-here. It is the state of human being which initiates a yearning to be, a for-itself, which flees the in-itself towards the self possession it feels itself to be, but which it can never accomplish.

Heidegger had accepted Nietzsche warning of the latent disciplines inherent in the idea of spirit and its mystical relation the transcendent, and therefore looked to Nothing as the root of a new Being, that is, the problemization of the world which is ours but which we have mystified. Sartre's disposition to realism persuaded him to accept a much more ordinary idea of the world. Sartre's 'consciousness' can only be as objective as it chooses to make itself, only as historical as it itself permits. Heidegger viewed the notion of choice to be too loaded with brutality to be able to bear such a philosophical burden. The essential difference between Heidegger and Sartre lies in the concept of the *cogito*, the translucidity of the immediate consciousness which gives it an autonomy, a power to govern itself. Nothingness, translucidity and freedom are interchangeable terms in Sartre's work and they are all the possession of the individual. For Heidegger such autonomy was itself deeply implicated in the structures of abuse.

However, Sartre took a great deal more from Heidegger's essay *What is Metaphysics?* than the idea of *nothing*. For Heidegger concludes the essay with something approaching a manifesto. It is the subversive tone of the work; its ambition to drag man from complacency, to waken him from his sleep which most impressed Sartre. *Nothing* puts us, the enquirers in question. In order for us to accept the challenge of metaphysics we must permit ourselves to 'go into Nothing, that is to say, freeing oneself from the idols we all have and to which we are wont to go cringing' (WM 380). This remark, reminiscent of Nietzsche, calls us to our courageous fate. It invites us to become unsettled.

Heidegger insists that the point of *What Is Metaphysics?* is to make our questioning more genuine to inspire a renewed originality.

Readiness for dread is to say "Yes!" to the inwardness of things, to fulfil the highest demand which alone touches man to the quick. Man alone of all beings, when addressed by the voice of Being, experiences the marvel of all marvels: that what is is ... The clear courage for essential dread guarantees that most mysterious of all possibilities: the experience of Being.

(WM 386)

In *Being* even the will, the exact feel of the volitional deed, will be questioned. The sharpness of the will, its aggressiveness was one of the main concerns of Heidegger's philosophy. Science and the will are partners in the current brutality. Modern science – as a method of objectivizing what-is by calculation – is a condition imposed by 'the will to will' through which 'the will to will' secures its own sovereignty. While for Heidegger the attack upon this perverse order would have to destroy the conventional idea of the self, for Sartre such a destruction and re-orientation rests upon a more natural and down to earth insistence. In essence he is arguing that we must not confuse the character of man with the nature of things. While Heidegger's philosophy is more radical in that it challenges our power to question, its very philosophical radicalism is its political weakness, it is too deeply challenging to offer a new relation to man – this is seen as something that must come about through confrontation with the shallowness of questioning. In the political sense Sartre is more radical because his concepts are more ordinary and his work is, therefore, more accessible.

Heidegger sees the quest of metaphysics as a renewal of our openness to *being*. In the essential question, in an inwardness that eschews the ordinary purposefulness of life, we refresh our relation to being as a gratefulness, an act of homage which is worthy of our guardianship of *being*. 'Original thinking is the echo of Being's favour wherein it clears a space for itself and causes the unique occurrence: that what-is is' (WM 389). Heidegger's hope of a gentle 'thanking' of nature can be considered as the apotheosis of the Romantic Movement. But his political quietism showed that his thought belonged to a more contemplative tradition than the original Romantics would have thought seemly. Sartre redresses this balance. Sartre who in *Nausea* had set out a vision of man condemned to dwell in a creepy and distasteful alliance with the natural world, to freely place himself in a dungeon of reality in order to feel his freedom, adjusts his argument in order to examine and explode a more conventional servitude; that of man to man.

4
The Playful Project

In his essays of the 'thirties Sartre had established the outlines of his thought; the self was a construct, it was phenomenal, it belonged to the world and like the world was beyond our true immediacy. This immediate self-possession is not a self in the traditional sense of a personality or soul, but was an evaporative power, the capacity to withdraw from any content, to deny itself any identity. This unconditional negation Sartre labelled 'nothingness' [*le Néant*]. Sartre's great work, *Being and Nothingness*[1] is an attempt to explain human experience in terms of nothingness. Despite its obvious indebtedness to Kant, Hegel, Nietzsche, Freud and above all, to Heidegger, its achievement is unique and impressive and in the immediate aftermath of the Second World War it brought Sartre great fame.

Significant to the work's success is its reduction of the technical, the social and the psychological aspects of its account to one idea, that of freedom. We will see that the *Néant* and Sartre's concept of freedom are inseparable but also that the *Néant* cannot be understood without reference to the idea of translucidity and the *cogito*.

For Sartre, freedom marks the paradox of the human condition, we are not free not to be free, this is our unvarying condition, we must choose in order to *be*. Life has character only insofar as character is made, and each of us must accept responsibility for the world we encounter. Moreover, we have no guide for there is no reason to do this rather than that, if by reason one means external justification.

Sartre's work opens with a very technical essay which purports to show how 'nothingness' [*le Néant*] can be described as the ground of human awareness, how it gives the root categories of space, time and reflection. It is essential to state at the outset that the basic equipment of mind is constructed by the *Néant*, which is universal and precedes any concrete individuality; the categories it creates are, therefore, innate and unvarying. For this reason his thought has been described as 'rationalism'. What makes Sartre's phenomenology distinct from that of his nineteenth century fore-bears is the element of 'translucidity' the transparency of con-sciousness to itself. This reversion to the simple substance of Descartes and Kant means that consciousness can never surren-der its immediate power of self-possession, which is to say the individual person is the ground of all phenomena. Thus while the structure of mind is universal the content is particular and unique. To understand Sartre's notion of freedom it is neces-sary to appreciate this paradoxical structure of universality and particularity.

Probably most significant element of the work rests upon Sartre's reading of Heidegger and reflects Heidegger's view that the world we encounter is a response to our endeavours, our ambitions and intentions. When subsumed into Sartre's system rooted in the *cogito*, it places the reality of the world in the sphere of the particu-lar individual – all phenomena are produced as a consequence of the designs of the *Néant*. As the *Néant* is always simple, particular and individual, it is fair to say each man dwells in a world of his own making. In short, Sartre's system is a most beguiling mixture of rationalism rooted in the idea of the simple substance and a subjectivism rooted in a radical interpretation of Heidegger. Sartre offers us a stark freedom which is both metaphysical, for nothing-ness is the ground of consciousness, and ethical, for freedom condemns us to accept responsibility for the world in which we find ourselves.

* * *

Historically speaking *Being and Nothingness* developed in the context of war. The outbreak of war made Sartre feel that his earlier essays had been too academic. He had, he reflected, retreated to an inner sanctum of consciousness.

> I was like someone who, amidst the most dire of adventures, scarcely feels the threatening reality of the tortures being re-served for him – because he always carries with him a pellet of deadly poison, which will deliver him before any one can lay a finger on him ...

> So he's great only when he gives the poison to comrades. It seems to me at that moment he's truly human reality, because

nothing holds him outside the world: he's fully inside it, free and
without defence.

The passage from absolute freedom to disarmed human freedom
– the rejection of the poison – has taken place this year .... It's the
war and Heidegger which put me on the right path.

(WD 324)

Heidegger's *Being and Time*[2] presented Sartre with the seminal idea
that the problems of philosophy, the issue of what constituted an
authentic or proper life, could be treated in terms of one concept,
that of being. Sartre discovered in *Being and Time* the extended
metaphysical structure he had sought and unashamedly used it as
the outline for his own work. Whether Sartre understood but rejected Heidegger's ideas or misunderstood them and erroneously
adopted them it is difficult to judge. He appears to have had an ingrained suspicion of Heidegger's philosophical project and his political motives. Nevertheless he set out to write his own account of
being, one which was to prove involved, intricate and original. For
these reasons it is necessary to preface a discussion of Sartre's *Being
and Nothingness* by a brief account of Heidegger's work.

Heidegger's philosophy should be understood as an attempt to
restore the wonder and inspiration of the pre-Socratics, it aims to
revive the original vigour of humanity, discarding ways of thinking
which have become habitual, mere mimicry, making each person
face the most radical questions with unlimited earnestness. The
opening remark of *Being and Time*, establishes the theme:

Do we in our time have an answer to the question of what we
really mean by the word 'being'? Not at all. So it is fitting that we
should raise anew the question of the meaning of Being. But are
we nowadays even perplexed at our inability to understand the
expression 'Being'? Not at all.

(BT 19)

As a manifesto *Being and Time* holds that we have forgotten
being, this forgetfulness looms over our lives, penetrates deep into
our 'humanity', we are alienated, our lives so dulled and blighted
that we have become brutish, barbaric and vicious towards the
natural world, towards each other and towards ourselves. We must
answer the summons of *being* and cast off the forgetfulness which

has brought us to wretchedness. Heidegger's belief was that a renewed determination to live would come about by instilling a fresh astonishment in men, a wonder at *being*. Such an intellectual endeavour, a new age for philosophy, was no mere academic exercise; it was the preparation and instigation of a new age for man.

Heidegger argues that our type of being, the being that 'does', 'manipulates', 'knows', 'worries' and 'dreams', is an imperious type of being which distributes meaning, value and worth to the world it encounters. By investigating the collective project, or *Dasein*,[3] the world or totality is revealed (BT 36). In practice it is the way *Dasein* is fascinated with the world, the way it exerts itself or invests its concern that governs the nature of the world we encounter. In short, the project of *Dasein* sets the parameters for the problemization which profiles our encounter with the world.

> The Greeks had an appropriate term for 'Thing': *pragmata* that is to say, that which one has to do within one's concernful dealing (*praxis*) .... We shall call those entities which we encounter in concern as 'equipment' (or 'tool') .... Equipment is essentially 'something in order to ...'
>
> (BT 96)

Meaning enters the world as a condition of *Dasein* and comes to attention in our concernful dealings with things and with others. This leads to the general observation that the types of involvement into which we become drawn format the being one finds in the world.

As truth is deeply infected with our manner of brutishness, our 'humanity', Heidegger must make us ask new questions by giving us a new motive and a new vocabulary, that is, a new agility. This is expressed in particularly tactile terms so that in our projecting into the world we find the world as easy to hand '*Zuhandenheit*' or awkward to hand '*Vorhandenheit*'. In the *Zuhandenheit*, in the dextrous dealing with the world, we have the thesis of Heidegger's philosophy; meaning, understanding, purpose, and authentic being are products of our encounter with the world, itself the outcome of our adventure. Heidegger wants this adventure to be guided by a new wonder and a sense of care.

Concernful dealing is the agency or shaping force of phenomenalization. Invested in our concernful dealings are found 'meaning', the 'known' and 'values'; and from concernful dealings emerge the significance of personhood, the sense of responsibility, i.e. what is it for an act to be voluntary, the appropriate response to other actions – reward and punishment – and the types of control that seem to be required – organization of the law, its creation and enforcement.

The crucial project of *Being and Time* is to draw us out of the comfortable averageness and restore in us the most intense awe of being through resoluteness. Ultimately death brings us to the most earnest open-ness to being. Death confronts us with the unconditional inevitability of ceasing to be. In being-towards-death, what Heidegger describes as 'our most resolute, ownmost possibility', we become naked before being. It transcends all our abilities, 'Death, as possibility, gives *Dasein* nothing to be 'actualized', nothing which *Dasein*, as actual, could itself be (BT 306). This 'overwhelming possibility' robs the self of its inherited arrogance and, Heidegger held, brought us into the presence of being.

What Heidegger, like Kierkegaard, wants to achieve is an authenticity which will confront the rational, a calculating, deliberating agent whose way of thinking has been inherited. He wants to avoid taking the self as it has been formed by the forgetting of being, the isolated 'abstractive and appropriative' *cogito* of Descartes and Kant. Such a self incorporates the very ailment which authenticity seeks to overcome.

* * *

While many of the themes of *Being and Nothingness* are obviously inspired by *Being and Time* – the concentration on being, the idea of the world as characterized by instrumentality – *Being and Nothingness* nonetheless is a work which stands in its own right. Sartre's absolute reliance and dependence upon the *cogito* means that the person he seeks to rescue from inauthenticity is more immediately familiar and apparent than the rather mystical being of his predecessor. Sartre has a different philosophical agenda, his aim is to give strength to the individual, to hold out against tyranny and totalitarian fervour.

For both Heidegger and Sartre the outlook or 'project' of man is the primal shaping force of the world. The phenomenal appearance of the world rests upon the adventure to which we are wedded. The profound distinction between Sartre's version of this instrumental world and that of Heidegger is that for Sartre the person, the actual concrete individual, is the ground of phenome-nalization whereas for Heidegger the person was a product of col-lective, social and 'objective' forces. For Sartre, authenticity lies in acknowledging that we are the authors of our lives shedding the illusion that anyone or anything else can move us without our complicity. Sartre's ontology confronts us, as individuals, with the awareness that we are the ground of the world, that all that is experienced in our lives bears our imprint upon it. This is the project of *Being and Nothingness*. It bears the simple thesis that to live well, to live together, we must face up to reality. It is an essay against fantasy and reverie and in favour of an frank openness to the awkwardness of being.

Sartre's re-assertion of the *cogito* means that his sense of being-here is immediate and particular and hence lacks the critique of individuality that we find in both Hegel and Heidegger. For Sartre the isolation of consciousness is real, that is, incapable of develop-ment or change, the 'self' is phenomenal because it is constructed, but the power upon which the self is grafted, consciousness, is radically atomic.

At the centre of the argument is the tantalizing but obscure notion of 'nothingness' [*le Néant*]. Understanding Sartre's idea of freedom, indeed, understanding his philosophy entails grasping what he meant by nothingness, and one cannot grasp nothingness without comprehending his philosophy.

The *Néant's* vacuity is the vital principle of consciousness and of intelligence. Essentially we are not, that is, we are not caught up in the causal structures of the world, our way of being is by making ourselves be what we are not. The *Néant's* quest to give itself sub-stance initiates an infinite cycle of attempting to be what it is not in order to identify itself and obtain a semblance of self-control. Consciousness is the product of the *Néant's* attempt to be what it is not, that is to 'be'. Being for the *Néant* means setting aside its own natural character, 'negating the negation'. Only the *Néant* can set a limit upon its own power of evaporation, this 'setting a limit' means no other force can intrude upon the sovereignty or 'auto-nomy' of the *Néant*. This alone accounts for the unassailable power of self-control.

The importance of the atomized character of the *Néant* cannot be over-emphasized as it grants an inalienable sovereignty to the natural individual. Each individual possesses clear and distinct command of the enterprise of having to be what they are not. This accounts for the clarity of mind, for its *translucidity*; for the specifically Sartrean aspect of this argument.

The entire structure of mind rests upon the elaboration of the primary paradox of the *Néant's* wanting to be what it is not ('being') in order to be what it is ('nothingness'). This individuality of structure associated with the clarity of self-possession is the source of Sartre's account of mind. His rationalism rests on the fact that all minds, at all times and in all places throughout the history of mankind, are composed of one necessary and essential structure which can be known and which accounts for all the operations of thought and experience and governs the formation of all the phenomena of our awareness. The distinct difference between this 'phenomenology' and Hegel's is that here each particular person is the ground of their reality; history, culture and intellectual traditions can never themselves intrude into the primal self-possession of the *Néant*.

It is not possible to comprehend the thesis of *Being and Nothingness* without recognizing its total dependence upon the premise of the Sartrean *cogito*, that dynamic of being and of nothingness first described in *The Transcendence of the Ego*. Sartre neatly summarizes his position:

> The necessary and sufficient condition for a knowing consciousness to be knowledge of its object, is that it be consciousness of itself as being that knowledge. This is a necessary condition, for if my consciousness were not consciousness of being consciousness of the table, it would be consciousness of that table without consciousness of being so, in other words, it would be a consciousness ignorant of itself, an unconsciousness of being conscious – which is absurd.
>
> (BN xxviii)

Much has already been said about both the *Néant* and its 'consciousness', that is, what is referred to in *Being and Nothingness* as the for-itself, but something must be said about being, that is, the 'in-itself'. Being is defined as the condition of all revelation, as resistance to the for-itself, indeed, as resistance per se. The in-itself is 'full positively' and 'knows no otherness' (BN xlii). Being is outside of time, it is outside of movement. Being in-itself possesses neither possibility nor necessity, it is dead, fixed and complete. It must be immediately apparent that this is not the being we find in Heidegger.

Before freedom the world is a plenum which is what it is, a vast swill. After freedom, there are differentiated *things*, because freedom has introduced negation .... It is the foundation of transcendence, because – beyond what is – it can project *what is not yet*.

(WD 132)

Being in-itself in its abstract nature may be said to be super-abundance or chaos, as such the in-itself is a centre of resistance to the transparency of consciousness, it is a region of opacity, it resists nothingness's attempt to be immediate to itself, a challenge to its self-possession (BN xxvii). In reaction the *Néant* projects itself in attitudes which shape the world and attempt to fix it in ways that will permit it to better possess itself. This is ultimately a self-deceptive drive towards a stability which is contrary to its nature. The world as we know it is ordered by mind at a pre-reflective level in an attempt to secure self-possession within a perplexing environment.

The alienness of the in-itself means that immediate consciousness must find its own 'being', its self, its own deeds and character as separate, as not alive in the way that the *Néant* is alive, as simply thus so, as contingency. All meaning found in the world is the product of the for-itself and its quest to be.

The characteristic of human reality ... is that it motivates itself without being its own foundation. What we call freedom is that it is never anything without motivating itself to be it. Nothing can ever happen to it *from outside* .... It motivates its own reaction to the events outside, and the event within it is that reaction ... it is thus free in the sense that its reactions, and the way the world appears to it, are integrally attributable to it.

(WD 109)

The tormented relationship between *Néant* and being, that is, between being for-itself and being in-itself, is illustrated by Sartre in the concept of vertigo. Vertigo is the manifestation of the fact that being can never quell the utter flight of the *Néant*. Sartre gives the example of a man walking close to a cliff edge, he might resolve to keep a careful distance from the edge, but must always be aware that the current resolve cannot bind consciousness into the future, and at the next moment he might abandon his caution. Vertigo is the giddiness of knowing that one must make and re-make the resolution and that one cannot bind one's future will.

Similarly, with regard to past determination. I might be proud to have sustained a personal resolution not to drink or gamble, but suddenly I am aware that the achievement means nothing, it must be reasserted at each moment. I can never be sure that I have 'broken the habit' each moment is a fresh challenge. I am always in the position of having to choose again. Awareness of having to do in order to be marks the spine of Sartre's work. The nature of the *Néant* means that man has no essence, he is nothingness, he is what he is not and is not what he is. Being for man is a constant effort which cannot be set aside.

Anguish is the manifestation of freedom ... man is always separated by a nothingness from his essence. We should refer here to Hegel's statement: 'Wessen ist was gewesen ist'. Essence is what has been. Essence is everything in the human being which we can indicate with words – that *is*. Due to this fact it is the totality of characteristics which *explain* the act. But the act is always beyond that essence; it is a human act only in so far as it surpasses every explanation which we can give of it.

(BN 35)

The for-itself never has the option not to choose. 'To be is to do', Sartre remarked, we make our being by doing, we are doomed to this unconditional responsibility. The problem for us is to identify what this 'making' actually entails and to understand what exactly is the quality of the freedom which it *enjoys*.

In Sartre's phenomenology there is only one substance: being, this is why he calls it an ontology, nothingness is the complete absence of substance, the interface is consciousness, it is the world as meaningful. The *Néant* is utterly parasitic, it must be what it is not in order to be. Sartre's philosophy has the universe as constructed of two primary forces with man lying at the centre. Human consciousness is the epicentre of the cosmic rift between the two ontological categories. Man is placed in a privileged position in the universe, this 'privilege' being manifest as 'intelligence', that is, as awareness, reflection and worth. Sartre never tells us what intelligence belongs to animals, or to what degree our fellow creatures experience nothingness.

* * *

In the last chapter we noted that Sartre had distanced himself from Husserl because he believed Husserl's Phenomenology had as its principle and moving force a self with an innate and substantial character. This, Sartre argued, created the same problem of solipsism we find in Descartes. Such a concept deprives us of a coherent account of our recognition that others are 'selfs' in the sense that one is oneself a 'self'. Sartre felt that a philosophy that rescued the *cogito* from solipsism would be able to counter the type of objective determination he thought Heidegger had advocated. *The Transcendence of the Ego* and *Being and Nothingness*, therefore, sought a concept of self which is necessarily, that is, metaphysically atomic and individual whilst avoiding the philosophical pitfalls of such isolation. For Sartre, individuality is necessary, innate and universal – a *Néant*, while the self is a construct – a phenomenal product of our projects. It is these projects we are now going to investigate.

For many of Sartre's readers, particularly those not familiar with the work of Hegel, one of the most startling ideas presented in *Being and Nothingness* is that the self is a product of our relations with others. The transformation of the *Néant* into a 'self' produces the most impressive passage of *Being and Nothingness*. Here we find the *Néant's* paradoxical dynamic, its yearning to be what it is not etc., develop into the stark and tragic account of human relationships which dominates Sartre's thought.

Self-hood is the awareness of being in the presence of the other's nothingness. The other, being for-itself, is the centre of a world of meanings subject to an alien design, beyond the immediacy of my *Néant*. My actions in the dead world of things gives me awareness but no thematic sense of self, I am simply thus and thus. But in the presence of the other my deeds adhere to me, I become the principle of their authorship. I see a new phenomena in the world, me being for myself. In place of being immediately free, a freedom that evaporates in the instant, I glimpse a for-itself being for itself, a phenomenal freedom.

The sense of being in a world of alien meaning creates an identity more pervasive than any I am able to construct in my own immediate consciousness, an identity we refer to as a self. Solipsism is overcome because the other is the ground of there being a phenomenon of self. Other selfs are not deduced from an analysis of consciousness but are the precondition of a certain form of awareness, one characterized by self-hood.

Sartre argues that being in the context of the other opens a new and more manageable sphere of operations, a sphere of being for-oneself. But unlike the *Néant* which is immediately for-itself, the self is a for-itself mediated through a world which rests upon the freedom of the other. It offers the prospect of being free, but this more substantial being lies in the gift of the other and if I am to freely be in this more vivid way I must take charge of the other such that he becomes a for-itself for me. If I am to be for-myself I must hold the freedom of the other. For Sartre the meaning of all human relations emanates from the single project of taking hold of the other's ability to grant substance to the *Néant's* freedom, all other characteristics are products of this project; love, hate, slavery and justice are all phenomenal outcomes of this primal need to give being to the for-itself.

As the other seems to offer me a tangible freedom, a realized freedom, I seek to have the other's freedom for-me. The other offers a sense of life richer than that obtained in the loneliness of the *Néant*. This project of captivation has two strategies which Sartre calls 'appropriation' and 'indifference', a project of charm and a project of violence These are not separate or distinct strategies but inter-linked and interchangeable and have the same objective; to obtain the freedom of the other as a freedom for me. Whether one employs one or the other is a matter of choice, one may alternate the project by the hour, use them schematically, or one may operate the same project for a whole lifetime but this project is what is manifest as 'personality'.

The strategy of 'appropriation' is dominated by the scheme to draw the other into making me the being through which they live their lives, to dedicate themselves to me. In this way I obtain a me, mediated through the other's freedom, that is for myself. I seek to be their object of devotion, I love them, I occupy myself with the project of being for them such that they cannot be without me and freely choose me as I would choose myself. But it is their freedom one must have, mere devotion, robotic and predictable, would not be acceptable – the other would collapse into an in-itself and I would be confronted once again with my immediate freedom. The dialectic of captivation is extremely intricate but for Sartre the generosity of love is a scam which has as its true end the colonization of the other's freedom. But the other is a *Néant* and as such can always escape any being-for-me I may engineer. Love is a project fraught with disappointment and loneliness returns more stark and cruel than ever.

The alternate and parallel project is one of 'indifference'. In this I affect a blindness to the significance of the other I seek to use the other's freedom transparently for myself. To use the other as a thing while maintaining the notion for myself that he freely mediates my identity. This is a project more crass than that of 'appropriation' but more readily available, I dominate the other, subject their life and body to violence to be for me that I may find my life through the agency of their abused freedom. But even here, Sartre insists, I can achieve only transient satisfaction for 'I can make the other beg for mercy but I always lose the meaning of this act for the other's freedom'.

Our concrete relations with others are necessarily doomed. The ambition of being really free by capturing the freedom of the other as a for-itself for me achieves only tragedy and disappointment. For in Sartre's system each is a *Néant*, the other's freedom is not for-me but for itself and I must embark on strategies of increasing desperateness in order to have this freedom for myself. In attempting to take hold of their freedom I embark upon a strategy which is by turn morbid and vicious, a strategy of obsession and then, when confronted by the emptiness of devotion, of increasing manipulation and violence.

Sartre sees relationships as ultimately destructive because he sets as their objective an end which his presuppositions make impossible, for if it is not possible for the for-itself to *be* for-itself then it, ultimately, cannot be possible for one to be for another. For Sartre individuality is a metaphysical truth we are particular, isolated and atomic. This is part of the universal and necessary structure of the *Néant*. The depth of the root of isolation means that all attempts to overcome it will be futile. All human relationships are constructed on a project which must end in failure and conflict. No matter how devoted I am to the other I can only assist him be this or that, something he is not.

On a more mundane level our attempts to help others fills their lives with our projects. Even assistance and comfort deprive the other of 'the free possibilities of courageous resistance, of perseverance and self-assertion' which he would otherwise have had. With these thoughts Sartre discloses an attitude reminiscent of Nietzsche's contempt for 'pity' and distrust of 'love'. Indeed he manifests the general characteristic of those writers for whom 'authenticity' is paramount, namely, that all help, even generosity is in some way manipulative.

For Sartre relationships are fundamentally exploitative and ultimately futile. The dynamic of trying to be free through the agency of the other lies behind much of what became known as French Existentialism and dominates much of Sartre's literary output. It also created the bind which deprived his work of any real moral theory, in the conventional sense, a lack which was to fracture his output until the 'fifties and his adoption of Marxism.

* * *

We must pursue what exactly 'authenticity' means for Sartre. What is good in Sartre's system is taking charge of freedom. We cannot really say, 'What is morally right', since both ethics and morality have an objective, collective character and Sartre has placed man outside such collective forces. By returning to the *cogito* he deprives custom, morality and convention of any inherent legislative force, all value and meaning are created within the confines of individual determination, one can never escape from the fact that one is oneself the origin of the meaning of all that occurs.

But the question then arises: If freedom is our nature, and is unassailable, how can we be inauthentic? How can there be a proper project, one Sartre seeks to promote, if we are free regardless of any intrusion or privation? Surely nothing can deprive us of our self-possession.

The crux of Sartre's case is that while we are free in the sense that we are nothingness we are also free to deceive ourselves to pretend to a way of being that mimics the in-itself. This leads us to the most significant of Sartre's ideas, to what we might call the moral core of *Being and Nothingness*, the notion of bad faith [*mauvaise foi*]. Sartre gives us some vivid examples of what he intends by this term.

A woman on a first date finds her admirer holding her hand, because she wishes to deny the man's intentions she leaves it there passive and inanimate as though she has lost control of it, neither deliberately holding on in reciprocation nor actively indicating her displeasure by taking it away. She becomes a thing in order not to choose, in order to 'be elsewhere'.

A waiter at work, performing as a waiter, acquiring mannerisms of a waiter, the walk, the posture and the attentiveness of the stereotypical waiter. He loses himself in the role, becomes mechanical and *is* a waiter, deceiving himself that he has the capacity to surrender his immediate self possession. So bad faith is succumbing to the illusion that one is a being like a table is a table, defined, characterized and externally fixed. It is an attempt to deny what Sartre believes to be the natural truth of mankind, that he is only by his own decree, man is self-legislating, the *Néant* is self-finitizing.

But this leads to the altogether more difficult issue of what is 'good faith', the proper attitude to being which give real expression to our freedom. Unsurprisingly 'good faith' is Sartre's attitude, the outlook of his philosophy; to conduct oneself in good faith is to have absorbed the lesson of *Being and Nothingness*, it is to have learned to be free. So now we must look at what Sartre actually understands by freedom.

Sartre, like Kierkegaard, holds that we should act for no reason other than that the act is truly mine, which is to say 'authentic'; full of value, honesty and limitless commitment. The nature of freedom means that to act for the good is unqualified by circumstances and moral convention, it is unrelated to place or to culture and immune to fashion, it expresses only one thing, what one is. *Being and Nothingness* requires us to choose, mindful that we are nothingness, that is, that our choice of being is all we are and what we are is our choice. We must look to ourselves as the source of this world and never attempt to think of events as accidental. I am the author of my world and bear responsibility for *all* that I find. This we shall call Sartre's realism. We accept our circumstances as the revelation of our true being, our choice and resist the delinquency of delusion, fantasy or immobilizing reverie.

Technically Sartre's philosophy has been held to proclaim that existence precedes essence, or that one must do in order to be. Man as *Néant* is without essence; he must engage his world in order to give himself a character. In order to understand this extreme individualistic anthropocentricism it is necessary to briefly return to Heidegger's notion of intentionality, the theory of *praxis*. For Heidegger human experience is rooted in the way we engage the world, our 'concernful dealing' is the shaping force of phenomenalization, of all meaning and values. Concernful dealing is not, however, something we choose as individuals but a way of choosing inherited and drawn from the past of our culture.

Sartre's philosophy is distinguished from that of Heidegger by the re-introduction of the Cartesian *cogito* which breaks the hold of history, of inheritance upon the self. Our individuality is a consequence of the *Néant* and is part of the universal, necessary and unchanging structure of being. We are not products but arbiters, each one of us stands at the pivotal point of determination. And this one point divides *Being and Time* and *Being and Nothingness*. It also accounts for the fact that in terms of the history of thought Sartre is something of a maverick of the twentieth century placing the individual's determination before all objective, collective or historical forces; making the atomic person the court of reality.

So for Sartre the 'doing' which precedes 'being', is an individual deed made deliberately, it is a choice. It is now necessary that we try to understand the nature of this individual choice which produces the world.

When we think of freedom we have a tendency to associate it with the will, with the faculty of volition. Sartre's first task is to remind us that his view of freedom is much more radical than this. The will is one manifestation of the original freedom of the *Néant*, but it is no more free than our other faculties, say the passions. He gives us the example of two differing responses to a life-threatening event; to run away or to remain and reflect how to save one's life, and remarks that the end to be achieved is the same in both cases only in the latter case 'the methods of attaining it are more clearly conceived …. The difference here depends on the choice of means and on the degree of reflection, not on the end.' (BN 443) What Sartre appears to be saying here is that there is a double element within choosing. First, what he refers to as the end, that is the goal, e.g. self-preservation, pleasure, etc., something which demands a changed state of the world. Secondly, there is the mode of consciousness in which this is to be achieved, here volition is one, passion is another.

For Sartre we choose in a radical sense in that we choose just how reflective and deliberate our choosing shall be. The will to will is merely one manifestation of our radical freedom. In this sense when we act passionately or spontaneously we 'choose' not to deliberate. A correlate of this is that what we normally refer to as a choice, that is the deliberate opting for one alternative against another, is not what it seems. 'Voluntary deliberation is always a deception' (BN 450), the elements which influence my choice, my reasons and motives are themselves products of a more radical choice. We try to think of our motives and reasons as thing-like elements with an existence of their own, but in truth, they stem from our original freedom and our basic choice of end.

Causes and motives have only the weight which my project – i.e. the free production of the end ... to be realized – confers upon them. When I deliberate, the chips are down. And if I am brought to the point of deliberating, this is simply because it is a part of my original project to realize motives by means of *deliberation* rather than by some other form of discovery (by passion, for example or simply by action ... as language reveals thought) ....
When the will intervenes, the decision is taken, and it had no other value than of making the announcement.

(BN 451)

The significance of this statement, that 'the chips are down', is that we must not believe that we must wilfully 'choose' in order to be free. Sartre's philosophy is not 'rationalistic' in that sense. Rather we must accept that the world we find ourselves in is our world, that this is chosen in the more radical sense.

The will is not a privileged manifestation of freedom but ... a psychic event of a peculiar structure which is constituted on the same plane as other psychic events and which is supported, neither more nor less than the others, by an original, ontological freedom.

(BN 452)

In this regard it is helpful to recall that Nietzsche is one of the thinkers to whom Sartre is most indebted. The radical nature of 'choice' in Sartre's thought corresponds with the *amor fati* in Nietzsche's work; it is the demand that we accept this world as ours, and do not attempt to waste time dividing every situation into what I intended and what is fate, misfortune or chance, in this sense all is chance and all is destiny, we must learn to acknowledge that the reality of the world, however hostile or obstructive it may be, belongs to us. Every situation mirrors my being, my intentionality, my enterprise of being and my way of life. This alien other world is my being. The requirement of good faith is that we rise to this recognition. The fact that I and I alone must make the values of the world, that nothing beyond me justifies my adoption of one project instead of another leads to the recognition that I am unjustifiable.

The primal fact of our being, of our nothingness, is manifest in anguish, awareness of our freedom. For Sartre anguish is the mood in which we cast off the ordinary illusion that we are positioned by society and by convention and in its place find ourselves as the source of ourselves. Like Heidegger and Kierkegaard, Sartre sees anguish as the outcome of man's willingness to accept himself as the ground of his existence. Even if he lives a life fully positioned by others, by topical affairs and conventional habits he must at times see that this has come about as a consequence of his complicity.

> Anguish is opposed to the mind of the serious man who apprehends values in terms of the world and who resides in the reassuring, materialistic substantiation of values .... In anguish I apprehend myself at once as totally free and as not being able to derive the meaning of the world except as coming from myself.
>
> (BN 39)

For Sartre, freedom is not an aspect of the world but the frame in which the world is set. The world which confronts me is itself my choice.

It is Sartre's thesis that each person is a whole of which each act is a demonstration. This whole is itself a project, a sort of choice. Sartre believes we have access to this original choice, that we can maintain it only by re-enacting it, moreover, his view of consciousness leads him to the conclusion that we have the capacity to alter it. This will lead to what Sartre calls existential psychoanalysis, but at this stage his concern is that we acknowledge this world to be ours, actually and practically, that we reject the bad faith of attributing its character to forces beyond ourselves, it is as it is because we are interested in it being this way. In this sense choice and consciousness are the same thing, indeed, he goes as far as saying 'one must choose in order to be conscious' (BN 462) and we choose the world by choosing ourselves.

> The value of things, their instrumental role, their proximity and real distance do nothing more than to outline my image – that is, my choice. My clothing whether neglected or cared for, carefully chosen or ordinary, my furniture, the street on which I live, the city in which I reside, the books with which I surround myself, the recreation which I enjoy, everything which is mine, all this informs me of my choice – that is, my being.
>
> (BN 463)

For Sartre nothing is gratuitous, the whole is meaningful, but we flee from this recognition under the weight of responsibility. This is our world, our being, our choice but it is simply ours, without exterior justification, it rests upon no cause but ourselves. Our world is a reflection of ourselves.

The sovereign power of the *Néant* can justify only one conclusion; the world as I experience it is mine. I may wish to hide from this, I may want to say that I am something else, that I do not 'deserve' my fate. But Sartre's claim is that I must resist all temptation to abstract myself from my world we must, rather, look to it and find ourselves in it untainted by delusion and cowardice. Only then can we live totally, fully and vitally.

Now the concept of choice appears to have been extended beyond any recognizable everyday sense. Ordinary reflection reveals not our total freedom but the extreme marginality of choice. Sartre's response to this is to remind us that the 'coefficient of adversity of things' only arises within a world which is ours, things are resistant to an end established by us. Resistance is not hostile to freedom but is the child of our freedom. To be free does not mean 'to obtain what one has wished' this would be to restrict freedom to one mood of self-realization, i.e. the will. It is at this point that the paradoxical nature of the *Néant* reaches its full significance. The *Néant* desires to have the world as the ground upon which it frees itself. It does not want a fabrication or a partially distinguished world, it wants the world actual, complete and whole. It draws reality into its sharpest focus in order that it be the ground upon which it may free itself.

> There is a being which freedom has to be in the form of non-being. To exist as the fact of freedom or to have to be a being in the midst of the world are one and the same thing, and this means that freedom is originally a relation to the given.
>
> (BN 486)

Sartre uses the term 'facticity' to refer to this necessity of the *Néant* to be what it is not in order to have itself. Facticity is the world as it is for the for-itself, not only the world around it, the product of its own end, but its being, its skills and capacities, its past. The for-itself makes this world but it does not immediately possess the power to make or invent the details. That would be to fall into mere dreaming. Rather this facticity arises like a chemical compound where we mix a known element, our end, with an unknown element, the 'brute being'. This 'mixture' is what Sartre refers to as the situation. It is our reality, again like Nietzsche's *amor fati* we must not be lured into trying to distinguish our part and that of fate, what we know as the world is ours.

> The *datum* never appears to the for-itself as a brute existent in-itself ... it is revealed only in the light of an end which illumin-ates it. Situation and motivation are really one. The for-itself discovers itself as engaged in being, hemmed in by being, threat-ened by being; it discovers the state of things which surrounds it as the cause for a reaction of defence or attack .... Thus we begin to catch a glimpse of the paradox of freedom: there is freedom only in a *situation* and there is a situation only through freedom. Human-reality everywhere encounters resistance and obstacles which it has not created, but these resistances and obstacles have meaning only in and through the free choice which human reality is.
>
> (BN 487–9)

It is the project of the for-itself, its end, which governs just how the world is experienced and there is literally nothing which can deprive us of our role as the fulcrum of reality.

> It is our freedom which is responsible for the fact that there are things with all their indifference ... [The project] causes them to be things; that is, precisely, realities provided with a coefficient of adversity and utilizable instrumentality.
>
> (BN 509)

The clearest example is that of the mountain which will only be an obstacle if one determines to be on the other side. Ultimately all the arguments offered are developments of the notion of the instru-mentality of the world in relation to one's project. An example is his attitude to our personal past.

> The meaning of the past is strictly dependent on my present project. This certainly does not mean that I can make the meaning of my previous acts vary in any way I please; quite the contrary, it means ... I alone can decide at each moment the bearing of the past. I do not decide it by debating it, but by protecting myself towards my ends, I preserve the past with me, and by action I decide its meaning.
>
> (BN 498)

And he reaffirms, 'we chose our past in the light of a certain end, but from then on it imposes itself upon us and devours us' (BN 503). This relates not only to our own, personal past, but to the collective. The past which surrounds us in language, habits and in institutions can have only the hold on us we grant it. Sartre moves towards his major thesis: 'it is in this world and no other that the for-itself's freedom comes into play; it is in connection with its existence in this world that it puts itself into question. For to be free is not to choose the historic world in which one arises – which would have no meaning – but to choose oneself in the world what-ever this may be'. (BN 521)

This leads us directly to what must be considered the most daunting test of our freedom, others. Even though the other is a freedom applying itself to our freedom, a power which, to Sartre's view is unique in its capacity to undermine our self realization, the same rule of facticity is maintained. Here Sartre is at his most belligerent 'even torture does not dispossess us of our freedom; when we give in, we do so *freely*' (BN 524). Sartre insists that regardless of how intrusive the other might be, it is still for me to use my freedom to live that situation.

> The race, the infirmity, the ugliness can appear only within the limits of my own choice of inferiority or of pride, or of any other choice of my ends; in other words, they can appear only with a meaning which my freedom confers upon them ... I do not choose to be for the other what I am, but I can try to be for myself what I am for the other, by choosing myself such as I appear to the Other – i.e. by an elective assumption.
>
> (BN 529)

The example Sartre offers is that a Zionist Jew can 'resolutely' and concretely assume the permanent alienation of his being a Jew. The more one is confronted and oppressed the more one may be drawn to acknowledge one's situation, Sartre's point is that one ought to attempt to capture the full actuality of the situation. There is a greater danger than being tortured into betraying one's colleagues; it is living life in the mode of fantasy. In this horror of the shallowness of life, Sartre follows Kierkegaard and Heidegger, but whereas Kierkegaard found authenticity in faith and Heidegger found it in being towards death Sartre seeks it in 'reality'.

Freedom is unassailable, but this is the source of our fragility, we do not need to contemplate death to feel vulnerable we should simply recognize our responsibility for what is. We find this in 'the situation'. Living in 'good faith' has as its concrete ambition that we should come to acknowledge the truth of the situation, that the 'for-itself is nothing other than its situation'.

> Being in situation defines human reality by accounting both for its *being-there* and for its *being-beyond*. Human reality is indeed the *being which is always beyond its being-there*. And the situation is the organized totality of the being-there, interpreted and lived in and through being-beyond. Therefore there is no privileged situation. We mean by this that there is no situation in which the given would crush beneath its weight the freedom which constitutes it as such – and that conversely there is no situation in which the for-itself would be more free than in others.
>
> (BN 549)

Thus for Sartre our freedom, and hence our responsibility, is categorical; there are no accidents in life for 'the peculiar character of human reality is that it is without excuse'. Sartre's version of *amor fati* binds freedom to its situation. We are so intimately joined to our age, to the times in which we live, that we can not exclude ourselves from responsibility for any event. It is 'a waste of time to ask what I should have been if this war had not broken out, for I have chosen myself as one of the possible meanings of the epoch which imperceptibly led to war' (BN 555). One must accept responsibility even for the vile outcomes one would never have imagined oneself to have intended because this world is what we are: each person absolutely belongs to their time.

We live in bad faith insofar as we attempt to conceal from ourselves our inseparability from the concrete content of our life, our dependence upon it, its dependence upon us. Bad faith denies responsibility, for Sartre this is inexcusable.

> Man being condemned to be free carries the weight of the whole world on his shoulders; he is responsible for the world and for himself as a way of being. We are taking the word 'responsibility' in its ordinary sense as 'consciousness (of) being the incontestable author of an event or of an object'. In this sense the responsibility

of the for-itself is overwhelming since he is the one by whom it happens that *there is* a world.

(BN 553)

Acknowledging that one is the author of even the most hostile situation is the burden which 'existentialism' places upon us. We must 'assume the situation with the proud consciousness of being its author'. Only then can we find ourselves, for man is nothing but his situation and the situation is nothing but the response of being to our project however remote from deliberate consciousness that project might be.

But like Nietzsche, Sartre does not intend that we should respond to this responsibility by passive acceptance or resignation, rather, we are encouraged to take command of what is ours. We live in an entirely human world; 'the most terrible situation of war, the worst tortures do not create a non-human state of things'. Sartre's work requires us to face up to the humanity of the world, we are encouraged to eschew the erroneous notion of the non-humanity of our world and thereby to stop alienating aspects of ourselves.

It is only through fear, flight, and recourse to magical types of conduct that I shall decide on the non-human, but this decision is human, and I shall carry the entire responsibility for it. But in addition the situation is mine because it is the mirror image of my free choice of myself, everything which it presents to me is mine in that it represents me and symbolizes me. Is it not I who decide the coefficient of adversity in things even their unpredictability by deciding myself.

(BN 554)

This is one of the most important quotes from *Being and Nothingness* for it asserts not only that our responsibility rests upon our being the adventure upon which all events are profiled, but that by altering our attitude, by accepting responsibility, by ceasing to delude and weaken ourselves by inventing occult causes, we can begin to revitalize the world to which we are bound.

The claim of absolute responsibility takes us to one of the more original and remarkable elements of Sartre's work; his psychoanalytic theory. In many ways this is the kernel of Sartre's early work, the point where he offers us a path to existential salvation, to taking hold of our lives. This is the opportunity to put into practice the merely theoretical assertion that we are the origin of the world as we find it. Here his Cartesian rationalism is used to transform all he has learned from Kierkegaard, Nietzsche, Freud and Heidegger.

We have already grasped that for Sartre being is never passive or neutral, it is characterized by our project, the end we pursue. This end is not something cerebral or transcendental, not anything beyond this world, it is this world. We are to be identified with the world we inhabit, we may protest that this world is merely accidental, unconnected with our real being, but such an attitude is itself an option purposely undertaken, its inauthenticity lying in the self delusion that it is not itself a strategy.

The totality with which we are to be identified is the total accumulation of our expressions, our deeds, preoccupations and habits, as such we would be wrong to seek the individual's character in some selected odd, eccentric or 'neurotic' detail, there is no character separate from the deed, and there is no type or species of deed more revealing than others, all are equally significant and all are part of the same project.

> If we admit that the person is a totality, we can not hope to reconstruct him by an addition or by an organization of the diverse tendencies which we have empirically discovered in him. On the contrary, in each inclination, in each tendency the person expresses himself completely, although from a different angle.
>
> (BN 563)

The aim is to reveal the fundamental project evident in all activities.

The *Néant* governs Sartre's psychoanalysis as surely as it does his politics and his ethics. Sartre rejects Freud's notion of an underlying structure of consciousness, an unconsciousness which governs our actions but which is not part of our awareness. This is incomprehensible for Sartre for two reasons: firstly; man is the desire to be, there is no abstract state that exists before he makes himself be. Secondly; as man is essentially nothingness all power over him comes from him, there is no secret which is not a secret made to be, and no obscure forces except what is made obscure by design. The *Néant* is master of its own territory, all else is bad faith.

The existential psychoanalyst will look for the individual in all his deeds. But a mere catalogue of such deeds is not enough – they must be placed in order, each used to illuminate the whole and the whole used to decipher each act. Unity must be found in the detail, in all the ways the individual uses to express himself, even the most insignificant and most superficial behaviour: a taste, a mannerism, all human acts are revealing.

> Its point of departure is experience; its pillar of support is the fundamental, pre-ontological comprehension which man has of the human person. Although the majority of people can well ignore the indications contained in a gesture, a word, a sign and can look with scorn on the revelation which they carry, each human individual nevertheless possesses *a priori* the *meaning of* the revelatory value of these manifestations and is capable of deciphering them.
>
> (BN 568)

The method is one of collection and comparison. The covert meaning, the project or way of being of the person, hides but is manifest in the gathered totality. Sartre says:

> Since each example of human conduct symbolizes in its own manner the fundamental choice which must be brought to light, and since at the same time each one disguises this choice under its occasional character and its historical opportunity, only the comparison of these acts of conduct can effect the emergence of the unique revelation which they all express in a different way.
>
> (BN 569)

The method is strictly objective. The individual has no 'privileged position' to inquire into himself. As with Freud's analysis the reflective level of introspection is a secondary structure which, while it provides us with material for analysis, cannot rely upon its own resources for revealing the fundamental project of which it is one manifestation (BN 571). What is sought is not some universal force or power, a libido or will to power, but 'a choice' which unites all the various manifestation All the details of behaviour express or particularize this choice. Sartre tells us that this choice is 'nothing other than the being of each human reality'. A particular behaviour 'expresses the original choice of this human reality since for human reality there is no difference between existing and choosing for itself'. This allows Sartre to define his psychoanalysis as:

> A method destined to bring to light, in a strictly objective form, the subjective choice by which each living person makes

himself a person; that is, makes known to himself what he is. Since what the method sees is a *choice of being* at the same time as a *being*, it must reduce particular behaviour patterns to fundamental relations – not of sexuality or of the will to power, but of *being* – which are expressed in this behaviour.

(BN 574)

Sartre's belief in the *cogito*, in the translucidity of consciousness, in the *Néant*, means that these ultimate ends of the individual are on display. They have a pervasive quality and are continuously manifested. As such while there will be as many choices of being as there are individuals, and the proper form of analysis will be the biography, it is, however, possible that we could form a general classification of human ontology. Indeed, in a rather speculative frame of mind, Sartre attempts such a general theory of the project of being. This returns us to the opening thesis of the work, that consciousness is created from the demand of the *Néant* to be what it is not in order to not be what it is, for the for-itself to exist in the permanently stable and self originating form being 'in-itself-for-itself'.

Here Sartre speaks of being as a compromise between the solidity of being and the vapidity of non-being. He out-lines the symbolic manifestations of this relationship; entering into an enclosed space, the exploration of holes, the joy of ski-ing and the revulsion of the sticky, all manifestations of being's unwillingness to let nothingness *be*. The 'ethical' ambition of the work moves towards a mood, a radical alternative to 'seriousness', this mood, the attitude embodying 'good faith' Sartre calls 'play'.

The idea of play represents a way to possess the world without compromising the for-itself. In play man holds to himself as the original source of his situation, he takes each moment as the setting for the implementation of his own rules, his self legislation, and is not distracted or diverted by the fact that anticipation is not realized but always begins again; he always finds himself at each moment even in moments of great environmental hostility. It is a courage in the face of facticity, a recognition that facticity is our only being. On the other hand, seriousness is the attitude of those who come to know themselves in terms of the world, it involves 'starting from the world and attributing more reality to the world than to oneself; at the very least the serious man confers reality on himself to the degree to which he belongs to the world' (BN 580). Serious thought is spoken of as 'thickened' as 'coagulated', man has given himself the existence of a rock. Yet the for-itself is not free not to be free; it can only deceive itself by binding itself to a series of in-itselfs hence the original project is characterized by the structure of viscosity. The for-itself's project is to attempt to by-pass its freedom, to bind itself to facticity as though it is simply given and not made. Sartre's work sets for itself the legislative project of making this self-binding unattractive. To make manifest the effort involved in giving viscosity to being.

'The first principle of play is man himself; through it he escapes his natural nature; he himself sets the value and rules for his acts and consents to play only according to the rules he himself has established' (BN 581). Play is the for-itself conscious of itself as for-itself. It is a living awareness that to be is to do. Sartre expresses this in the image of the skier.

> To *ski* means not only to enable me to make rapid movements and to acquire a technical skill, it is also to enable me to *possess* the snow ... That means that by my very activity as a skier, I am changing the matter and meaning of the snow .... In the descent I do not consider it in itself, bit by bit, but am always fixing on a point to be reached beyond the position which I now occupy, it does not collapse into an infinity of individual details but is *traversed towards* the point I assign myself.
>
> (BN 582)

The opposite existential possessiveness to ski-ing and sliding is to live the slimy. The slimy is the revolting confusion of for-itself and in-itself 'as ink is absorbed by a blotter' (BN 610). It is consciousness as embroiled in a world less human than the serious. Sartre tells us that 'the slimy offers a horrible image ... the slimy is a soft clinging, there is a sly solidity and complicity of all its leech-like parts, a vague, soft effort made by each to individualize itself, followed by a falling back and flattening out that is emptied of the individual, sucked in on all sides by the substance' (ibid.). In a very real sense *Being and Nothingness* is an essay rooted in the flight from the slimy. A horror and revulsion of 'a consciousness ... transformed by a thick stickiness of its ideas'. If we seek a final emblem of Sartre's view of freedom it is contained in the statement:

> The freedom of the for-itself appears as *being*. The freedom of the for-itself is always *engaged*, there is no question of a freedom

which could be undetermined and which would pre-exist its choice. We shall never apprehend ourselves except as a choice in the making. But freedom is simply the fact that this choice is always unconditional.

(BN 478)

The *Néant* represents the fact that man is a cause which is itself not caused. It therefore represents the same strain of thought as the *cogito* and the noumenon. Sartre's genius has been to re-work this idea so that we are thrown into reality as our reality. It is a paradoxical philosophy, on the one hand declaring choice to be the ground of the world, and on the other committing us to a resolute acceptance that our choice is what is real, a demand that we eschew an abstract or fantasy based notion of our lives. Abstract ideas of a self, a destiny, a character, of fate or divine intrusion must be recognized as exotic ideas imported in order to cloud our responsibility for the being of the world. 'Good faith' ultimately is the willingness to accept the world as ours. It sometimes appears to be a quietistic philosophy but this, I think, is an error, it merely reminds us that the results or outcomes of our dealings with others are essentially unpredictable but no less ours for being so.

The fact that *Being and Nothingness* is so closely related to *Being and Time* makes Heidegger's response especially pertinent. Regrettably Heidegger's *A Letter on Humanism* is based only upon a reading of Sartre's short lecture *Existentialism is a Humanism* which is a harshly abbreviated account of Sartre's thought. Still Heidegger's *Letter* remains one of the most perceptive treatments of Sartre's return to the *cogito*. Heidegger chooses 'humanism' as the centre of his attack because he believes that Sartre's work is a continuation of the radical arrogance of man. Heidegger believes that 'humanism' begins with a concept of our relation to the world which is over-developed and cluttered, it locates man amongst things rather than in being. Sartre has failed to recognize that we cannot think ourselves into being for 'thought' is too contrived, too loaded with disinterest.

Humanism is opposed because it does not set the *humanitas* of man high enough. However, the essential dignity of man does not lie in the fact that he is as the 'subject' of beings, their substance, so that as the despot of Being he may let the character of beings dissolve into an 'objectivity' that is much too loudly praised.

Man is rather 'cast' by Being itself into the truth of Being, in order that he, ex-sisting thus, may guard the truth of Being; in order that in the light of Being, beings as beings may appear as what it is. Whether and how it appears, whether and how the God and the gods, history and nature, enter, presenting and absenting themselves in the clearing of Being, is not determined by man. The advent of beings rests in the destiny of Being.

(LH 203)

'He [Sartre] stands opposed to the openness of Being, an openness which is Being itself' (LH 215). Heidegger sees Sartre as siding against 'being' in favour of the man produced by alienation and believes that Sartre's humanism places man against the world, he has joined forces with the prevalent strand of the history of thought in seeing man as the master of being and not its servant. The placing of the negating force 'in man', that is, in the subject as we have come to speak of him, misses the very point Heidegger had attempted to make, that we must first escape from the way we think of ourselves as thing-like in order to find things anew.

Nihilation unfolds essentially in Being itself, and not at all in the existence of man – insofar as this is thought as the subjectivity of the ego cogito. Dasein in no way nihilates as a human subject who carries out nihilation in the sense of denial; rather, Da-sein nihilates inasmuch as it belongs to the essence of Being as that essence in which man ek-sists [i.e. stands out].

(LH 221)

By employing the *cogito* Sartre incorporates a great deal of what Heidegger sought to challenge. Heidegger dislikes the crudity of the confrontation of the *Néant* and being, he views it as perpetuating that heavy-handedness which has made man the creature of 'science', turned him to barbarism and set him on the path to the ruination of the planet. Heidegger sees Sartre as having forgotten the fundamental community of man with his world, before we can be a negation we must become an articulation of place. Man is historical before he is logical. Sartre's notion of consciousness is part of the sickness of man; as a symptom not a remedy.

Heidegger had hoped that *Being and Time* would help us remember, and would make us turn to our heritage with awe and anguish. That it would help us regain that awakening which gave man finitude. Instead Sartre had developed a philosophy which was an invitation to pursue with greater rigour the forgetting of being, which placed man amongst the very entities which were fashioned from his indolence. In Sartre's philosophy there is too much 'thought', and his ambition for thought makes man strong again at the expense of being. This ontology is part of man's delusion not part of the veneration of being. With the return to the *cogito* Sartre had made alienation part of the permanent structure of being, the idea of the *Néant* made isolation an inalienable condition of being. Sartre's 'realism' had fixed man in his forgetfulness, crystallizing the subject–object division; the very stigmata of our hostility to being. It was nothing short of an indulgence of forgetfulness.

Heidegger claims that like the Idealists before him, Sartre displays little respect for the life that is beyond the intellect, indeed, life for Sartre means the human endeavour. This is part of his shutting off of man from the world, the arrogance of this logical creature, his contempt for the cleverness of the world beyond man. Sartre has set aside the loving inclination to the ground which must be the start of the new metaphysics, he places alienation first, his concept of play is no more than an act of contempt, an unconcernful dealing. It is an invitation to violence, to abuse the world.

But if Sartre's man-centred philosophy has forgotten being and reduced nothing to a mere metaphor of logical negation, still its greatest weakness is to forget that man's alienation is of historical origin and has an historical solution. Heidegger looks to being as the homeland from which we are expelled. Our task is to become close to being again.

> In this closeness the decision, if any, is reached as to whether and how God and the gods deny themselves and the night remains, whether and how the day of the Holy dawns, whether and how in the rise of the Holy an appearance of god and the gods can start anew .... But the dimension for the gods and the God only comes into appearance when, first and after long preparation, Being itself has been cleared and been experienced in its truth.
>
> (LH 208)

Homelessness has become the world destiny. Here Heidegger sees value in the work of Marx, for Marx deriving the historical from Hegel has recognized 'in an essential and significant sense' the alienation of mankind. 'Marx, in discovering this alienation, reaches into an essential dimension of history, the Marxist view of history excels all other. Because, however, neither Husserl nor Sartre recognizes the essentially historical character of Being, neither phenomenology nor existentialism can permeate that dimension within which alone a productive discussion with Marxism is possible .... From the point of view of the history of Being, it is indisputable that in it [communism] an elementary experience has been made manifest of what is world-historical.' (LH 209)

I said in the Introduction to this work that the issue of freedom rests on our idea of artificiality – the degree to which we create ourselves. Where the 'create' and the 'we' awaited clarification. For Sartre in *Being and Nothingness* the 'we' is our natural being, the me confronted by others and 'create' is an outreaching to 'what is' which respects what is as ours in its very formulation. The constructive role of our end, of our project in fashioning the world as we find it, develops the Kantian notion of the constructive consciousness to its fullest outreach. The question Heidegger raises is how much this dream of self-creation is an indulgence of a certain mood. An indulgence which is arrogant, dangerous and destructive, one which kills the earth and draws men into an over-expansive taking for himself which inevitably leads to war and cruelty.

5

The Sources of Fragmentation

If someone knows only one thing about Sartre it will probably be that Sartre held man to be unconditionally free but lived to change his mind, to believe almost the opposite. There is no doubt that he believed in unconditional freedom, the difficult issue is to what extent he ceased to believe in it. Unquestionably his style and vocabulary did change, demonstrating a much greater respect for the complexity of social relations, acknowledging that the past, transmitted through the forces of convention and propriety, has a vital hold on our consciousness.

Perhaps we should begin by looking at how Sartre himself visualized the 'change' in his treatment of freedom. In a famous remark made in 1969 he said:

> The other day, I re-read a prefatory note of mine to a collection of plays – Les Mouches, Huis Clos and others – and was truly scandalized, I had written: 'Whatever the circumstances, and wherever the site, a man is always free to choose to be a traitor or not ...'. When I read this, I said to myself: it's incredible, I actually believed that!
>
> To understand how I could have done so, you must remember that there was a very simple problem during the Resistance – ultimately, one of courage .... The militant in the Resistance who was caught and tortured became a myth for us ... the problem then was solely that of physical endurance – it was not the ruses of history or the paths of alienation. A man is tortured: what will he do?
>
> (IT 44)

Sartre identifies what he refers to as 'German Existentialism' to be the philosophy of 'failure and pessimism', an attempt to

101

revive the transcendent, an 'exquisite subjectivity' fascinated with the ineffable, a 'philosophy of the bourgeoisie of the decadent class' (PM 15).

But how radical is Sartre's conversion; does it represent a different notion of man? Speaking a decade after the completion of the *Critique*, Sartre offered a summary of his view of freedom. Although anxious to stress the degree to which personal autonomy is circumscribed he reveals that self possession and self-determination remain his ultimate concern.

> The idea that I have never ceased developing is that, in the last analysis, each of us is always responsible for what has been made of him – even if we can do no more that assume that responsibility. I believe that a man can always make something of what has been made of him, that is, the definition I would give today of freedom, the little movement which makes of a totally conditioned social being a person who does not reproduce in its entirety what he received from his conditioning.
>
> (IT 45)

Sartre in the 'fifties began to look for an opportunity to re-express his thought in a way that would be inclusive, which would understand the individual as an element of a dynamic whole, but which would recognize this 'element' as vital and decisive. In a revealing passage in the *Problem of Method*[1] he says: 'we have confused the totality with the individual' (SM 20). We might conclude from this that he had embraced the criticism levelled at him in the *Letter on Humanism*. Person-hood, Heidegger argued, was the product of a practice of division, of finitization, of *self*-finitization whereby the totality is fractured and part is designated the private zone, the self. Heidegger says.

> So-called private existence ... adheres obstinately to a negation of the public. It remains an offshoot dependent on the public and nourishes itself on its mere retreat from the public .... So it is a witness against its will to its subjection to the public.
>
> (LH 198)

Heidegger felt that Sartre had failed to recognize that the *Néant* was not innate and natural but a practice, a way of being learned, acquired and socially formed. To treat the individual as the first principle was to grasp the product rather than the production.

Sartre's response, evolved in the *Problem of Method* and the *Critique of Dialectical Reason*,[2] is to develop an account of the human situation in which social forces are given a measure of control over the *Néant* or, more accurately, in which the *Néant* behaves as though it is controlled by such 'objective' forces. Explaining why the *Néant* is so willing to be duped and how it can be drawn into a 'radical conversion' is the task of Sartre's latter work.

Sartre seeks an understanding of the patterns by which man is objectively situated in order that man may have greater command over his life. In short, his philosophy becomes part of the genre which seeks to discover and rescue the whole man. Indeed, Sartre is a Marxist because he holds social organization to be the source of mystification, alienation and violence and because he believes intellectuals possess the power to detect in the society of their own time the ailment which is the cause of chaos and strife. In short, he stands with Marx in holding conflict and enmity to be human constructions open to human abolition, that re-organization offers the prospect of restoring whole being and self creativity to the individual.

While accepting Marx's analysis that man will be free when history is made by a single class he is concerned by the fact that under Marxism, theory has become stultified and regimented. The history of Soviet Marxism has shown that Communism itself has failed to redeem its promise of emancipation and has, instead, itself become a system of alienation. Sartre's work is primarily guided by the intellectual need to explain how the abolition of private property and the rule of the proletariat has managed to retain a system of exploitation.

Sartre seeks to liberate thought from the binds of liberal humanism which he believes to be the root of contemporary alienation and to offer an account of the process of alienation which challenges Marx's reliance upon private property. The *Method* and the *Critique* are an attempt to find the free man, to give an outline as to how and why intellectuals can see beyond the conditioning of their epoch, that is, the humanism which has produced the isolated and estranged individual and its perverted and destructive view of freedom. They also seek to explain the responsibility of intellectuals to align themselves with and give assistance to those whose existence is an attempt to escape the conditions of oppression. The comparatively short book the *Problem of Method* is among the most important of Sartre's works, in fact, the much larger *Critique* can be best understood as an attempt to clarify and refine the arguments presented in the *Method*.

＊＊＊

Sartre viewed Marxism as the greatest nineteenth century attempt to construct a human society which would be able to make its own history (SM 31). While this must remain the task of philosophy, we now live in a world where Marxism had failed. It had fallen into the service of a new elite, its interest was to understand the world in terms which maintained the regime rather than pursued the emancipation of humanity (SM 133). Soviet Marxism as a state philosophy has become 'a terrorist practice of liquidating the particular' (SM 28). The task of philosophy is to restore to Marxist theory the task of liberation, to find the whole man, the force that makes history.

The ossification of Marxism has given existentialism a new responsibility, 'Marxism has re-absorbed man into the idea, existentialism seeks him everywhere where he is, at his work, in his home, in the street' (ibid.). Existentialism can emancipate the being which lies at the pivotal moment of creation. The task of emancipation remains, as Marx intended, that man should make history with full self-awareness.

The positive quality of existentialism was its commitment to the whole individual without definition or restriction. We must comprehend the conditions of each individual before we can understand him as his own project of self-creation, that project which is his alone, and through which the world is changed. Marxism as an ideology has reduced the individual to an object, a product of conditions, it deliberately ignores that 'small margin' which transforms and humanizes the world. In so far as the world is human it is through that lacuna in objectivity, i.e. the *Néant*, which is man. In a much quoted remark Sartre summarizes this synthesis: 'Valéry is a petit bourgeois intellectual but not every petit bourgeois intellectual is Valéry' (SM 56).

As in *Being and Nothingness*, action is the creative source of all meaning. We cannot analyse a person by resorting to generalities; they must reveal themselves through their deeds. Sartre says; 'each of us escapes history to the extent that we make it'.[3] We come to know the individual's condition through their life; this understanding requires that we find the true meaning of what has been done, made or used, by reference to the situation which it completes, in short, a hermeneutic method.

> Man, irremediable singularity, is the being through whom the universal comes into the world; once fundamental chance starts to be lived, it assumes the form of necessity. Lived experience [le vécu] ... is made up of non-significant accidents of being insofar as they are surpassed towards a significance they did not possess at the beginning.[4]

Thus, the true significance of the *Method* is that it sustains this existential agent as its primary presupposition but understands it as articulating the prevailing conditions. Manifest conditions are certainly viewed as being grounded in the project, but now the project is viewed as arising within a world attitude which is social and collective. These conditions are recognized as having real legislative power over the self-finitizing consciousness. It is the nature of this 'real power' which is the issue Sartre wants to clarify.

In this new existentialism, exterior or 'objective' relations or practices are part of the positive constitution of our being, that is, of our 'totality'. Sartre never abandons the idea of self-finitization, of the *Néant*, rather he incorporates it in a dialectic whereby its way of being is the origin of its own mystification and the alienated individual is an outcome of a way of being–doing which is infected with self-disrupting elements. He holds that no philosophy of liberation can be founded upon anything less than the revelation of man as a being who is in the act of self-creation, the political emancipation of mankind rests upon our determination to demand the full vital human being in his unabused creativity.

Sartre employs what he calls the progressive-regressive method. This attempts to comprehend the situation through the individual's manifestation of himself. It reads the event as revealing both the conditions and the project of surpassing those conditions. The regressive aspect of the technique reveals the individual's conditions as they are disclosed through their deed. The example Sartre offers is someone moving to open a window, by which we understand their prior condition as being 'too hot'. The regressive analysis should employ all the analytic tools available to us, to act along side the agent, to know the world as they find it, anthropology, sociology and psychology must be used to emancipate the full knowledge of the agent. This is important because only by exhaustively examining the agents prior conditions can we isolate the agent's future expectation which provoked this unique and specific deed. In an era of alienation separating out the agent's bewildered interpretation of his world is an exacting procedure, the biographical works of Sartre are extended efforts to apply this method in practice.

The progressive analysis rests on man as the being who works for his future. Conduct can be comprehended only by relating existing conditions to the future project to which it attempts to give birth. Only the project as mediating between moments of objectivity can account for history as the manifestation of humanity.

> This material being perpetually goes beyond the condition which is made for him; he reveals and determines his situation by transcending it in order to objectify himself – by work, by action, or gesture.
>
> (SM 99)

In his surpassing of the given, in his creativity, man makes himself known, hence, it is in his creativity we must seek him. Yet his creativity takes its meaning from his circumstances, from his world as comprehended, or 'totalized' and as surpassed. This dynamic of transformative self creation is what Sartre calls *praxis*.

> Praxis is a passage from objective to objective through internalization. The project, as the subjective surpassing of objectivity toward objectivity, and stretched between the objective structures of the field of possibles, represents *in itself* the moving unity of subjectivity and objectivity, those cardinal determinants of activity. The subjective then appears as a necessary moment in the objective process.
>
> (SM 97)

Praxis is the being-doing which responds to the needs of the situation and generates an understanding which maintains self-possession. The important point is that man remains self-finitizing, the pivotal moment of the dialectic. The individual, as project, recreates the world, is the source of meaning and value. Man defines himself through his own *praxis* by means of changes suffered or provoked and the interiorization of such changes, and then the surpassing of that internalization (SM 167). Our significations are recovered and, in that very act of recovery, surpassed as our own total signification.

Thus far this account could be merely a revision of the earlier existential theory. The distinct difference of his later ideas rests in the degradation of the capacity of the individual to autonomously take command of the situation – to repossess or take charge of his innate power of self-finitization. For our practice of being individual, being responsible and choosing are already imbued with elements which bind us to the dead world. We practice a perverted sort of choosing which leads us to impoverishment. For while only man can humanize the world, and man is the outcome of this humanization of the world, it is perversely the case that this very history is the shackle which binds man to his fate of oppression, exploitation and cruelty. Man's humanity is disturbed by his human inheritance.

The problems which dominate Sartre's later thought are characterized by the idea of self-inhibition: Why is humanity the origin of so much that is a denial of humanity? The substance of Sartre's later thought is how our way of life has been turned against our most human capacity, that of self-creation. To understand Sartre's attitude to this it is necessary to look first at Karl Marx's theory of alienation which Sartre considers to be the inspiration of his work.

* * *

The shibboleth of German Idealism is that man is the outcome of his own creative power, that history has been an adventure of self-discovery and that our humanity, our intellect and ability are its product. Phenomenology, particularly the phenomenology of Hegel, is the most cogent and complete statement of this creed, but Hegel's work is not the most influential. That distinction belongs to the thought of Karl Marx.

All phenomenologies achieve their coherence by dividing the world into appearance and reality, where the world we know as our day-to-day reality is appearance and where the thesis of the phenomenologist discloses the reality. The phenomenologist offers a key to a truth that lies beyond our everyday dealings and reveals a previously obscured reality. Knowledge, understanding, social order and values are portrayed by phenomenology as products of a deeper structure. For Hegel this 'deeper structure' was the manifestation of the 'mind' through history, through the objective disciplines which were themselves internalized as our intellect.

For Marx this 'deeper structure' is man himself, or more dynamically, it is the emancipation of 'man's essential powers' (PM 130).

For Marx, man is always real, that is part of the material-biological world. Appearance or 'imagination', as Marx usually refers to our mystified thought, has come into the world as an unintended consequence of the way we have dealt with our needs. Specifically, the estrangement of man from 'Man', the fully real, is an outcome of the way we have arranged our productive life, that is, the division of labour or property relations. Like Hegel, Marx believes that social organization is the substance of history, the very stuff of our understanding of the world. Against Hegel, Marx argues that organization has succeeded in its objective at the grave cost of alienating man from his true, immediate and comprehensive, self-possession. It is Marx's contention that human artifice is not only the source of man's brilliance and dexterity but also the origin of cruelty, abuse and deception. He convincingly portrays organization as being equally capable of generating mystification and liberation, of having an ambiguous relation to man's reality, to his 'essential powers'. For Marx the evil in humanity has a human origin.

Let us return to the primary difference between Hegel and Marx – that of the driving force of history. For Marx, man's becoming, that is, history, is not the manifestation of some occult force or Mind but man becoming man. He is already what he will be. Man's essential nature is innate and universal subject to no variation by time or place. For Marx only thought is historically dynamic; man's true being, the bio-material, is unchanging. Both thought and social structures are the product of our attempt to meet our natural needs. While the governing dynamic of history is the quest to satisfy need it is our modes of organization made in pursuit of this quest which are the substance of history. It is these organizational adaptations; the division of labour or relations of production or property relations, which are the subject of Marx's philosophy.

It might be helpful to see Marx's work as presenting three essential facets:

1. A theory of knowledge which is rooted in productive activity which has come to be called *praxis*.
2. A theory of alienation which sees man's estrangement from his fullness of being as an unintended consequence of his own endeavour.

3. A theory of liberation which combines the theories of *praxis* and alienation in order to argue that man is capable of re-organizing productive relations so as to repossess his fullness of being and emancipate himself from both servitude to nature and servitude to others.

Central in understanding Marx's work is the point that for Marx alienation means 'going beyond' as in losing oneself or becoming hostile to what one really is whereas for Hegel it means 'going beyond', as in a moment of growth.

Although Hegel's thought uses the term *praxis* and is the original inspiration of *praxis* philosophies it is Marx who is the true initiator of this genre. For Marx, man's way of thinking is itself a practical activity which becomes estranged from the material creation of his life as an outcome of the increasingly abstract nature of his actual production of his life. This 'increasingly abstract nature' of self production is a consequence of our organization of production other-wise referred to as the division of labour which is itself an outcome of our instrumental abilities or the 'technology' of production.

For Marx human sensuousness is the primary ground and such things as knowledge and 'spirit' are its phenomenal products. It is impossible to understand Marx's thought without appreciating that consciousness is, for him, an aspect of this 'practical human sensu-ousness'. In order to recognize why man is alienated under capital-ism and what grants Marx the prophetic vision and diagnostic critique which has made his work so appealing, we must under-stand that the intellect has been produced by the way we deal with the world. In a key passage from the *German Ideology* he tells us.

[The] mode of production must not be considered simply as being the production of the physical existence of the individuals. Rather it is a definite form of activity of these individuals, a definite form of expressing their life .... As individuals express their life, so they are. What they are, therefore, coincides with their production, both with what they produce and how they produce. The nature of individuals thus depends on the material conditions determining their production.

(MSW 161)

The material production of our lives is the key to Marx's theory of knowledge, to his understanding of alienation and to his belief that man is within reach of the end of such alienation. It is important to recognize that for Marx neither need or scarcity is the source of alienation, for man, by nature, exists in a need relationship with the world, 'a being which does not have its nature outside its being is not a natural being' (PM 137).

According to the *German Ideology* man has lost his oneness with his natural being as a consequence of the division of labour, i.e. the way production is organized. As a refinement we are informed that the various stages of development in the division of labour are just so many different forms of ownership.

> The production of ideas, of conceptions, of consciousness, is at first directly interwoven with the material activity and the material intercourse of men, the language of real life. Conceiving, thinking, the mental intercourse of men, appear at this stage as the direct efflux of their material behaviour. The same applies to mental production as expressed in the language of politics, laws, morality, religion, metaphysics, etc. of a people. Men are the producers of their conceptions, ideas, etc. – real, active men, as they are conditioned by a definite development of their productive forces and of the intercourse corresponding to these .... Morality, religion, metaphysics, all the rest of ideology and their corresponding forms of consciousness have no history, no development; but men, developing their material production and their material intercourse, alter, along with this their real existence, their thinking and the products of their thinking. Life is not determined by consciousness but consciousness by life.
>
> (MSW 164)

This is not only as concise a statement of Marx's position as can be found but also a very fine outline of the genre of thought which has come to be referred to as *praxis* philosophy. Marx's *praxis* theory is intimately linked with his theory of alienation and we should now briefly study his view of this matter.

Alienation is not part of nature nor a 'necessary' aspect of man's being here. Marx considered alienation to be a phenomenon introduced into the world through human relations, more specifically through the organization of production. Alienation is phenomenal because it is produced within a system of self-creation. Its genesis is the partial involvement of each in his own life, the marginalization of the active role each plays in his own self-production. No longer is he the product of himself, nor does he dwell in intimacy with his production, thus his product takes on a sort of occult existence which is strange and abstract, 'the worker is related to the product of his labour as to an alien object' (PM 63). Moreover he no longer produces to his needs but to the specifications of his job, he must surrender power over his own productive will, 'the worker's activity [is] not his spontaneous activity, it belongs to another; it is the loss of his self' (PM 66). For Marx alienation is practical, the result of a certain style of artifice.

But by far the most intricate and politically influential aspect of Marx's thought has been its view that productive estrangement is not only a contingent fact of human organization but also, avoidable and unnecessary. Two important points relate to the matter; why alienation is avoidable in a certain sort of productive age and how Marx explains his ability to foresee this coming age.

Put in plain terms Marx believed that alienation would be avoided in some future – post revolutionary – age because the factory system rendered the old relations of production anachronistic. The division of labour which had manifested itself in private property and capitalism was out-moded. As private property was the key to the estrangement of the worker from the product of his labour, the abolition of private property and its replacement by the more natural and immediate practice of property being held in common and distributed according to need would return to man his full and complete self-productive awareness.

It is Marx's contention that, while consciousness is formed as a product of our material endeavour it is not produced directly by our labour but in the social relations which have emerged as a primary by-product of the division of labour, the property relations. These property relations govern consciousness. Such notions as value, right and propriety are all justifications of the current relations of production. As consciousness is intimately related to the organization of production even when the usefulness of that order has been surpassed by our productive ability, by the forces of production, consciousness remains dominated by the order of relations which has been technically superseded. Or, in other words, social relations which are the product of the division of labour have a sort of inertia, a power to sustain themselves even when the productive need of these arrangements have be surpassed.

The normative force of Marx's work rests upon the belief that while the productive need for private property has been surpassed, the institution was maintained by those who materially benefit from its way of organization. Their material interest was the conserving force which retained what were the effectively redundant social relations associated with capitalism and with its practical consciousness, bourgeois values and propriety. Consciousness, order, propriety and the values associated with private property were now archaic in real terms, i.e. the forces of production but were sustained as an anachronism. Alienation, estrangement and exploitation have survived beyond the technological circumstances which gave rise to them and, hence, their practical usefulness because consciousness had itself become estranged.

> Consciousness only arises from the need, the necessity, of intercourse with other men …. Consciousness is for that reason from the very beginning a social product …. Division of labour only becomes truly such from the moment when a division of material and mental labour appears. From this moment onwards consciousness can really flatter itself that it is something other than consciousness of existing practices.
>
> (MSW 167)

Like Hegel, Marx believes that the intellect attains its pattern from social order but he interprets the significance of this recognition very differently. While Hegel holds our insight into this process to be always 'too late', it is always an outcome bereft of the capacity to manage or alter those circumstances which form its nature, Marx believes we know the underlying guiding force, the end which governs developments. We have knowledge of a 'real' being; one not mediated by patterns of relations, i.e. which are not phenomenal. Knowledge of this natural, innate and 'real' being is efficacious, useful and of operative application it is a standard by which the phenomenal manifestations of man can be measured and criticized. Marx's system, unlike Hegel's, 'knows' the *raison d'être* of human struggle.

The belief that Marx correctly identified the underlying guiding force of history and that the 'reason' of our age is the product of an old, antiquated and redundant order and of its profiteers gives Marxism its power to recommend and its authoritarian structure. Those who dissent from Marx's revolutionary view can be dismissed as thinking in terms of the old order, of failing to appreciated the phenomenal nature of reason. It makes the philosophy tragically invulnerable to intellectual examination as well as from practical criticism. It also accounts for Marx's style of advocacy, for if social order, reason and justice were products of social relations, Marx could explain the need for his writing, characterizing it as a catalyst, one element in urging workers to ignore conventions, social rules and their consciences and dispute the ownership of property and wealth.

Indeed, in terms of his influence upon history, it is Marx's justification of the use of force which is most important. The old order must be physically removed because those who prosper by it will not see the need for change. Left to their own devices they will do all in their power to conserve and retain the archaic institutions, their morality and politics which all operate to their material benefit. The workers' suffering will not in itself inspire revolt for without Marx's help their minds will be governed by the prevailing relations of production, by private property and capitalism. Indeed, the demand for institutional reform will be irrational. It will appear destructive and disturbing even morally outrageous, but it will be the vanguard of the new age and new intuitions and hence a new rationality.

Marx's key innovation is that human organization is the source not of comprehension but of distraction and confusion. This is, ultimately, the justification of revolution. By comparison, nothing could be more abhorrent to Hegelian thought than that social order should be challenged and destroyed. For Hegel, the institutions, values and practices were the repository of human wisdom and skill, our ability to live well. To instigate the wholesale destruction of a set of practices would be to deprive mankind of part of his civilization. Because all concrete recognitions are phenomenal, Hegel would point out to Marx that the idea of the sensuous productive man that Marx thought innate and universal was just a phenomenon, a product of the institutional achievements of his age. For Hegel no structure is ever entirely archaic but is, rather, absorbed into a more complex order. The destruction of the achievement of a particular stage would return society to an earlier, less sophisticated order.

There are two points here. Firstly, to simply destroy a set of social practices is actually a very difficult thing to do, for the mental practices of the contemporary generation will not be so readily altered. The concepts which are valuable to a culture would seem to be quite resistant to synthetic, authoritarian manipulation. Secondly, if institutional practices are the antecedent of reason and order in the Hegelian way, we would have no foreknowledge of what sort of being, life and humanity would be created from any synthetically rearranged institutions. The new man might well be more violent and inhumane than the old.

Marx's primary presuppositions are:

1. That he has correctly identified the ground of human history; that is, the conquest of basic material need.
2. That in his age, the age of factory production and of world trade, such basic need can be met.
3. That productive processes and trade have made the private property stage of the division of labour redundant.
4. That such division of labour is solely and entirely the cause of human productive alienation.

The problem is what is it that gives Marx the confidence to claim that private property and nothing else is the locus of estrangement. It is one thing to say that private property has had its day, quite another to say that without private property man would no longer be alienated. The assumption of Marx's theory is that the division of labour is the sole source of fracture within our *praxis*, that is, the one and only origin of separation within the creative unity of our world.

So for Marx, human history has been the struggle to overcome basic need, the principle which world history is to emancipate is 'man', no more and no less than our actual being in the world. Since disorder and unhappiness have their origin in our activity, they may be dissolved within the sphere of human possibility. The theme of Marx's thought is that history is not a mystery, an invention or an accident, but is practical and all practicality extends from our immediate, ever-present and unchanging being; mystery is our creation, something we have imposed upon ourselves, an unintended consequence of the organization of production.

It is important to restate that, whilst need or hunger disturbs us, it cannot estrange us, for only estrangement from nature can be the cause of human conflict. For Marx, as need is part of nature it cannot be the origin of chaos and conflict. The belief that man has a natural oneness with the world that only artifice has fragmented the whole man – qualifies Marx's philosophy as a naturalism, though one of a very intricate and sophisticated kind. The ultimate distinction between the system of Marx and that of Hegel is that for Marx man's wholeness is always with man and available to him as a standard or norm, it may be obscured by the mystifications induced by productive practice but it remains within us. For Hegel the whole was something for which we had to reach out, whatever stage of sophistication man might have reached wholeness was always one step beyond us drawing us into change and danger. Hegel's work encourages us to recognize with magnanimity that we exist at the point of mediation of spirit and being, with all its attendant toil, strife and conflict and become reconciled to this plight. Marx found this view of human history unacceptable. The recurring point of his work is that if the quest of history had any objective other than attending to our actual needs then that objective was an obstacle to 'man' and represented a false demand, for if reason was rooted in social practices other than those which would accomplish the feeding, clothing and housing of the population then such reason was mystified and perverted.

However, the practical evidence of socialist countries seems to be that 'rational organization' of production contains many unforeseen consequences, such as a disinterested work-force, unmotivated and unambitious, creating products of poor quality. Even worse, on the demand side of the economy there was considerable disagreement over the prioritization of competing needs, many of which Marx would have thought frivolous or eccentric. The implementation of a 'rational system of distribution' proved more contentious than Marx foresaw, disagreements regarding which qualities ought to count in assessing need and disputes as to how to calculate merit were, in practice, divisive and destructive. Most discouraging of all for Marx would be the fact that the abolition of private property seems in practice to do nothing to the individual's sense of being at home in his world. Communist man appears as equally estranged from the world and from others as 'bourgeois' man. These observations led some on the Left to conclude that the character of human existence may not be exclusively determined by the character of ownership and that liberation from estrangement might rely upon aspects of life other than property ownership. It is just such a *praxis* theory and just such a remedy which Sartre seeks to offer us.

* * *

The *Critique* is Sartre's most extensive attempt to deal with the matters which he feels Marxist thought has handled incorrectly or insufficiently. Sartre is a Marxist to the extent that he holds: (1) organizational practices cause alienation; (2) we can know what re-organization is required for emancipation.

For Sartre, need, scarcity and other people are natural elements of our circumstance. None of these could in themselves determine that we must be competitive rather than co-operative, greedy rather than generous or acquisitive rather than communal. The viciousness and cruelty of modern society is the outcome of a specific historical project, not one chosen by us but one we, nonetheless, have created. It is a destiny we maintain, nurture and develop despite our distaste for much of what it involves, a destiny we have made for ourselves and which we are, at any point, capable of changing. For Sartre, as distinct from Marx, there is no age of liberation, no epoch that is more privileged than any other, transformation has always been and will always be at hand. Yet only the determination to rid ourselves of mystification will emancipate man and restore the capacity to be the self creator of our own history.

We have seen that Marx's argument does not assume that man is alienated from nature *per se* but, rather, alienation is a consequence of contemporary organization. However, we are forced to acknowledge that a naturalism is implicit in his 'optimism'; that we are capable of living free of alienation. This assumes that there is a real, innate and universal state for man, a situation of being at home in his world. It is this 'being at home' which is the real problem, for how can we be sure that man has the potential for such 'wholeness', that it is in his nature to be at one with this world?

As in his earlier work, Sartre's presupposition is that man is essentially self-possessed. He says that 'the epistemological starting point must always be consciousness as apodictic certainty (of) itself and as consciousness of such and such an object' (CDR 51). This could easily have come from the *Transcendence of the Ego* or from *Being and Nothingness*. It reaffirms the principle of translucidity of consciousness and the ultimate incorruptibility of the *Néant*.

For Sartre the process of alienation is redeemable because man – as consciousness – is always the source of his own experience. Recognition and control of this self-possession has been lost through our participation in a way of life, a way of thinking which obscures the vital fact that man is the creator of man. For Sartre, the process of self-creation belongs to us always, even alienation is a product of a chosen way of being. The illusion of impotency is a situation made to be, the *praxis*, the self-making or consciousness making activity, alone determines meaning. In the key remark of his introduction he tells us that

> If dialectical Reason is to be possible as the career of all and the freedom of each, as experience and as necessity, if we are to display *both* its total translucidity (it is not more than ourself) and its untranscendable severity (it is the unity of everything that conditions us), if we are to ground it as the rationality of *praxis*, of totalization, and of society's future ... if we are to determine its significance, then we must realize the situated experience of its apodicticity *through ourselves*. Its goal is simply to reveal and establish dialectical rationality, that is to say, the complex play of *praxis* and totalization.
>
> (CDR 39)

Sartre sees the adventure of man as a unity, that consciousness is its own ground. Only self confusion is responsible for the ignorance of this power. This again refers us to Sartre's clarity of mind, his rationalism. The aim of the *Critique* is to avoid the claustrophobia of *Being and Time* where thought is always a part of its age, Sartre seeks to explain how 'reason' has the power to construct a critique of the current *praxis*. He aims to justify how, in the midst of a *praxis* that is partial and numbing, intellectuals can offer mankind a path to liberation. The tragic yearning of being in-itself for-itself described in *Being and Nothingness* is viewed by the *Critique* as a part of the mystification of our way of organizing our relations. Sartre seeks to abandon the idea that our metaphysical state of being nothingness can of itself be the cause of dissatisfaction – unhappiness is no longer seen as part of the universal and necessary structure of being, but a phenomenal outcome of one way of organizing our way of being.

The attitude of resignation – that self-possession is impossible – is a consequence of alienation, indeed, the 'useless passion' of *Being and Nothingness* is a human product of human fragmentation not our inevitable condition. Only mystification clouds our intellectual self-possession and mystification created by man can be abolished by man. An appreciation of alienation then will explain why man lives chaotically, under regimes of oppression, and how this mesmerism can be broken.

Sartre tacitly admits that the error of *Being and Nothingness*, of his existentialism, was to take translucidity as personal, ignoring that the person is a *praxis* loaded with destructive elements. Bourgeois humanism, of which the private individual is a part, is a *praxis* of fragmentation and alienation. More significantly, whilst the otherness of the other is a product of our way of being, it is not an inherent aspect of being.

Sartre sides with Heidegger in viewing the self as a practice learned from the collective resource, that is, the individual is a product of the common *praxis*; the particular is now viewed as one aspect of an objective adventure. If we are to seek our home in the world, overcome oppressive practices and the vicious handling of scarcity, then it is this objective adventure which must be clarified, for it is the collective *praxis* which is mystified, and it must be the collective that is emancipated. This is the political programme of Sartre's later period.

Sartre learned from Heidegger that choice is itself a practical product of the cultural adventure, operated at any one time within a complex of inherited assumptions. In the *Critique*, the power of self-finitization is absorbed into the common practice of finitizing the world. Sartre always remains loyal to the idea that each individual is the self-defining principle of their world, but in the *Critique* the resources the individual uses to shape his world, his faculties, are acquired from the way the world is ordered. Our way of orientating ourselves to our world comes as a complex containing within its both the idea of 'self' and, intimately associated with it, the mystifications which embroil us in the processes of inhumanity.

This inhumanity and estrangement is created and maintained by man, but is so deeply ingrained in our *praxis* that for the concrete operative individual it is sewn into the very fabric of his being-here. It is an inherent aspect of the individual's understanding of 'self-hood' and 'world', and is a condition only to be escaped in madness. Alienation is our way of managing our lives, but this alienation grasps our way of living so radically that we are not free to dissociate ourselves from it. Man is estranged from his product, where man is the product of himself. What is required in order that he might be liberated from the grip of this self-estrangement is that his product, his self, be returned to him as his own creation. We must find a way of turning the cycle of reciprocal alienation into a cycle of reciprocal emancipation. How can we transform the forces which are preventing humanity from being the master of its fate?

The essence of our alienation is that we have lost the knack of true self possession. Each individual has lost the power of self-creation because each operates a structure of denial of the full humanity of both themselves and every other. The individual's practical encounter with himself is mediated through a world given meaning by a regime, or social practice, which clouds their innate clarity. Sartre said, 'If history escapes me it is not because I am not making it but because the other is making it as well' (SM 88). My life is not my own because any designation I give to it can be countermanded by any other. I am in the situation of constantly having to re-determine myself in a landscape not of my choosing and adapt to a world which fails to reflect my intended determinations. We have, in short, lost our grip upon ourselves. We are a 'totality' which is populated by alien forces.

Initially it might appear to be a mere commonplace that others deprive me of possession of the world. Since we share a common environment they must inhibit me just as surely as my project must make demands upon them. However, Sartre holds that such conflict is not natural but created; it is part of human artifice. The intrusion of one upon one another is avoidable. The scarcity which causes me to intrude upon the other and *vice versa* is not natural, essential and unavoidable, but a product of our way of living our project.

Sartre is adamant that natural scarcity has no direct charge upon our lives. The simple fact that some resource is limited does not dictate how it should be managed, still less that we should form relations of conflict as a consequence. Sartre acknowledges that in an age of alienation this might be difficult for us to accept, for that very alienation requires us to believe that we are bound by nature to struggle and to live in need. It is the constitutive role of the individual in the maintenance of this regime of mystification which is the key to our liberation. The *praxis* of conflict antecedes scarcity and strife. It is not natural material need which determines that we should negate the existence of the other, rather, the practice of the negation of the other produces scarcity. Sartre's problem in the *Method* and in the *Critique* is to explain this structure of action and belief, this *praxis*, and to provide us with the incentive and the means to end this regime of self mystification.

If chaos and oppression are to be remediable they must not only be created by us, we must also be capable of living without creating them. This Sartre believes to be the case. He holds that estrangement is an outcome of our *praxis*, that is to say, is fully located within the adventure of being-here. The argument is really very similar to Marx's. For Marx alienation was an avoidable and destructive loss of human self-control brought about through archaic and inessential structures of organization. Sartre argues that man's estrangement is produced by us in a process of self-inhibition, of living in a way that permits inanimate things to rule us, of giving licence to dead matter to control our being. This argument resembles the for-itself's bad faith, its willingness to pretend to be in-itself. In the *Critique* this empowering of a thing-like deadness within our lives is referred to as the 'practico-inert'. They are practices which make man dead to himself and entail the illusion of impotency.

We can summarize the argument of Sartre's later philosophy by saying that man, the bearer of the *Néant*, is alienated from his world, from his lucidity, by practices, objective and collective, which are the foundation of his knowledge but which also delude and bemuse him by involving him in avoidable acts of self-abuse. It is the nature of the self-abuse, the genealogy of this unnecessary and avoidable alienation which the *Theory of Practical Ensembles* attempts to elucidate. Sartre assumes the elucidation of alienation is itself enough to enable us to liberate ourselves from alienation because it is only alienation which keeps us from self-creation.

To recap, we can say that in acquiring the habits and arrangements which govern our 'here-being' we inherit mystification and bewilderment incorporated within them. The crucial point, however, is that for Sartre, this mystification is a distinct and specific process, a canker within *praxis* which can be distilled and siphoned off. The *Critique* is dominated by his account of how this germ enters the practical ensemble and how we may begin to live without it, that is, how we might come to live at home in our world.

The key to man's critical grip upon his fate rests with the practico-inert, that aspect of our *praxis* which drags us into a fumbling awkwardness. This impediment is inflicted upon us by ourselves and is avoidable. However, for man in alienated society counter-*praxes* are an inherent part of *praxis*. Each project has costs, however, the practico-inert, the subject of 'practical ensembles' is a cost of a different order. It appears as already wedded to our very way of being-here, of being a self, of being free, of being truthful, responsible, etc. The practico-inert, therefore, possesses a necessity, a feeling of unavoidability and seems indistinguishable from the *praxes* themselves.

In the counter-*praxes* of practical ensembles, our actions take on meanings foreign to our intentions, where the dead world haunts our projects as though emulating the intentionality and freedom of other agents; it brings opacity into the heart of the *praxis*. It is the project of the *Critique* to enable us to distinguish the aspects of our *praxis* which give life to the dead world, and which thereby make the present hostage of the past.

In order to comprehend the structure which is to be presented it is necessary to return to the idea of scarcity. Man exists in need and while the exact nature of this need might vary, with technology and organization it remains the *a priori* condition of our being-here as a functioning being. It is a simple fact of being that to use a finite resource here and now is to negate alternative possibilities, i.e. later, elsewhere. While scarcity cannot of itself specify concrete social arrangements it does provide the motive force of human organization, for however men arrange their affairs, they must do so under its auspices. As a consequence, all human arrangements are constructed with the implicit awareness that one man's well-being can be the occasion for another's destruction. Even the most socially co-operative organization must cope with this fact – it is a living possibility of the human predicament.

What Sartre offers us is a way of understanding human history as a cycle of co-operative and competitive patterns of behaviour. In place of the class struggle of Marx's material dialectic, Sartre erects a dialectic whose component parts are spontaneous unity and destructive antagonism spiralling through history as a natural consequence of the threat each man poses to the other.

Of the two elements of the dialectic of practical ensembles, series and group, neither is prior or superior to the other. They are mutually dependent and evolve one from the other. Each develops as a disruptive and ultimately destructive element of the other. The spontaneous unity of the ensemble Sartre refers to as the group and its negation, the solitary individual, Sartre calls the series. These two forms of 'practical ensembles' stand in historical tension and it is the relation between them which dominates Sartre's work.

The series is a way of being here such that the other is specifically viewed as a negation of one's possibility. Sartre describes it as solitude; a lived structure of exclusion. The example that he offers is that of the bus queue. Here each individual is interchangeable, they are all demonstrating the same need, and they each deprive each other of attaining their goal exactly to the extent that they

themselves succeed in obtaining their own. The principle of distribution, of satisfaction, is entirely extraneous to the actual need.
There is no inherent human quality which distributes the good,
one's access to the bus is regulated by one's place in the queue,
itself simply a matter of exclusion and contingency, without reference to the individual need being satisfied, the urgency of the
journey the value of the trip, each is set to stand in silence in the
express project of negating the possibility of the other. Respect for
others is purely negative. Sartre points out that many sub-projects
will permit the agent to succeed in denying that the other has a
valid need, reading a newspaper, thinking of some diversion, all of
which helps him to sustain his project which has at its heart the de-
humanizing denial of the other's humanity. We treat each other as
things and act so as to cement the dynamic of human existence to
the dead world. Serial behaviour establishes and sustains attitudes
and behaviour which effectively privatizes humanity and permits
us to designate the other as inhuman, as negative to my being here.
The essence of serial behaviour is the reification of the inert, we
submit humanity to the inert order. The *praxis* of each gives to the
finite world a power to control the relation of each to the other. In
the serial ensemble humanity has been ruled out as the ordering
principle, in the bus queue only the mechanical fact of the number
of places on the bus decides whether someone will travel or have to
wait longer. This illustrates how inertial facts are brought to life,
are given significance in our relationships, what Sartre calls the
practico-inert.

Sartre speaks of the passage from serial behaviour to the group
as being accidental and contingent. It is not so much a project as an
event occurring in response to the perception of peril. There is a
sense of suffocation, the situation so fraught with danger that a
reaction is sparked, people become a crowd, a mob, a unity acting
spontaneously and in unison. Series becomes a group. The classic
example is the Storming of the Bastille, but any insurrection would
exemplify the mood which Sartre is trying to isolate. It is the disin-
tegration of group into series which occupies most of the *Critique*.
This necessary structure holds the key to human alienation and
misery; it is the story of the counter-*praxis*.

The point of fusion is reached when the collective, finding their
condition untenable and insufferable, are driven to break free from
the existing order, destroying the atomizing *praxis* of the series.
This apocalypse must be made by the determination of particular

men in specific circumstances, only human determination can create such a revolution. This is significant as it accounts for Sartre's own political activities, his articles, petitions and demonstrations; indeed, it in part accounts for the *Critique* itself.

In the moment of fusion the *praxis* of the ensemble is jolted into clarity, into self-possession. At this point there is no synthetic otherness, it is a moment when humanity is taken as the sole guiding principle. The project of all the members is homogeneous and ubiquitous, their *praxis* is framed solely by their adventure and the inertia of the world. While as an historical phenomena the insurrectional group is sporadic, transient and fleeting for Sartre, it is a glimpse at the true root of all *praxis* because as a *praxis* it has humanity as its animating principle. Its profound significance is its clarity of adventure which sweeps away all the inherited inertia and opacity in a breath-taking display of confidence and adequacy.

The group-in-fusion annuls the distinction between projects so that each agent's understanding of the situation is limited only by the inertia of the resistant world, i.e. naturally, and not by introduced and artificial projects of manipulation or exclusion. In this *praxis* the gap between self and other is merely formal, I find myself in the world as I am in myself, hence the pessimistic paradox of human relations offered in *Being and Nothingness* is replaced in the *Critique* by an immediate and practical reciprocity. This transparent reciprocity is the real theme of Sartre's life's work. It was Sartre's ambition, manifest since *Transcendence of the Ego*, to reveal that mood where man could make himself without depriving others of their humanity; the theory of practical ensembles was undoubtedly considered by him to be the fruition of this vision, its most complete formulation. And the account of the degeneration of this moment of hot-fusion is the story of how humanity is usurped by inhumanity, of how the project of exclusion comes to dominate human life. It is also Sartre's explanation for the 'pessimism' of his earlier work.

Sartre presents us with a paradigm of self-mystification. The agent voluntarily and purposefully surrenders part of his immediate freedom for the greater concrete freedom of a co-operative ensemble, this initial act draws the agent into a web of ever increasing confusion and self-betrayal, into a complex of self-inhibition and de-humanization.

The burden of the thesis of the *Critique*, i.e. that alienation is artificial and avoidable, rests on the decay of the group, for its dissolution is the origin of the ghostly force of inhumanity secreted within human *praxis*. The initial germ of the dissipation of the group's unity lies in the individual consciousness, each agent is an individual comprehension, autonomous and distinct. This produces an awareness that there are goals other than those represented by the group. The individual experiences this discord as an awareness that the group adventure is not the entirety of his being, as a fear of freedom. The individual must deny part of himself in order to retain the group project. This denial is the ground of all alienation.

The group's unanimity and spontaneity has, then, an intrinsic disposition to slacken, rooted in the atomized nature of man. Insecurity and the potential for perfidy are built into the group as primary structures. The first moment of degeneration is not due to treachery itself but to the fear of treachery, a fear rooted in an intuitive awareness. In the more relaxed environment which follows dilution of the original threat, the completion of the project becomes a more reflective issue, a matter of commitment, of wanting the group to survive.

There is a sense that the potency and freedom found in the moment of fusion ought to be preserved and should be placed beyond the destructive reach of others, that is, it leads to a determined project of conservation. The group becomes an end in itself and an object of concern. The adventure of the group must itself become the common interest and a limit to individual self-determination. Sartre speaks of this in terms of a pledge or an oath [*le serment*], initially tacit and vague but ultimately manifest and specific. It is, in fact, the first moment of discipline; the limitation of freedom. I freely limit my freedom in order to be assured of continuity and predictability. The pledge is an act of reassurance by each member of the group to all others that the group will persist. Each demonstrably assuring the others that their being is defined by the common *praxis*. One tacitly declares the group to be the true worth of one's life and sets aside one's capacity for spontaneity. By the same token one receives from all the others of the group the pledge that they will control their freedom so that the project of the group is their true substance.

This discipline, this morbid fear of individuality, is the ground of our degenerate type of ensemble; the society which uses natural scarcity in the same way it uses abundance, and which uses technology as it uses all its sophistication to deny the humanity of the other. For the pragmatic and voluntary determination to control *praxis* becomes the pattern for regulation of all threatening liberty. A project is established which has a goal of its own, the group sets itself a task quite separate and distinct from human need. Inhumanity creeps into *praxis*. This project is the foundation of the cruelty, viciousness and terror of bourgeois society.

The next moment in the decay of the group, the loss of the dexterity of our *praxis*, occurs when the pledge itself becomes the object of concern. At this point the group members seek manifest proof of the loyalty of the others in the group. In actively pursuing evidence of the future trustworthiness of the other, a *praxis* is developed which rests upon a mutually specified performance. Conformity with one's pledge has to be manifested by compliance to a publicly recognized discipline. At this point *praxis* becomes performance. It acquires a character of its own distinct from any inner truth or real need, it becomes a requirement and compliance with this *praxis* becomes a matter of compulsion. Maintenance of the group takes priority; immediacy is lost and order becomes a requirement with its own *raison d'être*. The particular members of the group find themselves drawn into the grotesque pretence of authenticity which we recognize as society.

The pledge, at first spontaneous and unanimous, becomes an ossified group *praxis*. Social unity becomes tenuous and the object of nervous anticipation; in short, it becomes the object of concern, and establishes a conditionality of group membership. Each member of the group trades security for spontaneity and obtains order at the price of the terror of non-performance. As *praxis* becomes a discipline it establishes a dark region of peril, one's own prohibited freedom projected into the world as the threat to the common *praxis*. An out-group is established which is the embodiment of the group's decay, its loss of potency and efficacy. This out-group acts as a regulator of performance, the group requires as a sign of membership a manifest display of disassociation from the out-group.

At this stage the group *praxis* is increasingly self-obsessed and remote from the real, from the immediate needs of individual members. It is largely concerned with anxieties of dissolution rather than projects of satisfaction. Such a *praxis* is, for Sartre, a counter-*praxis*, that is, it is a virus which enters the constitutive *praxis* of each group member, loosening their hold upon their world, increasing the auxiliary concerns which each must include in their dealings. Each is increasingly drawn into a being-here which is mediated through ever more abstract and convoluted considerations. Thus the counter-*praxis* is a type of disease in the life-body of the group's *praxis*, a set of manoeuvres designed to signify the group's continued well-being rather than attend to its members' actual needs. Consequently the generations of mankind find themselves in a *praxis* which is mannered and regimented, they find themselves designated by a concept of 'self', of 'freedom' and of 'responsibility' which is ever more distanced from their own need.

As concern and anxiety increase, the introversion of the pledged group leads to ever more complex arrangements, dominated by functionaries whose task it is to attend to the growing needs of organization; rulers, administrators, officers of various kinds who represent an ever intensifying interest in formalizing the project of the group as it is established. This increasingly important and eventually dominant cadre comes to be the defining order of the group, its *praxis* becomes the common project. This sub-group's well-being comes to dominate and a legislative order is set in place. As such, the group-*praxis* becomes an ever greater burden of discipline and constraint upon the non-governing members and conflicts of interest finally become manifest and articulated. Sartre argues that it is at this point the fear of terror becomes actual terror in the 'purge'; an increasingly bitter and vicious attempt to isolate and condemn enemies of 'good order' within the group, to specify the out-group and ritualize its destruction.

The degeneration of the group continues to the point where the only thing the group can agree upon is that they should be a group and their sense of unity is sustained by this one belief. The solution to the ever increasing chaos and sense of helplessness is the formation of an identifiable elite, even a single monarch, whose interest is taken to be the project of all, one person is sovereign, that is, possesses original freedom. In such an organized and institutionalized state the group's adventure has been wholly usurped to the secondary function of resolving the anxiety of dissolution.

Each member finds himself possessed of a *praxis* which separates him from his own needs and capacities, subjected to the total rule of his sovereign and to the vicious and often violent attention of his peers. The group is now obsessed with need to display their commitment, to reassure the collective that all are equally restrained and oppressed by the inertia which has descended upon them.

Thus there develops a sort of collective neurosis where a prurient and 'moral' majority; officious and intrusive, are determined to achieve absolute observance of a discipline entirely devoted to maintaining the group. Each member is forced to deal with others via a set of practices and considerations dedicated wholly to the needs of a derelict structure, one utterly removed from and alien to their natural spontaneity. All relationships serve the preservation of a wholly degenerate *praxis* and all group members become participants in a ritual dance of self-denial.

Under the domination of these 'inertial' relationships regulated by the dead world of the counter-*praxis* we have returned to seriality. The idea of self is saturated by competitiveness and by vulnerability. It is the self of responsibility and of privacy. *Praxis* has become dominated by the reification of the inert; whole and part are totally mystified.

Sartre's discussion of the development of practical ensemble reveals the growing clumsiness of our concernful dealing with the world. It attempts to demonstrate how *praxis* becomes increasingly convoluted and distanced from the original dexterity, or clarity, of adventure. The theory is really a retelling of Sartre's theory of the translucency of consciousness portrayed as a fall, or expulsion. Opacity is brought into the world as part of a primal conflict between freedom and order, between self and other. Viewed from the point of the constitutive *praxis*, that is, the individual consciousness; what began as practical or functional self-denial of freedom has evolved into a systematic practice – self denial. Each group member lives an artificially impoverished humanity.

This practice of self-denial is the root of inhumanity. It enables each member to steel themselves in order to deny the humanity of the other and to treat other men as though inanimate. Self-denial is the essence of the counter-*praxis*. Indeed, the practico-inert is functionally a process of denial, one denies the richness of life in order to sustain one's own poverty. One decries the liberty of the other as an indulgence, an excess. Most dramatically one seeks evil in humanity in order to sustain the 'good' in oneself. This is, for Sartre, the root of our way of life, of class society, of the staggering inhumanity which mankind displayed in Sartre's own lifetime.

Capitalist society is oppressive not because of the practices associated with surplus value, but because we have fallen into the trap of managing scarcity within a general comprehension of exclusion of the marginalization of freedom. We are separated from our power of self-creation not because of private property, but, rather, we cling to private property in order to sustain our discipline of self-denial. A denial sustained by the anxiety inherent in the common *praxis*; a nervousness contained within the way of thinking, of being and of doing. We are not living in a state of alienation as a consequence of archaic social relations, rather, retain archaic relations in order to sustain our alienation.

Sartre considered that for contemporary man both freedom and society are constituted from within a *praxis* which has alienated itself from its natural self-possession. Freedom is the serial freedom of accomplishing my project in the face of the opposition of others, limiting myself to a practical notion of self which is reduced to its operative minimum. 'Community' is a synthetic togetherness actuated by a thinly veiled recognition of the others as alien and hostile. It is, for Sartre, merely a pretence at real community which has been obscured by the counter-*praxis* borne out of self-alienation.

Soviet Marxism had failed to emancipate men because abolishing private property was simply too superficial a change to the social order. The proletarian revolutionaries easily established an exclusive discipline, an order of manifest commitment, loyalty and terror. Soviet order has repeated serial relations rapidly because so much of their interpretation of Marxism bonded man to the inert, to his conditions. Marxism had proved to be a catalyst for serialization of the group-in-fusion, and the hope offered to the world by the Bolshevik Revolution was, almost enthusiastically, destroyed.

Again, merely intellectual notions of community or freedom cannot rid a state of its serial performance. It is necessary that the mass of ordinary people feel the violence of their *praxis*, feel its irrelevance; they must feel that they are capable of dis-abusing themselves of this estrangement. This is the moment which can destroy serial *praxis*, the moment of fusion, the point where individuals decide to strip all that is inhuman and hostile from their world. The moment of recognition is marked by men taking back their being in order to become the product of their deeds and not mystified by the mediation of the counter-*praxis* of the ensemble haunted by its own anxiety.

One might remark that this paradigm of history has some resemblance to Freud's theory of personal neurosis. Relationships developed in order to manage specific problems become anachronistic as the set of conditions under which they were formed change but they do not evolve. These remnant practices take on a rationale of their own and though freely sustained by the individual they are a bind. They inhibit the person's capacity to relate to the real world yet the individual cannot escape from these practices of self limitation without assistance. It is quite fair to say that Sartre's theory in the *Critique* belongs to the set of social theories created in the middle of the twentieth century which can be described as 'therapeutic' in the sense associated with the 'talking cure' of Freud.

I have argued that Sartre's 'second phenomenology' is very much like his first in that freedom is the driving force, the major difference being that here freedom has to be concrete and inclusive and as such inevitably deteriorates, becomes inert in order to be a collective reality. Perhaps in response to the criticism levelled in Heidegger's *Letter on Humanism*, Sartre acknowledges that what we call freedom is an abstraction, an exclusiveness which severs each from their concrete whole, deleterious and enervating, a surrender to the practice of self-alienation. A practice which makes a virtue of inwardness, isolation and solitude. Sartre had always believed bourgeois isolation to be a perverted self-hood but in the *Critique* he was able to express this view in the most coherent terms.

The *Critique* is an attempt to show that human history has been created through structures of organization, that the practice of thinking, of reflecting, is derived and learned from social practices. There is one outstanding difference between the *Philosophy of Right* and the *Critique*, namely that whereas Hegel sees the critical intelligence as always entering too late, as always being coherent only when the problems which it identifies have already been surpassed, Sartre believes that the intellect has a role to play in the construction of the future. The principal reason for this grip upon the theme of human history lies in the idea of counter-*praxis* and the practico-inert, for man's organization is not simply constructive but also destructive – it not only creates structure but also creates inhibitions to itself. This 'self' is innate and universal, it is naturally free and self-possessed. Sartre, like Marx, rejects Hegel's scepticism because Sartre believes we have lost or misplaced an ability and capacity which is ours in essence one which can be recuperated. In short, the *Critique* no less than *Being and Nothingness* is the story of the *Néant*, our innate, free, self-possession. Both accounts rest upon that translucidity which is self-evident in and proved by our being consciousness of consciousness.

Ultimately the radical assumption of this account of the historical liberation is the *Néant*, for man must become what he 'is'; the self-making product of himself. The 'real' of Sartre's phenomenology is nothingness. The substantial difference between *Being and Nothingness* and the *Critique* is that in the latter the otherness of the other is created and can be dismantled. For Sartre it is still the particular individual who is the origin of finitude in the world, but there is no *a priori* reason why the multiplicity of centres of finitization should lead to the denial of the other, no reason why humanity could not be dealt with as utterly objective, mutual and 'clear'. In this sense the *Critique* fulfils the ambition expressed in the final pages of the *Transcendence of the Ego* to find a way of being in which the reciprocity of mankind is utterly manifest and open, where nothing is discrete.

When we come to draw some conclusions about freedom in Sartre's work, we are returned to our original point that for Sartre freedom is synonymous with nothingness, our way of being. Freedom is our metaphysical condition. The question is not whether we are free nor even how we become free but rather how we handle the freedom which is our essence. Sartre offers two accounts as to how man may take charge of his life and his world. In *Being and Nothingness* this self-possession was to be found in the 'situation', the reality which though phenomenal and though produced by our project was, never-the-less, the only truth of our being. Sartre's point was, briefly, to destroy the idea of a stable self, an inner innate character or a soul with a divine destiny, to point out the fabricated nature of our being and to take away the inauthenticity of pretending that our being was thing-like, solid and responsive to causes other than itself. It attempted to take away the stiffness of existence. This, Sartre's original phenomenology, had the dual purpose of situating us in our reality and of explaining that this reality is a construction grounded upon our way of being, that this fluid and transient world is all we have as our substance and that we are nothing else. Hence we ourselves are transient: fragile, vulnerable and constructed and must learn to accept and enjoy this fact. We must come to love this, our fate, and with the awareness of this mechanism, that is, with reason make ourselves more in the cast of our freedom, live closer to our essence of not being externally defined but self-defining and self-creating.

In the *Critique* this atomic scheme is replaced by a collective programme for self-mastery, indeed such mastery is viewed as impossible without the prior reformulation of the collective institutions of society, institutions which pervert our awareness of our own being. However, I have argued that the basic mechanism is, in both major works, the same, that it rests upon the *cogito* the self-possession of the immediate particular consciousness, the atomic individual. It is the belief in the translucency of mind to itself which is the root of Sartre's work. It is the principle of his ideas of freedom, both the original notion of absolute personal responsibility and the Marxist variation of institutional reformation as the preface to the new age.

The presiding question of Sartre's work is then; has Sartre accurately described consciousness? Is it true that only mind limiting itself, as in the negation of the negation or the Kierkegaardian self-finitization, structures the World? Does the actual phenomenal shape of the world depend upon the operation of the mind? Obviously there can be no answer to these questions, indeed they are not real questions in the ordinary sense. The real question is; What can we knowingly or deliberately make otherwise, and here I think lies the weakness of Sartre's thought, for ultimately Sartre's work is just another intellectual system. It recommends that we do not think of ourselves in terms that we think of the things of the world, a Kantian point, but goes beyond that to claim that our relation to what is can be dramatically different from its present state. The point is, this is not what we want or what we ought to want; what we want is happiness, health and security, peace and social justice. Sartre simply offers us too much.

The real problem with Sartre's work is that translucidity does not appear to conform to common sense. There is a remarkable persistence in the being of the world, of the things in it, but of much more damaging significance to Sartre's view of the world, there is an astonishing persistence in our experience of ourselves. The radical vulnerability of personality, the fragility of human character presented in his work simply does not comply with ordinary experience. We are not, I think, as open to the opinions of others, as vulnerable to the will of those around us, as he suggests. Whether we dwell with people who love us or with people who hate us there is a remarkable persistence in personality. Indeed, one of the 'problems' of humanity is that we are genuinely stuck in our characters. Our memories impose a past upon us as a possession more valuable than the present, our emotions seem to have a way of their own and whether it is genetic make-up or childhood experience, we find or discover in ourselves a set of ready-made dispositions, likes and dislikes, strengths and weaknesses which prefigure any actual ability we can be said to actively possess. At night our dreams, blissful and terrifying, impose themselves upon us revealing phantoms we ignore at the cost of their returning as part of our future. Such is the nature of reality. We make ourselves passive to it not because we have deluded ourselves about the nature of being human, but because we know that we maximize our power over the future by anticipating that it will be much like the past. Sartre is simply wrong when he argues we are essentially characterless; the dreams we have in sleep are there to remind us that we are not free.

Oakeshott

6

Understanding Experience

As with Sartre, the thought of Michael Oakeshott[1] is essentially concerned with political and moral issues. However, Oakeshott's way of proceeding is very different from that of the thinkers we have been discussing for he is as troubled by the authority of the intellectual as by any other form of authority. He views the academic to be a potential source of regimentation, as threatening to the vitality of man as any political or moral dogma.

In one of his early essays he says that it is the task of religion to 'give life in abundance',[2] and while he abandoned religion as a source of inspiration he never let go of the idea that men should be permitted to forge their own way of life – to make an adventure of being here. This he saw required not only restriction of the powers of the state but limitation of the pretences of the intellectuals, who since the Enlightenment, have fulfilled many of the functions of the medieval clergy.

Oakeshott's political thought is characterized by the awareness that the authority of the thinker is limited by the resource at his command. Our first task must be to understand these constraints. Oakeshott made three distinct attempts to articulate this view:

1. A work of epistemology which viewed practical affairs to be only an aspect of thought and, therefore, not the source of an unqualified truth. A theory opposed to the clarity of *praxis*.
2. A political theory rooted in Hegel's notion of *Sittlichkeit* of the *Philosophy of Right*.
3. A political theory based on an original understanding of law.

There is no question that Oakeshott was profoundly influenced by his reading of Hegel and his thought, certainly his early work, owes a great deal to Hegel. His idealism belongs to the form referred to as British Idealism – a hybrid of the work of Kant and Hegel. However, Oakeshott's thought also discloses an interest in the thought of Aristotle and Hobbes, and his work displays the eloquent earthiness characteristic of their work. However, more marked and more obvious, particularly in his early work, is the influence of the British Idealist F. H. Bradley.[3] As it contributes to an understanding of Oakeshott's thought, we begin with a brief outline of Bradley's work.

Hegel's genius is to have seen that patterns of organization and habits of thought are intimately linked. Thought reflects our concrete skills of arranging ourselves and manipulating the world-skills which are themselves a manifestation of the human principle – mind – intruding into the stuff of the work. Hegel's work sought to reconcile man to the laboriousness of this emancipation and to disabuse us of the occult belief that reason was inspired by some resource other than our actual competence in dealing with the world, an augury which could guide, advise and recommend a new skilfulness.

Bradley offers us a species of idealism which differs from the Continental variants in that it binds itself to a truly earthly absolute. This absolute is referred to as 'experience' and is nothing other than our immediate predicament. It is the totality of experience. In Bradley's thought there is no governing principle entering the world through human agency. Mankind copes with problems as they present themselves. History has no tendency and no theme. There is no transcendental destiny becoming manifest in a 'growing' body of truth. There is no actualization of the absolute as there is in Hegel's thought.

Bradley's thesis can be stated quite succinctly – the absolute, whole or totality is immediate and present to man, it cannot be alien, foreign or remote, the absolute is not transcendent but is simply inclusive of all that is real. But this very proximity and intimacy makes it elusive and difficult to identify. However if we refer to this totality as 'sentient experience' we will at least have communicated the degree of intimacy, that is, man's vital acquaintance with this totality. The measure of truth and reality – the only measure we have to hand – is the whole or total, that is, 'experience'. We can only disable and confuse ourselves by believing that there is something more than experience.

In the history of thought it is said that Boethius taught the Schoolmen that the distinction between Plato and Aristotle lay in the fact that for Aristotle there were genera external to thought.[4] In this classical sense Bradley is Aristotelian. Thought is viewed as something which works on the world rather than being seen as being the world itself. It is not misleading to say that the motto of

Bradley's philosophy is that the real is always more than our thinking can reveal. For Bradley, Hegel's identification of the real and the rational gave thought a content it could not meaningfully possess.

Appearance and Reality[5] is an attempt to think through just what can be known about ultimate reality, it anticipates disappointment, or at least 'very partial satisfaction' but Bradley confidently asserts that 'I am so bold as to believe that we have knowledge of the Absolute, certain, and real, though I am sure that our comprehension is miserably incomplete' (AR 3). Metaphysics is an eccentric though not perverse activity, it is an attempt to know reality. It is eccentric because it places an undue stress on one aspect of life, setting aside more common-place satisfactions. Its enthusiasts seek the fulfilment of a mystical strain in our nature. In a famous remark Bradley says that 'Metaphysics is the finding of bad reasons for what we believe on instinct but to find these reasons is no less an instinct' (AR xiv). It is therefore 'not perverse' for to seek the truth is part of our nature, though it is not intrinsically more valuable than poetry, art or religion only different from these (AR 3).

Bradley's philosophy rests upon our possessing an intimate acquaintance with the whole. Again I should repeat that for Bradley the real is the totality, it is present to us, nothing can be usefully described as being beyond us. The question as to how we can know thought to be partial rests upon our possession of an absolute criterion for knowing what is real (AR 136). To be real is to be self-complete, to be truly individual, anything which cannot support itself, which relies upon something other than itself is not fully real, it is 'abstract' (AR 140).

The standard we are to use in our critique of ordinary experience is, then, self-completeness. We know that it must be one, complete, substantive and harmonious. The fact that it is harmonious is derived from its unity and singularity, for where there is conflict, there must be plurality. Harmony, consistency or coherence is the standard of reality, each of the disparate elements of human life, including thought, have the harmony of the real as their end.

Before we continue we should make some attempt to specify what it is that Bradley means by 'thought'. Thought is relational, to think is to discriminate, to identify, to attribute a quality to an existence, thought is essentially discursive. It is, in short, judgement. 'In judgement', Bradley tells us, 'an idea is predicated of reality'

(AR 164). This gives thought its ordinary, instrumental identity and saves it from the fate of being the 'transcendental ground' as it is for the German writers.

When we come to think about thought in terms of reality it always appears inadequate. Thought constantly finds itself excluded from the substance of the subject it tries to grasp. It finds a part of reality which is not thought. If thought is to be the substance of our actual world it would be something other than what we actually use as thought. Bradley perceptibly points out that whatever such an experience would be it is no more thought than any other kind of experience.

In a positive attempt to identify what is 'other' than thought, Bradley describes other aspects of experience – besides thought there is feeling and volition (AR 144). We know that thought is a part of experience and not the whole, for if thought is taken as the essence of experience then perception and feeling would be absorbed into thought. Thought cannot be identified with feeling without ceasing to have its usual meaning (AR 383). In a sense then we may trust our feeling that judgement is not the whole, for 'if [feeling] does belong to thought then "thought" is different from thought discursive and relational, its goal would be other than truth.' Bradley insists 'I dissent from the view that nothing other than thought exists' (AR 167). However, while thought is not the whole it is a manifest part of our experience and as such it must be part of the whole for everything which appears is to some degree real. For all its conditionality it is a functional part of human life. As part of the whole it strives to be whole. If thought attained the end for which it yearns, the unity of truth, it would abolish itself for thought relates things which are distinct; pure unity would be suicide. It is the crucial character of Bradley's metaphysics that thought to be thought must retain its inconsistency, as such it is satisfactory for all ordinary purposes but not for metaphysics.

We have viewed the whole formally as the *totality* and as harmonious *unity*, as *real*. Our aim now is to develop a concrete picture of the 'real'. As whole it must include what appears, it must be the totality of all its parts: it, therefore, includes thought, feeling, perception and volition; we also know that it is not reducible to any one of these. This unity is a mystery, it coheres in a way which is never immediately brought to mind, it cannot, of course, be thought. 'We never have, or are, a state which is the perfect unity of all aspects: and we must admit that in their special natures they remain inexplicable' (AR 468). Moreover, 'how these various modes can come together into a single unity must remain unintelligible' (AR 457). What we can say is that there is not one mode or aspect to which the others belong as products or into which they can be resolved (ibid.). For instance, Bradley is very hostile to the idea, he might have had Schopenhauer in mind, that thought and perception are governed by volition. He insists that such a concept is simple mysticism, 'an uncritical attempt to make play with the unknown' (AR 483). For we cannot know what will is except from the way it manifests itself through action, phenomenalization and judgement.

The burden of Bradley's case lies in the identification of the absolute as the real. This one idea is responsible for the originality and importance of his work. For the absolute viewed in this form is neither transcendent nor immanent but simply present. The whole is intimately ours, it is the felt background within which each identity is framed. The more we try to *think* about the absolute the more bound in abstraction we become, for we lose hold of the fact that the whole is immediate and concrete. It is the very essence of Bradley's philosophy that the absolute is concrete it is what we actually are.

> When we ask as to the matter which fills up the empty outline, we can reply in one word, that this matter is experience. And experience means something much the same as given and present fact. We perceive, on reflection, that to be real, or even barely to exist, must be to fall within sentience. Sentient experience, in short, is reality ... and what is not this is not real. We may say, in other words, that there is no being or fact outside of that which is commonly called psychical existence .... Anything, in no sense felt or perceived, becomes to me quite unmeaning .... I am driven to the conclusion that for me experience is the same as reality.
>
> (AR 144–5)

However, once we start to question experience we impose structures upon it which alter its immediacy and its inclusivity. Experience as *ours* is inherently finite, for the possessive aspect of experience is a division of the whole, a part separated and defined within an established purpose, orientated at specific satisfactions. To see the whole we must pass beyond that which is partial, we must acknowledge that which is other than thought.

Bradley's whole argument rests upon the belief that he has succeeded in defining thought as a part of experience, also that he has adhered to common sense when he condemns Hegel's identification of thought and reality, as extending thought beyond any defensible meaning. To think of anything which exists outside of thought is surely impossible but this does not mean that we lack awareness of a world that is more than thought, we can feel it, we can perceive it. Feeling, perception, goodness, and beauty all press beyond discursive thought, judgement is, hence, one aspect of the whole. We can no more comprehend the real than understand why it is we live in a finite world. The relation of the aspects of experience to *experience* whole and complete is, in the end, beyond us. (AR 527) It is a question which demands more of thought than it can give.

We may summarize Bradley's thought by saying that what is real is whole, total and unified, that which is divided, limited and finite is partial and possesses only a derived existence, it is abstract and as dependent is not fully real. The absolute, is the whole of our vital being, a whole which draws together the fragments which appear as sub-divisions. The absolute is a standard by which the aspects are measured, in it they are complete and lose the finitude and transience that they display in being thought, felt or perceived.

Bradley's vision of the totality does not conflict with the way it is usual to think, or deal with the world. The strength of his case rests largely upon the weakness of any alternative notion of what is real, self-complete and self-sustained. From this Bradley deduced that the real is one, a whole in which all externality ceases and in which all parts are finally arranged harmoniously. Reality satisfies our whole being (AR 159). As Bradley's absolute is real, it is positive. This is in direct contrast to Hegel's system which rests upon an active negation – mind's power to withdraw from any content. For Bradley man's existence is set amidst being not set against it; we find ourselves surrounded rather than suspended. It is a more claustrophobic attitude to thought.

The Bradlean man lacks the inclusive over-view or the transcendent perch which plays such an important role in continental thought. The vast systems of Germanic phenomenology constructed upon man as the source of the negation the self-finitizing force is set aside, the man of Bradley's philosophy is a more modest character. We find ourselves in a certain situation, a predicament to be dealt with. For each person the truths he encounters will depend upon his concerns and interests but this project is not the sole ground of the revelation of truth, reality or value it is merely an occasion of their expression. In these few remarks we have the germ of the very considerable genius of Bradley's work.

Like *Appearance and Reality*, *Experience and its Modes*[6] is a phenomenology of part and the whole. Although difficult and obviously a sketch rather than a complete philosophy it offers an interesting opening to a study of Oakeshott's work. It introduces us to the major elements of his thought, most notably, the marginalization of the technical thinker.

Bradley's remark that doing comes first and reflection follows[7] directs us to Oakeshott's problem; the relation between thinking and doing. For our purposes it is sufficient to say that it is concerned with the independence of the pursuit of life – its separateness from such activities as science, history and philosophy. Oakeshott follows Bradley using 'experience' to refer to the inclusive totality which is divided into dependent parts or modes. Where Oakeshott differs radically from Bradley is in his unwillingness to limit thought to an aspect of experience, for him experience is thought. In *Experience and its Modes* experience is a concrete whole, a self-complete world of ideas. Thought is both the measure of truth and reality, that is, the criterion of the judgement, and the substance of all being. In viewing thought as the sensuous concrete whole Oakeshott returns British Idealism to the mainstream of idealist philosophy.

For Oakeshott experience is a world of ideas inclusive and complete. Experience 'stands for the concrete whole which analysis divides into 'experiencing' and 'what is experienced' (EM 7). These two parts if 'taken separately are meaningless, abstractions; they cannot, in fact, be separated. Perceiving, for example, involves a something perceived and willing a something willed' (ibid.). To put this more plainly; there is no radical distinction between being and thinking, they are two species of our known world, distinguished and differentiated by acknowledged characteristics, but both, ultimately, thought. Thus, for Oakeshott, experience is thought.

> The view I propose to maintain is that experience is a single whole, within which modifications may be distinguished, but which admits of no final or absolute division; and that experience everywhere, not merely is inseparable from thought, but is itself a form of thought.
>
> (EM 10)

There is no experience which is not an idea, 'experience is a world of ideas' and each idea is an implicit reference to the whole.

Oakeshott's first task it to explain why we should accept thought or judgement as the synonym of experience. This is to be done by demonstrating that nothing can really dwell outside experience. There are, of course, different kinds of experience; 'it is not wrong to attempt an analysis of experience, to distinguish sensation, reflection, volition, feeling and intuition; the error lies in supposing that in so doing we are considering activities which are different in principle and can be separated from one another finally and absolutely' (EM 10).

> All abstract and incomplete experience is a modification of what is complete, individual and concrete, and to this it must be referred if we are to ascertain its character. And thought or judgement as I see it, is not one form of experience, but is itself the concrete whole of experience.
>
> (EM 11)

Oakeshott enquires why it is that we feel thought to be an inadequate expression of the whole. He holds that we believe that there is more to experience than thought because we have a tendency to allocate a specific character to thought, to express it too narrowly.

The first claim to be rejected is that sensation, that is, immediate experience is less than thought. We are tempted to separate sensation from thought or judgement because it appears neither sophisticated nor structured enough to reach the level of thought. Sensation seems to require no interpretation or reflection, its 'stuff' seems simply to obtrude itself onto consciousness without context or relation. Sensation it appears is isolated, simple, exclusive, transient, inexpressible, unsharable and impossible of repetition (EM 13). It is a shapeless 'thus' and 'thus', etc. Oakeshott rejects this for such simple, isolated moments could not be experienced at all.

Actual experience implies consciousness, and to be conscious of something is to recognize it. Recognition requires a continuous subject equipped with opinion, prejudice, habit and knowledge, that is to say, and a body of related experiences. Oakeshott insists 'experience is always significant' (EM 13). There is nothing, we are told, immediate or 'natural' in contrast to what is mediated and sophisticated, there are only degrees of such sophistication, or degrees of completion. Each moment in experience is a recognition.

Oakeshott informs us that 'my view is that in experience we begin and end with judgement', and what is given in experience and escapes significance is a contradiction. What is then held to be outside of thought is outside experience and is a nonsense.

But there is a second class of arguments against thought being experience, namely, that there is more to experience than thought. Two candidates for experience which might be more comprehensive than thought are intuition and feeling. Compared with these forms of experience thought appears defective; telling us something about experience and hence not itself the substance of experience. This, of course, is Bradley's argument – judgement, in this view, is inherently relational, it is the application of predicate to a subject. This view implies that direct and immediate experience is somehow more complete than that disclosed in the subject predicate relation of judgement. But Oakeshott says such a view is an erroneous understanding of thinking because:

> Thinking is not the mere qualification of existence by an idea; it is a qualification of existence by itself, which extends, in the end, to a qualification of the whole of existence by its whole character, judgements, in the sense of propositions in which predicate and subject are separate and remain separated from beginning to end, are the mere deposits of the current of concrete experience.
>
> (EM 24)

In separating a 'what' from a 'that' it is dissecting experience which is already recognized, signified, etc. it is reflecting upon thoughts achievements. A form of experience beyond thought appears necessary only if the whole scope of thought is restricted to the manipulation of explicit relations as in the Bradlean view, but experience is thought or judgement. This totality is 'a world of ideas' and all that occurs within it refers to this world. This introduces us to the central principle of Oakeshott's philosophy that we cannot resort to some primitive immediacy free from judgement. There is no simple substance, only experience itself, whole, developed and elaborate. We are returned again to the claustrophobia of Bradley's philosophy, man finds himself locked into his inheritance. More significantly, the thinker possesses no station or perch above or beyond the fray of life save that which he constructs for himself as an exercise, an effort of abstraction. We are hereby prepared for the major thesis of *Experience and its Modes*, there is no escape from the tumult except by mental exertion, by operation of a specific discipline, engineered in an effort to temporarily quell the flux, to make order.

Thought is not only the substance of experience it is also the measure of experience, that is, the criterion of validity and of such terms of commendation as 'truth', and 'reality'. We must start by recalling two primary points, firstly, that experience is composed of ideas, secondly that it is a totality, it is complete, a system or a world. The word 'world' is used by Oakeshott synonymously with system and simply means the whole, what is complete, or what is total. This is important because this totality or complete world is always and everywhere the criterion for what is true and real. It must be understood that this criterion is not itself stable, for Oakeshott the instability within this world of ideas, the change which requires adaptation and reformation, is always a mysterious process without extraneous principle or transcendent governing order. But within this given what is demanded is coherence.

The capriciousness of change and the ultimate shapelessness of the world which tumbles into our purview is an essential feature of Oakeshott's work. As was said earlier, there is no escape from the turmoil that is not itself an engineered and specific abstraction borne of our desire to abate chaos. Order is an achievement, it is artificial and tenuous. The understandings discovered in the world are human constructions imposed upon an infinite mass of available data. The principal paradox and motive force of the Oakeshottian system is that the achievement of shapes contradicts the essentially shapeless world, we possess the world only by deluding ourselves that what we have is actually it. Oakeshott neatly summarizes his view of reality for us by saying:

> What is satisfactory in experience is what is individual and therefore a whole in itself. And again what is satisfactory is what is universal and absolute. And these are the characteristics of what is real. Reality is a coherent world of ideas, and it is real because it is coherent, in experience, that is, there is always a reference beyond what is merely true to what is real, because what is merely true – a coherent world of mere ideas – is, in the end, neither complete nor absolute, but an abstraction.
>
> (EM 58)

Reality is probably the most demanding of all the aliases of the 'absolute', the 'system' and the 'whole', the 'truly individual' and the 'self-complete'. Oakeshott insists we require a philosophy which acknowledges 'even more thoroughly than Hegel's the fact that what we have, and all that we have is a world of "meanings"'. For even Hegel superimposed upon his axiom 'the real is the rational' an extraneous notion of becoming. By contrast, for Oakeshott, reality is given in experience in so far as that experience is obligatory, unavoidable and complete. To be is to be real (EM 61). Truth and reality are simply what experience compels us to believe by its presence. Oakeshott's scheme retains the almost romantic vigorousness and openness to life of Bradley's philosophy while avoiding its irrationalism.

However, this openness to experience is quelled in everyday life by our posing specific questions. It is not, therefore, 'normally' the case that in experience the whole of reality is explicitly given, or that in every judgement the whole of reality is asserted directly. Rather this whole is modified by our specific interests. The whole, however, remains the substance of what actually appears. We are told that we turn aside from the 'main current' in order to construct or explore the world from a restricted view point. We turn aside from the obligation of the whole in order to seek a lesser satisfaction than what is complete, we interrupt the flux by self limitation and restraint. We look for meanings here and there, localized and topical, instead of the meaning without limitation.

> To be satisfied with a singular judgement ... [is] to have taken up with a purpose which is satisfactory because it appears to be what is required in experience, and unsatisfying when this appearance reveal itself at mere appearance.
>
> (EM 71)

Here it is the word 'appearance' which should attract our attention. For, as we have previously noted, the phenomenological tradition rests upon establishing a relation between that which appears as the everyday reality and that which is truly real. Oakeshott's phenomenology, like Bradley's, is based on the part/whole distinction, but whereas Bradley's parts were moods of the sensuous whole, Oakeshott's are modes. An understanding of the nature of a mode is the key to his thought.

In the first instant a mode is a defective form of experience, and must be explained as a divergence, a modification or an abstraction, each mode attains its unique character by reason of the deficiency it represents. 'A mode of experience is experience with reservation, it is experience shackled by partiality and presupposition; and its character lies, not merely in the particular reservations and postulates which distinguish it, but in the entire world of ideas which these postulates imply, call forth and maintain' (EM 74). Each arrest is a determinate world of ideas, distinguished from every other world of ideas in respect of the precise assertion of reality it embodies. The significance of the arrest in experience lies in the character of the ideas it brings into being.

Such a limited world is a particular attempt at what is satisfactory in experience. It is part of experience, hence, it is measured by the criterion of coherence.

> No abstract world of ideas is independent of experience, for each is experience at a certain point. And no abstract world of ideas is independent of the totality of experience, for each derived its character from the whole from which it is an abstraction. And apart from that whole neither has meaning or significance.
>
> (EM 75)

Whilst the coherence of any modal reality is indebted to the true whole, each mode creates its own truth and reality rooted in its determinate presuppositions, that is, upon the style of its arrest. Each is absolutely independent of every other. One cannot pass in argument from mode to mode for the criterion of truth is specific to each. So, what is arithmetically true is morally neither true nor false, it is simply irrelevant (EM 76). Each mode is true as far as it goes, that is, assuming it is found to be coherent and one accepts the limits imposed upon experience by its presuppositions, i.e. if one is well disposed to that way of looking at the world. Viewed from the point of concrete experience the modes are dependent and surrogate, it possesses what they lack, for should they attempt total coherence they would abolish the limitation which provide for their existence. A mode cannot be whole and complete without ceasing to possess its modal character. At the heart of every mode there is, then, a paradox that the achievement of shapes, that is, meanings, is maintained by obscuring much of what is presented, it is a process of exclusion, we possess the world only by deluding ourselves that the part is the whole, a deception which frequently fails.

By way of clarification of this complex relationship Oakeshott reminds us that wherever the concrete purpose of experience is pursued there is philosophical experience, that is, experience without restriction or arrest. It is that experience which determines to be satisfied only with complete coherence. Thus philosophy is experience remaining true to its inherent purpose, that of becoming a world of ideas. Philosophy acquires its character in its refusal to accept the schemes of the modes. Though, as *Experience and its Modes* itself demonstrates, philosophy can help us to behave modally, that is, to conduct better history, or at least to do history with greater awareness of its discipline, to avoid trying to reduce experience to 'scientific logic' and to deprive philosophers of authority, that is, of a legislative role in life. 'Philosophy, experience for its own sake, is a mood, and one which, if we are to live this incurable abstract life of ours, must be frequently put off'.

In experience there is no limit to the number of determinate worlds we can devise or create. However, there are only a small number which are so well developed that they merit consideration. These are specified as being, historical experience, scientific experience and practical experience; poetry was added later. Little indication is given of what other modes there might be. This omission is a concern because there is reason to wonder whether Oakeshott's basic thesis, which rests on the relation between these modes, would have been sustained if modes other than these had been employed in the argument. There is considerable reason to believe that the central issue of the book is the inter-modal relationship. For it was the indiscipline of some historians; the imperious attitude of science towards everyday life; and the inability of philosophy to advise and direct the conduct of life which are the matters to which he most frequently returns.

We must now try to specify the character of a mode. Each mode of thought is itself a world of ideas, but a world viewed, as it were, through a filter which selectively blocks out all but part of the detail. One might say that it is the whole seen in a particular light, as though different shades of light illuminate different features. Another common analogy for the modal theory is a map. One should imagine an ordnance survey map, the key or legend of the map offers a number of symbols representing various details such as roads, paths, railways, the contours of the land, settlements, rivers and other named features, natural and man-made. One has the option of understanding the map – which for our purposes is not representing something else but is reality itself – as a whole rich in detail but confusing and unhelpful, or one can pick some particular element each one of which will reflect the shape of the whole, and will indicate in its own way the pattern of the totality.

The individual modes are themselves items of fashion. The devotion and enthusiasm of any particular culture or generation to a specific set of modes of experience is an expression of their civilization, for experience itself can offer no necessary modal division. And within each culture individuals will themselves have their own particular loyalties to certain abstract modes according to taste and disposition. The modes which Oakeshott chooses to examine are, we are told, adopted because they are particularly well developed and established. Such modes as science and history have become a part of our understanding of our world, but their importance is relative to our culture, they have not always been of significance and may not always be so. The mode of practical experience is rather different, because it is concerned with the conduct of life itself it must always command a profound degree of importance.

One of the aspirations of *Experience and its Modes* is to designate practical experience, that is, the pursuit of life, as an abstract point of view, and to isolate that which is not practical, in Oakeshott's meaning of the term, namely science, history and philosophy. The success or failure of the argument rests upon whether we are moved to accept his designation of practical experience as an aspect of experience. This is the matter we shall have to pursue. However, as this is to some extent dependent upon the character of scientific experience, historical experience and philosophy, we cannot totally ignore these other modes though they are ancillary to our main interest.

For Oakeshott scientific experience is a world of ideas; experience formulated upon the practice of semi-detached observation of the uniformities of the world. It is a world of experience upon which universal agreement was possible, which offered an escape from personal perception and sensation, one which was 'free from merely personal associations and independent of idiosyncrasies of particular observation' (EM 169). It was an attempt at an absolutely impersonal and stable world, that is to say, a selected aspect of our everyday world.

> Experience becomes scientific experience when it is a world of absolutely communicable experience. Scientific experience is based upon a rejection of merely human testimony; its master-conception is stability.
>
> (EM 171)

The stability, communicability and impersonality sought in scientific experience is found in measurement, in quantification.

Scientific experience is a world of ideas conceived under the category of quantity, it differs from other worlds on account of this governing notion.

Ultimately scientific experience rests upon generalizations abstracted from observed detail, but never wholly dependent upon such observations. It is a world abstract, incomplete and unsatisfactory. Such deficiency is unimportant whilst what we seek is a world of stable and communicable facts, however, if the world of scientific experience is portrayed as experience complete and unconditional then only error can follow. And any attempt to construct a philosophy upon this will create the dull pretence of a homogeneous world of ideas, narrow, uniform and alien to much of what actually comprises experience.

Historical experience has as its unique concern the past. Indeed it is the quest for the past simply for the sake of the past. As such it is an aspect of experience, one selected on the basis of the criterion of what is 'past', but it must be constructed from the experience we have.

> A past divorced from and uninfluenced by the present, is a past divorced from evidence (for evidence is always present) and is consequently nothing and unknowable …. The fact is, then, that the past in history varies with the present, rests upon the present, is the present. 'What really happened' (a fixed and finished course of events, immune from change) as the end in history must, if history is to be rescued from nonentity, be replaced by 'what the evidence obliges us to believe'.
>
> (EM 107)

Of what actually happened we can know nothing, we rely upon the evidence, and that is the past. The question of history is never what must or might have taken place, it is solely what the evidence we possess obliges us to conclude did take place. Such evidence is a constructed world of ideas, made by the historian upon the ground of experience, 'in historical inference we do not move from our present world to a past world; the movement in experience is always a movement within the present world of ideas' (EM 109). In truth there is nothing which is not present 'through and through'.

This might lead us to conclude that history does not really exist. Here 'reality' is being used in a totally mystified sense. For what really exists is the whole and history is one part of that whole selected and abstracted by its character as past. History, because it is experience, is present, its facts are present facts but because it is history it is the continuous assertion of a past which is not past and of a present which is incomplete. Therefore, history like all modes of experience is ultimately self destructive. It is a defective mode of experience. Historical reality is past reality yet to think of history as actually lying in the past is to suppose a world which is not a world of ideas, to entertain facts which are not part of our experience (EM 146). Historical experience represents a defective organization of experience, a renunciation of the full, unmitigated character of the whole.

Oakeshott draws two conclusions from the fact that history is an abstract experience. Firstly, it cannot reveal the whole truth, history is not the golden path to our understanding the world. Secondly, it is independent of other modes and can add nothing to those disciplines. History is by its modal nature a limited and defective view of the whole and, therefore, cannot be the key to experience as a whole. Furthermore to use the past as a guide to action is to pretend that the past is an extension of experience rather than a set of selective details abstracted from experience. History cannot contribute to the world of ideas used in everyday life, history cannot guide or advise the practical person.

This slight outline of Oakeshott's view of science and history leads us to the most significant mode, that of practical experience. A mode, we have been instructed, is distinguished not by what it attempts, i.e. coherence, but by what it achieves, a body of determinate ideas. For practical experience what is undertaken is the alteration of existence.

> Practical life comprises the attempts we make to alter existence or to maintain it unaltered in the face of threatened change, it is both the production of change and the prevention of change, and in either case it is not merely a programme for action, but action itself. Our practical world is the totality of such actions, together with all that they imply. Practice comprises everything which belongs to the conduct of life as such.
>
> (EM 256)

The fact that 'practice is activity … Inseparable from the conduct of life and from the necessity of which no living man can relieve himself', indicates to us that this is a mode of thought of a rather different character from the two others we are offered. There are principally two aspects of practical experience which are of interest to us: (1) practical experience is a mode, it is not experience proper, i.e. it is less than the totality; (2) practical truth is not only the 'truth that we can life by and act upon', but is also, 'the truth which can give freedom' (EM 308).

As a mode of experience practice is a world of ideas, governed by the principle of change. Practical experience is the only mode where what is true today can be false tomorrow. What is given is a world where change occurs and is significant and what is achieved is a world altered by our intervention. It is the power of intervention which makes the mode so much more opulent than the others. Practical experience is the mode governed by will, by our volition. Events and actions, the stuff of practical experience, are its world of ideas, recognized and made significant by their position in the integrated whole. We know from earlier remarks that it is impossible for action to be less than thought as nothing is less than thought. Action is not the outcome or product of thought but, rather, is itself a species of thought.

In the mode of practical experience what is attempted is the alteration of existence, and this felt need to alter is borne upon a felt discrepancy between 'what is' and what we desire shall be, i.e. 'it implies the idea of a 'to be' which is 'not yet' (EM 259). Volition attempts to make the experience more systematic, more coherent and more complete. The requirement of satisfaction is that of coherence and self-completeness. Although it must be acknowledged that 'nowhere is the criterion of judgement more negligently applied than in practical experience, nowhere else does the full character of judgement more frequently remain unrealized' (EM 254). None the less, like all other modes, practice has its own attenuated achievement of self-completion, its own practical reality.

As practical experience is a mode it is not experience as a whole. It is one of the more impressive claims of *Experience and its Modes* that life can be conducted only at the cost of an arrest in experience. To put this another way, it can be seen as the central thesis of Oakeshott's early work that experience is more than the conduct of life. Hence, willing is a species of judging rather than judgement being a manifestation of willing. It is one of the enduring features of Oakeshott's philosophy, in contrast to that of Heidegger, that our practical ways, our projects, do not shape the whole of our thought. A corollary of this is that the philosopher or theorist deals in categories that are neither transient nor topical but are true for all time. In short he stands in opposition to the influential school of thought dominated by Heidegger which places activity at the cutting edge of meaning and views the philosopher as the senior guardian of that achievement.

We must now review our treatment of practical experience in order to understand Oakeshott's idea of freedom. We have already acknowledged that *Experience and its Modes* as a work of philosophy seeks to offer definitions. It locates part in terms of the whole. Therefore we should expect to be told what freedom is in relation to the whole. This will be its definition. Freedom will emerge as the presupposition of practical experience.

Oakeshott tells us that, 'the question What in a mode is real? I have preferred to consider in the form What is in this or that mode of experience an individual or a thing', hence, the modal achievement of truth is a 'fact'; the modal achievement of reality is a 'thing'. The reality of practical experience is the practical thing, the part/whole relationship produced by the conduct of life.

> What is fixed upon is that which is self-contained, and not that which is self-complete. Whatever is required, in the conduct of life to be treated as separate, this (in practice) is a thing and is real.
>
> (EM 268)

In practical experience the category of separateness, that is, of reality, is of particular significance as it concerns not just practical things, whose shape is derived from our purposes, but the author of all such purposes the human person or self. The separateness of the self is everywhere designated by what is other than itself, by the world which changes and other people who bring about change. The self is known as contrary to and exclusive of the world. Such contrariness is the condition of action. The self and activity are corollaries.

> The conduct of life, involves a certain conception of the self or person. And this conception is ... a presupposition of action. The explicit problem of reality or individuality of practical thought is ... Where is there to be found a person or thing which is distinct, separate and unique.
>
> (EM 269)

What is found in practical experience is an instinct for separateness, what is to count as individual is, in this mode as in all others, presupposed and is not open to critical treatment. Such separateness is phenomenal; its reality is merely apparent.

Practice, change and action all identify each other and all depend upon the primary practical 'thing'; the 'self'. This is, of course, not just a thing subject to change but the instrument of change. The will, the practical aspect of judgement, is inherently free and self-determined, not by achievement or by arrangement but because such character belongs to it by definition. That is freedom is merely another way of expressing the character of the active self. The self presupposed in practical activity is a self-determined self (EM 270). The practical self is an 'end in himself' because this is required by the very character of practical reality. For reality in the practical mode is designated by the precept of the separateness and uniqueness of the self. That which conforms to the designated character of separateness and uniqueness thereby is an end in itself. To deny the integrity and reality of the self as an end in itself is to deny practical experience. Hence the practical self is the will and is inherently free and self-determined.

> Wherever an attempt is made to break down the separateness and uniqueness of the practical self, wherever its 'freedom' is denied and wherever it is replaced by an idea of the self based upon some other principle of individuality than separateness and distinction, the seeds of disintegration have been sown in the practical world ... The practical self and the conduct of life are correlatives; deny the one and the other becomes impossible.
> (EM 271)

Freedom for Oakeshott is a matter of definition for without such a notion determinate action would be impossible. This 'definition' is within the mode, that is, within experience designated by the criterion of practice which is whatever is required in the conduct of life. The self, the will and freedom surrender their character when subjected to the quest for the totality. Freedom is an idea which belongs uniquely and specifically to the practical world of ideas.

> If a man thinks to set himself free, in any save a vague and metaphorical sense, by the study of science or of history or by the pursuit of philosophy he is grossly mistaken. The only truth that makes a men free is practical truth, the possession of a coherent world of practical ideas, indeed, practical truth and freedom

seem to me inseparable; wherever the one is, the other will be found also.

(EM fn268)

For Oakeshott freedom is a postulate of practical life.

The vulnerability of freedom rests upon its modal character, there are many concerns which mitigate the pursuit of the separateness of the person. We may seek what is whole and complete rather than what is discrete and separate, we may attempt to lose ourselves in abandonment to another, or in an abstract idea such as the good of the whole. The attempt to achieve what is complete rather than what is separate will by definition constrain and hamper practical life. For practical experience, hence, freedom, is developed and sustained by our pursuit of 'self hood', the individualization of the self through the self-possession of the self.

The application of will to its task, i.e. to practical coherence, is always piecemeal, it is always a specific alteration in response to a particular discrepancy (EM 303). The only means which practice recognizes for this purpose is action, the actual, point-by-point qualification of 'what is here and now' by 'what ought to be'. The toil of the will is, therefore, never total or complete, each alteration throws up new discrepancies and new adventures of reconciliation. 'Every achievement brings with it a new view of the criterion, which converts this momentary perfection into imperfection' (EM 291). This is an endeavour without end for 'permanent dissatisfaction is inherent in practical experience' (EM 304). What is sought is the transformation of experience but what is achieved is simply change, the 'transformation offered does not touch the main structure of that world; it is a transformation merely of content' (EM 308). As with every mode the principle, in this case the principle of transience, lies beyond the reach of the modal adventure. There can be no final resolution of the dissatisfaction because we are working at the level of a mode of experience not experience itself.

> Practical experience, to gain the whole world, must lose its own soul. Not until we have become wholly indifferent to the truths of this world of practice, not until we have shaken off the abstractions of practical experience, of morality and religion, good and evil, faith and freedom, body and mind, the practical self and its ambitions and desires, shall we find ourselves once more turned

in the direction which leads to what can satisfy the character of experience.

(EM 310)

Practical experience, as modal, is ultimately counterfeit, it pursues what it can never attain, the world achieved in practical experience does not differ in principle from the given world, i.e. lack of satisfaction is the end achievement of each move to overcome a lack of satisfaction. From the standpoint of the totality of experience it is 'no more than a cul-de-sac, a regrettable mistake, perhaps a youthful folly' (EM 311). Practical truth is the truth that we can live by, it is the mode marked by change and by alteration. It seeks completeness but is willing to settle for the useful. As with all modes it therefore harbours a contradiction at its heart for what is mutable, vulnerable or transformable cannot be what is finally real in experience. For this reason life, i.e. practical experience, as a guide to philosophy is 'worse than useless – it is misleading' (EM 319). For philosophy is the pursuit of the truth without limit, thought that is critical throughout, 'without presupposition or reservation', and practical experience is only a mode of experience, determinate and restrained. Conversely philosophy has nothing to offer practical experience, it is an escape from the requirements of life

From the stand point of practical experience there can be no more dangerous disease than the love and pursuit of truth in those who do not understand, or have forgotten, that a man's first business is to live. And life, we have seen, can be conducted only at the expense of an arrest in experience. The practical consciousness knows well enough what is inimical to its existence, and often has the wisdom to avoid it .... It is not the clear sighted, nor those who are fashioned for thought and the ardours of thought who can lead the world. Great achievements are accomplished in the mental fog of practical experience. What is furthest from our needs is that kings should be philosophers. The victims of thought, those who are intent upon what is unlimitedly satisfactory in experience, are self-confessed betrayers of life.

(EM 321)

This quote accurately summarizes Oakeshott's early attitude to practical experience and its relation to rigorous thought. It is the crux of Oakeshott's argument that to live life well it is not required that we must pursue what is finally satisfactory in experience, indeed, such a demand makes practical experience as a mode lose its determinate strength and become incomprehensible. 'A satisfactory life does not depend upon philosophical knowledge; indeed such knowledge is irrelevant to it' (EM 339). Good and bad, right and wrong belong exclusively to the practical mode and not to ethics still less to philosophy proper.

Experience and its Modes is a book about philosophy, which is understood by Oakeshott to be the pursuit of experience self-complete and whole. It is the attempt to see each part, each abstraction, in the light of the totality of experience. The practical world must, as we have seen, carry out its business untroubled by such ultimate questions for they are inherently impractical. The actual judgements, beliefs and opinions by which we govern our lives are irrelevant to that view which has as its standpoint the whole of experience. Thus Oakeshott rejects the Heideggerean notion of *praxis*, and the practice inspired pattern of reason. For Oakeshott thought has many preoccupations besides the cultivation of life.

Oakeshott's position is then that philosophy cannot intrude upon the province of practice as practice. It may designate its region, it may define what way of thinking does and does not comply with its presuppositions, but it cannot partake in the business of that mode. It cannot advise, recommend or justify what should be done in actual practical situations. In practice the only power that may govern is life. It is life, complete and whole, which is the end we have in mind when we think practically. It is this whole we comprehend as freedom, for freedom is the truth of practical experience just as simply as error in such conduct enslaves us.

The philosophies we have previously encountered have all offered us views of freedom rooted in metaphysical endeavours. Both Bradley and Oakeshott deny that speculative thought may advise or inform us about life. Human existence, sensuous, vital and pathetic stands at the cutting edge of meaning, not because reason is composed of practice, but because useful reason belongs to practical experience. Freedom cannot be specified in philosophical terms except to say that it is modal, i.e. it belongs exclusively to one particular mode; practical experience. The idea of freedom cannot be explored by reference to philosophic categories; necessity, actuality and potential belong to the idea of the whole and as such are irrelevant to freedom.

Moreover we have learned from the modality of experience that freedom is both transient and tenuous. It cannot be said to be richer today than at earlier times. Whatever sophistication we may attain freedom is always as paradoxical an achievement as any other. All human circumstances give of moments of transient satisfaction. There is no recipe for contentment and it is to be thought that in all the millennia to come man will be as miserable and as happy as he was at the start of time. As with Bradley's thought there is no world progress only the diverse attempts to abate mystery.

The modal theory rejects the Hegelian idea of growing closeness to the absolute, to an age of self-possession but it also dismisses the concept of freedom originated by Descartes and developed by Kant. For the self is part of the conduct of life, and this is an open category. From the standpoint of the totality of experience, that is to say the field of philosophy, the self is an abstraction or perhaps even an illusion, a dream. The practical life demands that we act but even the most practical sort of person will occasionally glimpse the vagueness of self-hood.

> We are often aware of a self which, though it be unique, is anything but a unity. We are aware of a thousand selves within this single self; and what we are least able to do is to persuade ourselves of our practical identity. There are moods and there are activities in the conduct of life when it is scarcely an exaggeration to say that the separateness of the self is qualified, and its singleness is destroyed.
>
> (EM 272)

The 'I am' which, it has been alleged, accompanies all our thoughts is, to say the least, questionable. It is not that we are unaware of a continuity, it is simply that the possessive pronoun cannot be more than one of many options. For Oakeshott this 'mine' is certainly strongly placed in our experience, but it is a modification of experience.

Finally we must deal with the freedom of Sartre, the freedom of the *Néant* to transcend all contents, which Sartre took from Descartes and Kant. An innate and universal power granting to the individual the inalienable capacity of self determination. For Oakeshott, as for Bradley, only the totality is essential. Experience, the whole, is the ultimate, true and necessary. Comprehensive universals such as 'being' cannot offer us any additional insight, indeed, they lack any true identity being only the whole by another name. The exploration of 'being' can only return us to that sense of wonder we attain in pure contemplation of the whole. What concerns us is not being but being able, and that is a part of practical experience, a mode of experience.

These philosophies have no place for the metaphysically real elements of 'being' and 'nothing', they do not view the world as the dialectical show of non-phenomenal forces. They are grounded upon the interplay of whole and part, an endless process of selection and identification. There is no negation, no identifiable driving power to which life, or man may be reduced. For Bradley and Oakeshott it makes no more sense to characterize the life force in one expression than to express the world in one term, the whole. We know no more about our life force than we know why there is a world at all. Both life and world are a given, what matters to man is not life or world but the endeavour to make something of it.

Oakeshott rejects the Continental tradition which situates philosophy at the pivotal point of its experience, as an arbiter of experience. Philosophy becomes a specialist interest, perhaps a mania. The conduct of life is removed from its sphere of legislation. Where Heidegger had used metaphysics to rescue men from the blandness of life which is considered to be drawing us into an age of darkness, Oakeshott is happy to let life itself make its own demands. By giving life sovereignty in its own domain and dismissing the philosopher as moral advisor Oakeshott rejects the tradition inherited from Descartes and Kant, freedom is a parochial matter of importance in its own field, to be free one does not have to take charge of all knowledge one only has to be good at running one's life.

We find in *Experience and its Modes* the root ideas of Oakeshott's thought that meaning is projected onto an ultimately meaningless world, that all such shapes are human and are sustained as much by omission as inclusion. That man may no more be known than the world. The notion of a natural content is sheer bravado for 'nature' is but one structure we use to know the world, not one we should be satisfied with for ourselves. His scepticism is directly responsible for the main features of his philosophy; its liberal or indulgent character; its deep respect for ordinary life, and its hostile attitude to the intellectual; an enthusiasm tending to crab the vitality of actual life.

7

The Vigour of Inheritance

The image of freedom outlined in *Experience and its Modes* largely conforms with common opinion – freedom is held to be self-possession; the capacity to direct one's own life. In that work Oakeshott's primary ambition had been to distinguish the interests and segregate the achievements of different intellectual disciplines and, most importantly, restrain them from encroachment into the realm of the conduct of life. Having designated these regions of competence Oakeshott, in his post-war essays collected under the title of *Rationalism in Politics*,[1] moves his attention to the actual substance of thinking – how we come to know what we know.

In these essays he sets out to distinguish the type of thinking that is acquired and used in practice from an abstract or analytical type of thinking which he believes is actually corrosive and degenerative. Freedom, our self-possession, is revealed as a complex of skills, as a craft of living and the threat to life posed by the intellectual is seen not as the encroachment of one discipline upon affairs of another but as the actual impoverishment of our ability to live well.

Oakeshott employs the term 'practice' to designate all those activities, skills and crafts which are acquired and which collectively compose the substance of life. Normally, we contrast practice with theory – distinguishing the practical aspect of life from the cerebral – and Oakeshott is using the term, at least in part, in this sense. Each craft of life, practice or discourse is initially something done and learned in doing, but this doing includes the associated exercise of mind. Hence 'practice' refers not just to dextrous manoeuvres but to the series of recognitions, computations and observations which are an integral part of any such activity. Oakeshott holds that our understanding is itself an acquired set of skills, learned in use much as we learn a language but always learned in the context of undertaking an activity. Any practitioner be he a scientist, an historian, a cook or a citizen will find his activities directed by a pattern of learned procedures, considerations and habits of organization which together direct his attention.

> All actual conduct, all specific activity springs up within an already existing idiom of activity, and by an 'idiom of activity' I mean a knowledge of how to behave appropriately in the circumstances .... The questions and the problems in each case spring from the knowledge we have of how to solve them, spring from the activity itself. And we come to penetrate the idiom of activity in no other way than by practising the activity; for it is only in the practice of an activity that we can acquire the knowledge of how to practice it.
>
> (RP 101)

A practice, in this sense is, then, a way of approaching and challenging the world a way which governs the sort of questions to be pursued and the type of answers obtained. The human world is formed from a countless number of these 'practices', together they compose our understanding, the known world and ourselves. We find these practices to be at one and the same time resources already existing in our human environment, objective and communal and the structures we use to investigate and interrogate, the world and ourselves. They are, therefore, also the ground and fabric of the articulation of our selfhood.

One of the pervasive themes of the essays is the vulnerability of these concrete activities. For Oakeshott these resources are a treasure made by man, our historical inheritance, the legacy of the generations – but they are frail. Oakeshott wants to warn of a tendency, a growing habit of neglect of the actual sensuous activity in favour of abbreviated formulations of these activities. This formulation is referred to by Oakeshott as rationalism and may be considered as itself a practice, one which mistakes the nature of learning and of knowledge. It is an attitude which spawns incomprehension and inadequacy.

The problem put succinctly is this; the urge to possess quickly what in fact takes a long time to acquire means that an impoverished and abbreviated form of practice will often be paraded in place of the real thing. Where the reward is great so much greater is the tendency for the crib to masquerade as fluency. And nowhere is the temptation greater than in political life, politics is the true home of truncated understanding. Indeed, our whole understanding of politics has been affected by this attitude. Before we can move on to

Oakeshott's view of political life we must investigate the problem of depleted knowledge itself, the issue of rationalism.

The account of knowledge is given mainly in three essays: *Rationalism in Politics* 1947, *The Tower of Babel* 1948, and *Rational Conduct* 1950. We are told that a distinction may be made between 'two types of knowledge'. Actual knowledge is always some mixture of the two but at any time we may favour one at the expense of the other. These two types of knowledge are described as 'practical knowledge' and 'technical knowledge'.

Technical knowledge is the sort that can be learned from books, it can be learned by heart, repeated by rote, applied mechanically it is susceptible to formulation in rules, principles and maxims. On the other hand practical knowledge is not susceptible to formulation, 'its normal expression is in a customary or traditional way of doing things, or, simply, in practice' (RP 10). Practical knowledge can be neither taught nor learned but only imparted and acquired 'the only way to acquire it is by apprenticeship to a master – not because the master can teach it (he cannot), but because it can be acquired only by continuous contact with one who is perpetually practising it' (RP 11).

The real distinction between these types of knowledge lies in our ability to record and retrieve them. The character of technical knowledge gives it the appearance of precision, its susceptibility to formulation gives it a deliberateness and orderliness which practical knowledge can never emulate, it always appears to be mere opinion to be probability rather than truth. Technical knowledge, because of this ease of formulation, has come to be mistaken for knowledge itself.

> The Rationalist holds that the only element of *knowledge* involved in any human activity is technical knowledge, and that what I have called practical knowledge is really only a sort of nascence …. The sovereignty of 'reason', for the Rationalist, means the sovereignty of technique.

> The heart of the matter is the pre-occupation of the Rationalist with certainty. Technique and certainty are inseparably joined because certain knowledge is, for him, knowledge which does not require to look beyond itself for its certainty but begins with certainty and is certain throughout.

> (RP 11)

What is sought is knowledge which seems to be self-complete; possessing its own beginning and end. Here it is distinguished from practical knowledge which in its vagueness and impression has no beginning and no end, but is a continuous process of modification and reformulation of what is already there. The quest of the rationalist is for a type of knowledge which is given to precision, demonstrability and propositional formulation. The type of knowledge which can be formally taught and systematically learned, which can equip an unencumbered intellect with proper thinking processes. Its enemy is the merely habitual, the intuitive, the customary and 'prejudice' for the rationalists' reason is common to all mankind and anyone thinking honestly and clearly will think as the rationalist thinks.

As a manner of behaving 'being rational' is identified with activity which is deliberately directed to the achievement of a formulated purpose. To be recognized as being rational behaviour must be governed by a rule or a principle. Rational conduct is conduct 'springing from an antecedent process of reasoning' (RP 85). Mind is held to be most efficient when it is freed from its preconceptions, when it calculates from primary elements, liberated from unexamined habit and traditions of belief.

Oakeshott insists that such an instrumental mind is nonsense. Mind, he argues, is constituted of its activities there is no underlying structure which orders the in-coming contents.

> You do not first have a mind, which acquires a filling of ideas and then makes distinctions between true and false, right and wrong, reasonable and unreasonable, and then, as a third step, causes activity. Properly speaking the mind has no existence apart from, or in advance of, these and other distinctions.
>
> (RP 89)

The essays seek to dispel the illusion that thought possesses an innate and universal genius which, because it is prior to anything learned remains native, primitive and primal; a point of departure which would lack the residue of superstition and habit. Oakeshott condemns this view as itself a superstition and considers it to be an attitude inherited from the Romantic vein in our tradition. The rationalist has a distrust of time, a desire for permanence and for the eternally stable, there is an impatience with anything temporary, transient or topical. The rationalist has no confidence in what is merely accumulated, he 'has lost the capacity to accept the mystery of life, its uncertainty' and he has lost patience with the need to become acquainted with an institution or a skill.

Now we should turn from the negative argument – the attack on rationalism – to a more extended treatment of true, vital knowledge. Practical knowledge exists only in use, it is the ground from which subsequent reflection may produce the abstractions of the rationalist. True knowledge is acquired incidentally and in apprenticeship. To reflective examination it may appear imprecise, uncertain, probable and opinionated, but in execution it is proficient, undemonstrative and competent. It lacks the troubled self-examination of the more formal type of knowledge, it is un-neurotic and smart. Oakeshott frequently resorts to the analogy of the craftsman to describe the process of learning all social skills, moral and political. We acquire our habits of conduct by living with people who habitually behave in a certain manner, 'we acquire habits of conduct in the same way as we acquire our native language' (RP 62).

> There is no point in a child's life at which he can be said to begin to learn the language which is habitually spoken in his hearing; and there is no point in his life at which he can be said to learn the habits of behaviour from the people constantly about him …. This sort of education is not compulsory; it is inevitable.
>
> (ibid.)

We possess a collection of acquired patterns of recognition and organization, these are the resources of our survival and of our accomplishments they are also the ground of reflective intelligence. We may understand this as one version of the family we have called 'mimetic' theories of knowledge – the progeny of Hegel's phenomenology.

> Human activity, then, is always activity with a pattern; not a superimposed pattern, but a pattern inherent in the activity itself. Elements of this pattern occasionally stand out with a relatively firm outline; and we call these elements, customs, traditions, institutions, laws, etc …. They are the substance of our knowledge of how to behave. We do not first decide that certain behaviour is right or desirable and then express our approval of it in an institution; our knowledge of how to behave well is, at this point, the institution.
>
> (RP 105)

Here, as in Hegel's notion of *Sittlichkeit*; the shared, learned habits, order and sophistication of a people, are the substance of our intellect. The corruption of rationalism ought to be resisted because it actually diminishes our ability to live, it dissipates these sensuous patterns of engagement. Oakeshott's thesis is that the desire for a knowledge rooted in principles is leading mankind away from the real wealth of his culture. This depletion of our skills brutalizes both the way we manage this world and the way we deal with each other.

As to why this perverse enthusiasm has obtained such kudos Oakeshott tells us that it results from the urge to find perfection within a lifetime, to attempt to short-cut the nagging diversity of frustrations, indignities and chores with which he resents being presented. Rationalism takes hold because we are unwilling to undergo the tedious apprenticeship entailed in the acquisition of real knowledge. Historically, sixteenth-century philosophers, especially Bacon and Descartes, impressed by the success of science took it to be a model of thought. Oakeshott insists that both Bacon and Descartes are not guilty of rationalism but are part of its history. Their writings are early intimations of an enthusiasm which was coming to grip our civilization. Descartes 'perceived the lack of a consciously and precisely formulated technique of inquiry'. Their aim was certainty and certainty meant self-creation, man for the rationalist is his own master, the source of himself. To accept that one enters civilization at a mid point, that one inherits a set of activities more or less established is to accept dishonour and indignity, to insult the power of the mind, to deny its agility as a tool.

We have been seduced by the notion that behaviour ought to be guided by rules, by ideals selected in advance of their application and expressed in a system of abstract ideas. The aim is to set out our moral aspirations, the desirable ends of conduct, clearly and unambiguously so as to reveal a complete system of relations. These aspirations must be capable of a reasoned defence, i.e. they must be placed within a universally accepted system of ideas.

> In this form of moral life, then, action will spring from a judgement concerning the rule or end to be applied and the determination to apply it. The situation of living should, ideally, appear as problems to be solved ... [and] it will appear more important to have the right moral ideal, than to act.
>
> (RP 67)

Besides tending to stifle and to diminish our capacity to act ideal morality demands prophetic guidance, direction by someone who knows what life is for. Oakeshott associates rationalism with the growth of barbarism in Europe for while the tyrant has been a feature of all ages, the cruel authoritarianism of the visionary leader is a modern invention.

With the impoverished intellectual mannerisms of rule based moral conduct comes incapacitation of a community. Ideologies, principles, and rule governed behaviour are ill suited to coping with the diversity of predicaments which a society must, in time, confront. The stilted style makes societies attracted to this moral attitude less able to adaptation.

> A morality of ideals has little power of self-modification; its stability springs from its stability and its imperviousness to change …. It has a great capacity to resist change, but when that resistance is broken down, what takes place is not change but revolution.
>
> (RP 69)

Finally, rational morality seeks what it cannot deliver, for the very pursuit of one ideal excludes the possibility of pursuing some competing principle, we find ourselves plunged into interminable quarrels. Its rigid vocabulary mean that it cannot be the basis for social order, conflict and disaffection are inevitable as each moral ideal has its opposite or competing ideal which appears equally valuable.

> Liberty or order, justice or charity, spontaneity or deliberateness, principle or circumstances, self and others, these are the kinds of dilemma with which this form of the moral life is always confronting us, making us see double by directing our attention always to abstract extremes, none of which is wholly desirable.
>
> (RP 70)

Oakeshott contrasted this morbid attitude to conduct with the moral life of habit, custom and experience. Where this form dominates there will be a healthier and richer social life.

> Moral life in this form does not spring from a choice, determined by an opinion, a rule or an ideal … conduct is as nearly as possible without reflection. And consequently, most of the current situations of life do not appear as problems requiring

solutions; there is no weighing up of alternatives or reflection on consequences.

(RP 61)

This is to a great extent the Oakeshottian creed. It is a form of activity acquired in the flow of life, learned as a language and assembled piecemeal in practice. It is an education which gives us the power to act appropriately and without hesitation but which does not necessarily supply us with a capacity to explain ourselves in terms of rules, principles or any abstract terms. This kind of moral education engenders an individual whose 'moral dispositions are inseverably connected with his amour-propre' and 'the spring of his conduct is his self-esteem' (RP 63).

This form of moral conduct is stable in a way that rule governed is not because it subsists throughout change. Custom, Oakeshott insists, is adaptable and susceptible to the nuance of the situation it, in fact, has a history of continuous change. Moreover, Oakeshott believes the claim that formula morality protects against the superstitious and xenophobic isolation of customary societies, their fear of difference and diversity is false. Only societies confident of their stability and aware of adaptability can cope with such pressures (RP 65).

We must now turn to the issue at the heart of Oakeshott's concern – rationalism *in politics* – for here its impact has been greatest. Political activity is seen as the arena in which the values of life are forged and created. Rationalism promotes the role and extends the remit of the government while at the same time making political life abrupt, uneven and incompetent. Once again we are offered the contrast of a vernacular language, vigorous and resourceful with the homoeopathic qualities of adaptability and continuity and a rationalism derivative, shallow, impoverished and disorientating.

Oakeshott says he takes politics to be 'the activity of attending to the general arrangements of a set of people who chance or choice have brought together ... the communities in which this manner of activity is pre-eminent are the hereditary co-operative groups, many of them of ancient lineage, all of them aware of a past a present and a future' (RP 112). Politics is seen as learning how to participate in a conversation, it is an initiation into an inheritance in which we have a life interest and an exploration of intimations.

There will always be something of a mystery about how a tradition of political behaviour is learned ... the politics of a community are no less individual than its language, and they are learned and practised in the same manner .... It begins in the enjoyment of a tradition, in the observation and imitation of the behaviour of our elders, and there is little or nothing in the world which comes before us as we open our eyes which does not contribute towards it .... Long before we are of an age to take interest in a book about our politics we are acquiring that complex and intricate knowledge of our political tradition without which we could not make sense of a book when we come to open it.

(RP 128)

To understand what politics is we must first look at the habits, customs and institutions which belong to our political culture.

In politics rationalism is exemplified by the 'ideology', or the doctrine, principles which designate a path to be taken, an end to be pursued, 'freedom, equality, maximum production, racial purity or happiness' all have been offered as contenders for this goal. Here political activity is 'understood as the enterprise of seeing that the arrangements of a society reflect the chosen track' (RP 116). With admirable economy Oakeshott outlines the kernel of the style of thinking which he rejects.

It is supposed that a political ideology is the product of intellectual premeditation and ... is able to determine and guide the direction of the activity .... So far from a political ideology being the quasi-divine parent of political activity, it turns out to be its earthly stepchild ... it is a system of ideals abstracted from the manner in which people have been accustomed to go about the business of attending to the arrangements of their societies.

(RP 118)

Activity precedes ideology; principles and rules are abridgements of a concrete manner of behaving. They are a crib, 'what we do, and moreover, what we want to do, is the creature of how we are accustomed to conduct our affairs (RP 120). Ideals are merely the reduced remnants of activities which we enjoy and for which we feel affection and loyalty.

In politics, as in morality, vulgar rules disclose a decadence in the life of a community, a lack of confidence and of competence, perhaps a disenchantment induced by the inflated claims to which abstract ideas are prone. The paradox of rationalism is that it inspires dramatic ambitions whilst it impoverishes our actual social skills and deprives us of the capacities we need to manage our affairs.

The essence of political skill is its propensity to yield to the demands and strains which unfolding circumstances both social and natural place upon it. It is its ability to adapt which is its true resource. The inspiration of such change is always part of the existing resource, it is intimated in current practice. Our acquired activities are themselves the ground of a sympathy for that which is not yet developed, politics is 'the pursuit of intimations; a conversation, not an argument' dedicated to the exposure of specific inconsistencies in the arrangements of society. In this context there is a role for abstract ideas, for technical knowledge, as a supplement and a forum for criticism and reform.

> Every society which is intellectually alive is liable, from time to time, to abridge its tradition of behaviour into a scheme of abstract ideas .... And there is no harm; perhaps even some positive benefit, it is possible that the distorting mirror of an ideology will reveal important hidden passages in the tradition, as a caricature reveals the potentialities of a face.
>
> (RP 125)

Thus abridgement can play a part in the process of political evolution.

Oakeshott sees politics as an inheritance which intimates change. Our guide is our tool-kit of habits and customs, each crisis or troubled period tests the richness of this resource but we possess nothing beyond our skills. Our tradition of behaviour might be damaged or disrupted by disaster, by war, by invasion but, no matter what the difficulty, we have only our manner of proceeding to rescue ourselves. Oakeshott summarizes his thoughts on political understanding by saying that a 'political crisis always appears within a tradition of political activity; and 'salvation' comes from the unimpaired resources of the tradition'.

> Those societies which retain, in changing circumstances a lively sense of their own identity and continuity, are to be counted fortunate, not because they possess what others lack, but because they have already mobilized what none is without and all, in fact, rely upon.
>
> (RP 127)

The attitude which corresponds to this understanding of politics is what he calls 'conservative' because at any moment the number of arrangements which are used or 'enjoyed' will far exceed those which need attention. This form of government is appropriate for a diverse and free society. Oakeshott attempts to explain the apparent paradox that a restless and adventurous society requires a conservative attitude in regard to government.

Government is a specific and limited activity concerned with the provision and custody of general rules of conduct, as instruments enabling us to pursue activities of our own choice with the minimum of frustration.

> [Government] is not concerned with moral right and wrong, it is not designed to make men good or even better; it is not indispensable on account of 'the natural depravity of mankind' but merely because of their current disposition to be extravagant; its business is to keep its subjects at peace with one another in the activities in which they have chosen to seek their happiness. And if there is any general idea entailed in this view, it is, perhaps, that a government which does not sustain the loyalty of its subjects is worthless.
>
> (RP 189)

For Oakeshott, the image of the ruler is the umpire whose job it is to administer the rules of the game. This vision of government is part of our culture, it is not innately true or universal, it simply fits our attitude to life. Hence what we must understand is our culture and the reason why this style of government suits it.

Oakeshott detects in our culture a lust for change, a fascination with what is new and an appetite for innovation. There is a general carelessness with our identity and a prejudice in favour of what is untried. This attitude is so contagious that we are apt to believe that we can apply this enthusiasm to government as well; that we can be ruled in the same manner we rule our lives. Oakeshott's aim is to explain why this is undesirable.

Conservatism is an appropriate disposition where 'stability is more profitable than improvement, where certainty is more valuable than speculation, wherever familiarity is more desirable than perfection or wherever agreed error is superior to controversial truth' (RP 178). And while we are inclined to reject conservatism in respect of human conduct in general there is an aspect of life for which it is 'not merely appropriate but a necessary condition', that is, in the way we are governed where stability, familiarity and agreement are the primary virtues.

Oakeshott understands by 'conservative' the 'disposition ... appropriate to a man who is acutely aware of having something to lose which he has learned to care for'.

> To be conservative it to prefer the familiar to the unknown, to prefer the tried to the untried, fact to mystery, the actual to the possible, the limited to the unbounded ... the convenient to the perfect.
> (RP 169)

The conservative is aware that each innovation entails a certain loss and, hence, that the burden of proof lies with the innovator. He is also aware that innovation to be worthy of attention should appear to grow out of what is already familiar and that change ought to be a response to a specific, identified defect (RP 172). Most importantly for Oakeshott's thesis on government 'familiarity is the essence of tool using; and in so far as man is a tool-using animal he is disposed to be conservative (RP 179). When we look at craftsmen we see that their capacity to execute their craft depends upon their skill, the way they use their tools. In order that their skill may be variously and appropriately applied it is necessary to have familiar and reliable tools, 'a surgeon does not pause in the middle of an operation to redesign his instruments'. Oakeshott's point is that 'what is true about tools in general, as distinct from projects, is even more obviously true about a certain kind of tool in common use, namely, general rules of conduct' (RP 181). The familiarity that springs from such a relative immunity from change is supremely appropriate, to the institutions of government.

We have already acknowledged that Oakeshott views government as the 'provision and custody of the general rules of conduct ... enabling people to pursue the activities of their own choice'. The stability of political institutions is needed because of the character of our type of society, our way of life.

> Each of us is pursuing a course of his own; and there is no project so unlikely that somebody will not undertake it .... We are all inclined to be passionate about our own concerns .... This multiplicity of activity and variety of opinion is apt to produce collisions; we pursue courses which cut across those of others, and we do not all approve of the same type of conduct.
> (RP 185)

Oakeshott rounds off this passage by saying that the reason why our lives have come to take this form does not matter, it could be otherwise, it is simply our way. 'It is an acquired condition, though nobody designed nor specifically chose it in preference to all others'. This situation draws a variety of responses; where some see diversity others find disorder, where some find competition other find waste, and what may be a challenge to one is a frustration to someone else. They seek a discernible direction of movement, they have a vision of a condition in which conflict has been removed from our society, that activity should be co-ordinated and directed, in short, they desire that the whole should be a managed project. For these people to govern is to 'turn a private dream into a public and compulsory manner of living' (RP 186).

This is the antithesis of Oakeshott's view of government, for he holds that it is not there to impose a way of life upon the population, to educate or make them happier but, rather, to rule them, to hold the ground which is the occasion of their activities. For Oakeshott there is no need for elaborate argument against the more extensive visions of political life, it simply goes against the way we like to live.

> We are not children in *statue pupillari* but adults who do not consider ourselves under any obligation to justify their preference for making their own choices …. It is beyond human experience to suppose that those who rule are endowed with a superior wisdom which discloses to them a better range of activities and which gives them authority to impose upon their subjects a quite different manner of life.
>
> (RP 187)

Ultimately their designs on life are no more pure or divine than those of the rest and 'if it is boring to have to listen to the dreams of others being recounted, it is insufferable to be forced to re-enact them' (ibid.).

To be conservative in terms of government is to recognize that it is the task of ruling to quell the passions of its people, to 'inject into the activities of already too passionate men an ingredient of moderation; to restrain; to deflate; to pacify and to reconcile' (RP 192). This is not because moderation is a virtue but because it is essential if we are not to be locked in an encounter of mutual frustration'. The subjects are not to be invited to adore their government to look to it with devotion or affection, but to acknowledge its role and to regard it with respect, loyalty and suspicion.

Thus, governing is understood to be a secondary activity, not easily to be combined with any other because all other activities entail taking sides and the surrender of the indifference appropriate ... to the legislator.

(RP 193)

It is the task of government to encourage restraint; the spectacle of its indifference to the beliefs and substantive activities of its subjects itself encourages restraint by exemplifying a civilized lack of intrusiveness. Oakeshott tells us this is the form of government for a people who 'do not need to be inflamed, whose desires do not need to be provoked and whose dreams of a better world need no promoting. Such people know the value of a rule which imposes orderliness without directing enterprise (RP 194). This encapsulates Oakeshott's view of politics, it enables a lively population to pursue their own affairs without the need to convince everyone that it is right.

Politics has been more susceptible to rationalism than almost any other aspect of life furnishing us with a contemporary notion of government is that it is saturated with doctrinaire ideas controlled by a belief in getting results. We have great expectations of government and this has hardened the image of government as a collective project and produced a range of obsessions and quests entailing popular commitment, upheaval and war. Yet it is the talent we most need to survive, it is the skill that preserves us in times of adversity. If a single individual should experiment and fall he places only his own life at risk, but if a government should embark upon some scheme or project it risks everything, the life of the nation. Oakeshott thinks politics has succumbed to the charms of rationalism because of the historical emergence of new powers, a new class; merchants over aristocrats, and workers over merchants and the notion of politics as a career for those individuals willing to scheme to achieve power. This type of politics, the politics of doctrine and of ideology lead to disaster and to social chaos, indeed, the problem with rationalism in politics is that its consequences are so dire that we tend to consider it part of the tragedy of the human condition rather than as an outcome of our dedication to rationalism.

Most hostility towards Oakeshott's political views has been directed against the narrow remit he gives to government. The tradition of the twentieth century had been to grant to government an ever greater range of responsibilities. To the already awesome list, which include maintaining the necessary organs of the state, the army, the judiciary and the police, defending against external foes and migratory invasion were added the additional responsibilities of diminishing poverty, fighting disease, providing a basic education for all and promoting the prosperity of the land. This latter has seen government become increasingly concerned with economic performance and has introduced the language and ethos of corporate business into the sphere of government. The authority of the state has been used to tax the population in order to administer, co-ordinate and implement various schemes and projects, to construct and maintain a national infra-structure, to sustain the vital industrial base of the economy, and to establish various institutions of training and information which facilitate the nation's ability to compete against other nation-states which have governments which operate in this fashion.

Arguments against the narrow remit have two basic forms, the first is utilitarian in the sense that it claims the population will incur a cost for its government's lack of interest in welfare and economic matters, poor standards of public health, the diseconomy of an illiterate, recidivistic population with its permanent possibility of civil disorder and even revolution. The second is the ethical argument that it is improper for us, as a people to permit suffering, to neglect to provide education for the children of indisposed or inadequate parents, for the health of those incapable of providing for their own hospitalization, for those congenitally disabled, etc.

As to the first point it is difficult to argue against the fact that central and authoritative provision of the national resources does supply structures which would otherwise not develop. Also it appears that Oakeshottian government would not be permitted to offer the economic resources, transportation, information and instruction which would augment the nation's capacity to capture its part of world trade in competition with nations with more despotic traditions of government. As to the second, I think it is less sure that the Oakeshottian view of government would be indifferent to the residual needs of a 'lumpen-proletariat' as it is clearly a matter of political interest to avoid the creation of a criminal subculture. It is always important to remember that Oakeshott's arguments are not against communal political life or 'socialism', though few would doubt he personally disliked interventionist government, his interest in the essays is the quality of government rather than its responsibilities. His concern with the skill of those charged with the duties of government; to protect and maintain the order won through the toil of generations. His case is rooted in the quality of knowledge and skill, and his impressive critique of our notion of government stands not on the question of national prosperity but on the peace, security and stability of public life.

Those who see Oakeshott's work as an attempt to justify an aristocratic and elitist notion of government have a responsibility to provide arguments that the type of government they support does not, itself have dis-economies of a more severe nature, specifically that generated by planned upheaval, dislocation, war and civil disorder but also, more insidious but less obvious, the dulling of the genius of the people. It is this latter point that seems to be at the root of Oakeshott's real fear of governments of command systems or of interventionist tendencies. The essay which provides the real clue to Oakeshott's politics is to be found in his 1949 article on the work of the Chicago economist Henry C. Simons, *The Political Economy of Freedom*.

Oakeshott commends Simons for having composed a body of work that is a lucid account of the sort of society he, that is, Simons, would like without the pretence of 'making a desert of his consciousness before beginning to cultivate it for himself' (RP 38). He is proud of belonging to a tradition and describes himself as 'an old-fashioned liberal' in a world where 'liberty has become the emblem of frivolous or disingenuous politics', indeed, Oakeshott insists that it is the 'friends of liberty' who have posed the greatest threat to its healthy survival.

> We must be clear, they say, about what we mean by 'freedom'. First, let, us define it; and when we know what it is, it will be time enough to seek it out, to love it and to die for it. What is a free society? And with this question (proposed abstractly) the door opens upon a night of endless quibble, lit only by the stars of sophistry. Like men born in prison, we are urged to dream of something we have never enjoyed (freedom from want) and to make that dream the foundation of our politics.
>
> (RP 39)

But the freedom disclosed in Simons' work is quite different; 'He is a libertarian, not because he begins with an abstract definition of liberty, but because he has actually enjoyed a way of living (and seen others enjoy it) which those who have enjoyed it are accustomed to call a free way of living, and because he has found it to be good' (RP 40).

The English word 'freedom' has its meaning in our political experience, in a 'coherence of mutually supporting liberties, each of which amplifies the whole and none of which stands alone' and if we are to defend it we need to distinguish the arrangements which sustain it and those which would compromise it. Any 'freedom' which could not be achieved by the kind of arrangements which gives us our freedom must be acknowledged to be an illusion.

Of the arrangements which sustain our freedom the most impressive is the absence from our society of overwhelming concentrations of power.

> We do not fear or seek to suppress diversity of interest, but we consider our freedom to be ... threatened if any one interest or combination of interests, even though it may be the interest of the majority, acquires extraordinary power.
>
> (RP 41)

The freedom we understand lies in the fact that no-one possesses unlimited power. But this is a dynamic even 'precarious' situation for arrangements which once promoted the dispersion of power often come, in time, to assist concentrations of power. Normally government needs only enough power to counter the greatest of the range of interests which may be found in society. But in our experience of freedom by far the most effective moderator of government power has been the rule of law. Oakeshott views the 'known and settled protective structure ... of the enforcement by prescribed methods of rules binding alike upon governors and governed' to be the emblem of the diffusion of power.

> It is the method of government most economical in the use of power; it involves a partnership between past and present and between governors and governed which leaves no room for arbitrariness; it encourages a tradition of resistance to the growth of dangerous concentrations of power.
>
> (RP 43)

If the rule of law is the 'greatest single condition of our freedom' such freedom is amplified and secured by two species of liberty; the freedom of association and the right to private property, and there is no doubt that it is the latter which is of abiding importance. It is a diverse institution created by a host of traditions and customs from estate to patent law, but all have the same basic function to secure for the person the enjoyment of the skills and talents which are his by fortune, nature and application. It is this institution of liberty which Oakeshott finds the most difficult to specify and the most open to abuse in the prevailing political climate.

> There is no doubt about the general character of the institution of property most friendly to freedom: it will be one which allows the widest distribution, and which discourages most effectively great and dangerous concentrations of this power …. It entails a right of private property, that is, an institution of property which allows to every adult member of the society an equal right to enjoy the ownership of his personal capacities and of anything else obtained by the methods of acquisition recognized in the society.
>
> (RP 45)

Now a state may take certain designated goods out of the field of private ownership and Oakeshott acknowledges that there may be reasons for doing this, but it cannot be for the increase of liberty. The maximum diffusion has been impaired by the 'acquisition of extraordinary proprietorial rights by the government, great business and industrial corporations and by trade unions, all of which are to be considered arbitrary limitations of the right of private property'. This is certainly the most nakedly 'political' Oakeshott's thought ever becomes.

> That a man is not free unless he enjoys a proprietorial right over his own personal capacities and his labour is believed by everybody who uses freedom in the English sense. And yet no such right exists unless there are many potential employers of his labour. The freedom which separates a man from slavery is nothing but a freedom to choose and to move among autonomous, independent organizations, and this implies private property in resources other than personal capacities. Wherever a means of production falls under the control of a single power, slavery in some measure follows.
>
> (RP 46)

In the context of its composition this obviously refers to the legislative efforts of the Attlee government which Oakeshott unquestionably disliked. But we are soon reminded of the epistemological root of these thoughts, that no monopoly can be trusted and that it is 'mere foolishness to complain when absolute power is abused', for power 'exists to be abused'. This, perhaps more than any other expression in the essays, reveals Oakeshott's continuing debt to Hobbes.

Collectivism necessarily involves the mobilization of society for a unitary purpose and it can only be justified by a narrowing of the purposes of a people. Oakeshott acknowledges that there may be gains in such regimentation, at least in the short term, but the political economy of freedom rests upon the recognition that what is being attempted is freedom rather than prosperity, not the maximization of wealth but the political aim of 'the custody of a manner of living'. Our affection for this way of life may incur for us a price in a diminished capacity to produce, but it is worth paying in so far as we are permitted to cling to what we love and to what we have learned to recognize as liberty.

I take this to be the nub of Oakeshott's argument, the essential reason why he will grant government only a limited remit. We do not give much power to government because, granted such power it swiftly becomes a monomania, dominated by the ambitions of some one or some interest, it thins out the depth of life of the whole it choreographs in a way that is purposeful, even productive and effective, but which always has the cost of reducing the fund of life belonging to a people, the greatest and the most significant resource it has at its disposal. For in times of tragedy or of crisis it is this resource which will be needed to rescue the nation.

Now many people have viewed Oakeshott's notion of tradition, custom and habit as encouraging us to look to our past, to 'return to our roots'. This, of course, could not be further from the truth. We are encouraged to trust our own talents, to explore our strengths and to abstain from dabbling. The concept of tradition is ultimately a charm to ward off the undesirable attentions of the rationalist. The paradox of Oakeshott's thought is that respect for institutions is the condition of our self-possession.

The issue of the essays is the conservation of the full sensuousness of human conduct, the vitality of the various crafts of human self-discovery and disclosure. Life is seen as an adventure and politics is viewed as something which enables but does not assist this adventure. Indeed in what must be the most famous of all Oakeshott's remarks he says:

In political activity, then, men sail a boundless and bottomless sea; there is neither harbour for shelter nor floor for anchorage, neither starting-place nor appointed destination. The enterprise is to keep afloat and on an even keel; the sea is both friend and enemy; and the seamanship consists in using the resources of a traditional manner of behaviour to make a friend of every hostile occasion.

(RP 127)

The paradox that must be grasped if Oakeshott's social and political thought is to be understood is that it is habit and custom which provide the environment in which our adventurousness is possible. One cannot shrink from the fact that the overwhelming impression of political experience in this century tends to support Oakeshott's view. For surely the lasting image is that those nations that succumbed to bold, audacious and grand administrations, besides regimenting their populations, enslaving their work-forces and waging wars against their neighbours, have actually frozen the life-styles of their people in the era of their institution and have shown little capacity to adapt or innovate. Oakeshott attacks a way of thinking, one which impoverishes and debilitates the capacity of men to live vigorous lives and to live together civilly in the context of such frenetic activity. Oakeshott is impressed by the vulnerability of life to the canalization of rationalism and to the brutalization of politics because of the form of his idealism, its softer, looser construction than the vast Germanic systems and I want to end by saying something about this vernacular idealism, dominated by the metaphor of language and the image of the craft.

A brilliant insight into Oakeshott's attitude to politics and its wider significance is found in his contribution to the *Scrutiny* symposium of 1939 on the responsibilities of the artist; *The Claims of Politics*. Oakeshott introduces two significant themes, firstly, the artist as the inspiration of a culture the seminal element of its orientation, secondly, a vision of politics, an endeavour of marginal significance, administrative in character, secondary in the life of a people. Politics is viewed as being too shallow and narrow a part of life to be of interest to the artist, the author or the poet whose job in social life is to renew and vitalize the real ground of life, our civilization. He argues that we do real damage to our collective life if we think that politics is the most important social activity for we degenerate the real force of life. Politics is not the soul of communal life, it is not the crucible in which right and justice and all values and beliefs are forged. Politics is 'a highly specialized and abstracted form of communal activity; it is conducted on the surface of society and except on rare occasions makes remarkably small impression below that surface'.

> A political system is primarily for the protection and occasional modification of a recognized legal and social order .... Its end and meaning lie beyond itself in the social whole to which it belongs, a social whole already determined by law and custom and tradition, none of which is the creation of political activity .... A political system presupposes a civilization; it has a function to perform in regard to that civilization, but it is a function mainly of protection .... The things political activity can achieve are often valuable, but I do not believe that they are ever the most valuable things in the communal life of a society.
>
> (CP 148)

Government and political activity is of limited significance in our life as a whole. This leads directly on to a second very Oakeshottian theme that the exaggerated importance given to politics is corrupting to the life of a community. Indeed, the behaviour and attitude which such activity requires is flattened and impoverished.

> A limitation of view, which appears so clear and practical, but which amounts to little more than a mental fog, is inseparable from political activity. A mind fixed and callous to all subtle distinctions, emotional and intellectual habits become bogus from repetition and lack of examination, unreal loyalties, delusive aims, false significances are what political action involves .... Political action involves mental vulgarity, not merely because it entails the concurrence and support of those who are mentally vulgar, but because of the false simplification of human life implied in even the best of its purposes.
>
> (ibid.)

Politics may be important in some people's lives but this tells us nothing about politics only something about the psychology of those people. Politics does have an extended significance at times of crisis, for then the task of protection may well be of great significance, but Oakeshott insists that this is usually because of the poverty of the real creative activity of society, the real life of the community. Oakeshott warns us that the communal life is 'as often threatened by political success as by political failure' (CP 149). Rescuing an endangered society requires something 'more radical' than politics; the work of those whose 'true genius and interest lies in literature, in art and in philosophy' and for these people the callous superficiality of politics is a perversion of their gifts. Their business is with the horizons, ambitions, and affections which are the real life and character of a society.

Societies are in fact 'led from behind', it is in the work of artists and, perhaps, philosophers that society finds renewal. In their work society becomes conscious and critical of itself. For there is an evil greater than social disorder and that is the corruption of the consciousness of a community. Such a corruption would mark its demise, its loss of any capacity to rescue itself from ill fortune. Artists and poets are required to continuously save society from the exaggerated influence of the political. 'The emotional and intellectual integrity and insight for which they stand is something foreign to the political world ... their job is to mitigate a little society's ignorance of itself' (CP 150).

This theme is taken further in his remarkable article on Hobbes in *The Listener*. Oakeshott tells us 'we are apt to think of civilization as something external, but at bottom it is a collective dream .... And the substance of this dream is a myth, an imaginative interpretation of human existence, the perception (not the solution) of the mystery of human life'.[2] Here, 'civilization' is the inclusive, complete and vital totality which is the ground of our understanding. Underpinning the various idioms of engagement it is the climate of the age fashioned and remoulded by great artists and writers who set the scene for the more mundane operations of moralists and legislators.

> The office of literature in a civilization is not to break the dream, but to perpetually recall it, to recreate it in each generation, and even to make more articulate the dream-powers of a people. We, whose participation in the dream is imperfect and largely passive, are, in a sense, its slaves. But the comparative freedom of the artist springs not from any faculty of wakefulness but from his power to dream more profoundly; his genius is to dream that he is dreaming. And it is this which distinguished him from the scientist, whose perverse genius is to dream that he is awake. The project of the scientist, as I understand it, is to solve the mystery, to wake us from our dream, to destroy the

myth; and were this project fully achieved, not only should we find ourselves awake in a profound darkness, but a dreadful insomnia would settle upon mankind, not less intolerable for being only a nightmare.

The gift of the greatest literature – of poetry – is a gift of power. Its effect is an expansion of our faculty of dreaming. Under its inspiration the familiar outlines of the common dream fade, new perceptions, and emotions hitherto unfelt, are excited within us, the till-now settled fact dissolves once more into infinite possibility and we become aware that the myth (which is the substance of the dream) has acquired a new quality.[3]

Artists do not direct our ambitions rather they prepare the ground, create the heroes and the idylls which we come to treasure, artists are the true legislators, they create the affections which stand as our horizons or ends, which govern what we hold dear and the way we conceive life.

For Oakeshott, our understanding of ourselves is gathered from inherited human creations; language, literature, art, and history from the structures and institutions which are the context of our coming to question ourselves and our world. The skills in which we discover ourselves and which give fabric to the world we know exist only partly by our endeavour, for they are in large part the gift of our forebears, an inheritance which fortuity grants or denies. In the terms that we have previously identified, this is, at bottom, a mimetic thesis, though one lacking the teleology or the unity of Hegel's *Sittlichkeit*. The education of mankind is a rag-bag affair from which we may pick as we are inclined.

The key to the political attitude of Sartre we located in the romantic tradition of rescuing man from the perversity of institutions by constructing institutions which will emancipate his inner being. The quest for authenticity represented by Heidegger's maxim that 'we must free man from the idols to which he is wont to go cringingly', that is, give man the opportunity to determine his own idea of life. But this maxim also discloses how differently Oakeshott's views the world, for Oakeshott wants us to be permitted to hold on to our idols, the icons and totems created by the cultural genius of our people. He feels that it is destructive to separate men from their idols because these are all we have to give our lives direction and character, if these are destroyed or more likely damaged or degraded, then we would be put in the position of being without guidance in our lives or having to replace those idols we had acquired in the course of our lives with ones invented, that is, for the idols of some elite, most obviously a religious, political or intellectual enthusiasm. Such would be of impoverished quality and of dubious worth, and the community of men would enter a period of quarrelsomeness, instability and unpredictability.

Politics and rationalism are a closely linked pair, they both crab our dreamful self-invention, they both canalize and vulgarize the meandering affections of life. By the same token private property makes us free. It is the key to our self-possession and hence to our capacity to give substance to our fancies to make our world reflect our dreams. When his critics accuse Oakeshott of disregarding the power of man to manipulate the whole, to make man free by reorganization, it is to this poetic view of the totality they should be directed. For Oakeshott is not in doubt that it is possible to manipulate the whole, indeed the opposite he is most impressed by just how easy it is to manipulate, his point is that the dignity of man, as well as his capacity to survive depend upon the diversity, the opulence and the vitality of the accumulated crafts of life. And these are secured by our being able to make our own way in life, not by the obscene attempt to dismantle the folly of life only to find that there is nothing beyond the game.

8

The Achievement of Legal Order

Shortly after the publication of the essays Oakeshott appears to have recognized that a more comprehensive account of his views was required. His response to D. D. Raphael's critical review[1] centred on the need to distinguish between explanation and recommendation, a theme explored in *Experience and its Modes* and perhaps not one that would be immediately associated with *Rationalism in Politics*. *On Human Conduct*[2] is Oakeshott's attempt to make a clear statement of this distinction and to explain its significance for political thought. The work seeks to characterize the phenomenon of the modern European state and to explore its desirability as well as pursuing the more philosophical task of explaining the basis upon which human institutions may be examined and recommended. It follows the general theme of Oakeshott's output in having a dual purpose; specifying a narrow remit for government and circumscribing the authority of the intellectual.

In the preface to *On Human Conduct* Oakeshott informs us that the themes explored had been with him as long as he could remember. In fact, the book re-works familiar themes in an original and difficult manner. In *On Being Conservative* Oakeshott had attempted to characterize a type of government which was largely indifferent to the adventures of its citizens one where the rule of law 'imposed orderliness without directing the enterprise' (RP 194). *On Human Conduct* pursues this theme in a more rigorous and thorough fashion. The idea of law lies at the core of the work. Law is at once the product of and the instrument of the civil freedom which Oakeshott seeks to defend, inseparable from the character the 'modern European state' and from the expectations of life men in these countries have come to treasure.

The work develops and extends what we may take as the axiom of Oakeshott's thought, namely, that a real distinction can be made between those conceptions of government which 'hand over to the arbitrary will of a society's self-appointed leaders the planning of its entire life, and those which not only refuse to hand over the destiny of a society to any set of officials but also consider the whole notion of planning the destiny of a society to be both stupid and immoral'.[3] This dual phenomenon is the subject of *On Human Conduct*, what is to be explained is the origin and desirability of each form.

* * *

Oakeshott identifies the two ideal forms of the modern state as *universitas*, meaning a common enterprise, and *societas*, meaning an association of individuals under the rule of law, each person being largely responsible for their own well-being. The actual entities which we would give as concrete examples of the modern European state the Republic of France, the German Federal Republic, the United Kingdom, etc. cannot be specified as either *universitas* nor *societas* for these are 'the complex, ambiguous out-comes of countless historical contingencies; numerous acts of con-stitutional construction and reconstruction' composed of layer upon layer of traditions of government and national ambitions. But Oakeshott's point is that what is specific to them as states can be reduced to these two forms, these are 'ideal characters' which are actually manifest in various amalgams. In other words, we are dealing with abstractions.

Oakeshott argues that our inheritance offers us two traditions of national association, one being of significantly greater importance than the other because whilst the type of state founded on an image of an enterprise is common to man throughout history the type of state represented by the ideal form *societas* is the unique achieve-ment of modern Europe. It is special because it is unlike any other form of association, having only vague analogies in ordinary life. It is an achievement of mankind, not itself a deliberate creation but a by-product of our understanding of ourselves, our hopes and ambi-tions. As its identity has only been dimly distinguished it has been undervalued and undefended and its well-being neglected. *Societas* is, then, an emerging phenomenon, a developing mode of associa-tion ambiguously manifested in actual practice. Part of its evolution has been five centuries of more or less faltering attempts to compre-hend it, these often associated with equally diverse recommenda-tions aimed at preserving and enhancing what was found to be admirable.

While actual states are historical outcomes of largely contingent forces we can, Oakeshott argues, isolate certain tendencies and enthusiasms which are so characteristic of *universitas* or *societas* that we may identify them as essential elements in the development of the form of which they are a feature.

As regards *societas*, one such element is found in the image of man as an intelligent individual, one for whom it is a matter of dignity that he ought pursue his own life according to his own compunction. The origins of this individual can never be separated from the history of Europe in general, but it may be broadly characterized as an affection for personal autonomy.

> The self here is a substantive personality, the outcome of an education, whose resources are collected in a self-understanding; and conduct is recognized as the adventure in which this cultivated self deploys in its resources, discloses and enacts itself in response to its contingent situations.
>
> (OHC 237)

Its actual historical emergence was both gradual and ill-defined but 'like anything else in the modern European character this sentiment of individuality appeared there as a modification of the conditions of medieval life and thought' (OHC 239). It was an outcome of an evolutionary process:

> It displayed itself in the persons of younger sons making their own way in a world which had little place for them, of foot-loose adventurers who left the land to take to trade, of town-dwellers who had emancipated themselves from the communal till of the countryside ... in the lives of intrepid boys and men who left home to seek their fortunes each intent upon living a life for 'a man like me'.
>
> (OHC 239)

This was a gradually emerging tendency to cultivate the powers, abilities and fancies belonging to the particular individual, 'a reading of the human condition in which a man's life is understood as an adventure in personal self-enactment'. A view given embellishment in the legends and myths and in the great literary works that 'it is something almost divine for a man to know how to belong to himself and to live by that understanding' (OHC 241).

We may imagine that the opposing ideal form; *universitas*, the nation as a fellowship, a brotherhood or a race was promoted by a lingering medievalism. But while there were aspects of medieval life which favoured this collectivist notion, such as the need to maintain the nation, to generate solidarity at times of peril and bind together often disparate peoples, Oakeshott insists that the disposition associated with the collectivist state is as modern as that of autonomy. Indeed it is a direct product of the modern individualistic condition. For in a world being transformed by the aspirations of those who were excited by these opportunities there were some perhaps, a majority, who by circumstances or by temperament were less ready to rise to these new demands, for them the new liberties were a burden.

> The old certainties of belief, of occupation and of status were being dissolved, not only for those who had confidence in their own power to make a new place for themselves in an association of individuals, but also for those who had no such confidence .... In short, the circumstances of modern Europe ... bred, not a single character, but two obliquely opposed characters: not only that of the individual, but also that of the 'individual manqué'.
>
> (MRD 111)

This individual *manqué* is not a relic of a past age he is part of the modern character, it is this character's sense of loss and inadequacy that is the source and inspiration of the collectivist model of the modern state and which sees government as a managerial engagement. For while the sense of discomfort and failure provoked in some resentment in others 'it bred envy, jealousy and resentment' a victim with a victims conscience. This 'anti-individual' was a complete mirror image of the new free man, 'he required to be told what to think, to ask for, and to do, and in the course of time his natural submissiveness prompted the appearance of 'leaders' to perform this service for him'. (OHC P75, MRD 113)

With this disposition grew a moral identity associated with the idea of 'security', that is, defence against having to make choices for himself and against having to meet the vicissitudes of life from his own resources. In the eyes of this character 'to govern was understood to be the exercise of power in order to impose and maintain the substantive condition of human circumstance identified as "the public good", not of "public order" in an association of individuals pursuing their own activities, but the public good of a "community"' (MRD 117). The ruler was not to be recognized as referee to the collisions of individuals, but the moral leader and managing director of the community.

Oakeshott pictures this character as the source of much that has been evil in the developments of the modern state. Those leaders concerned with power, not particularly well disposed to place a limit upon their activities, would reassure the individual *manqué* of his superiority and use the disposition of the 'mass man', to impose upon all a uniformity of belief and conduct. From the individual *manqué* such leaders formed the determined 'anti-individual', 'one intolerant not only of superiority but of difference' one who could unit with his fellows in a revulsion from distinctness and create 'a therapeutic corporation devoted to remedying the so-called self-alienation with which they had infused their followers'. (OHC 279)

* * *

Turning our attention to a less rhetorical sphere of discourse, that of the various texts which attempt to understand the phenomenon of the modern European state, we find arguments that have promoted one or the other view of the underlying association. The ambiguous nature of actual states has, Oakeshott argues, been a major obstacle to their recognizing the distinction he believes it essential to make, i.e. that between *universitas* and *societas*. However, some historical theories may be positively identified as belonging to or, at least, favouring one or the other mode of association. Of those writers whose work seems to favour the ideal character *universitas* Oakeshott argues Francis Bacon to be the most clear-sighted and influential. Bacon, Oakeshott claims, understood the state to be, and not merely to have, an 'economy'. An understanding which had its root in the religious attitude that 'to win from the natural world its secrets and to exploit its resources is the chief (and perhaps the only) way mankind had of glorifying God' and hence the proper occupation of mankind was 'the unremitting and intelligent exploitation of the resources of the earth for the satisfaction of human wants'. Bacon felt that this task had been pursued with only limited enthusiasm and that a more resolute, determined and diligent attempt at the husbanding of the potential of the earth was needed, and this required the marshalling 'of the resources of the earth under central direction' (OHC 289).

The Baconian vision then is one of 'maximization' of yield, and the corporate pursuit of 'well-being'. Bacon's successors accepted that it was the proper occupation of mankind to subjugate nature, to make ourselves the master of the natural world and to exploit its resources to the utmost. The state was understood as a 'corporate productive enterprise, centred upon the exploitation of the material and human resources of an estate and managed by a government whose office it was to direct research, to suppress distracting engagements and to makes instrumental rules for the conduct of the enterprise, to assign to each of its 'subjects' his role in the undertaking' (OHC 290). That is, as an operation with a purpose and a destiny, where each citizen is a role player and the civil relationship becomes a managerial operation of education, planning and directing.

The greatest theorists of the association characterized as *societas*, we are told, are Hobbes and Hegel but the most impressive or influential are Montesquieu and Bodin. Of Montesquieu Oakeshott says that the value of his work is obscured by the fact that he used the vocabulary of constitutions while he was, in fact, dealing with the engagement of government. Oakeshott points out that the terms *despotism, republique,* and *monarchie* do not designate constitutional forms but modes of association. Each, he tells us, is an association of personae, that is, a moral identity or disposition and in each government is specified in terms of the performance of a certain office in relation to the associates. Oakeshott claims it is Montesquieu's main concern to 'specify what he thought to be the essential character of a modern European state'. In brief, the mode of association designated by the term *despotism* is held together by terror, the disposition of the associates is then fear of a ruler who is known only as a capricious will and whose utterances are commands and whose capacity to govern rests upon force and a cowering population. Montesquieu finds two important things to say about this form of government, 'First, it is scarcely recognizable as a mode of human association: it is an outrage against human beings, reducing them to slaves of another's will. Secondly, it is unknown in modern Europe' (OHO 247).

The second form referred to as a *republique* is said to be composed of associates 'distinguished by a disposition to prize *la vertu'*. This ideal of virtuousness is manifest in a communal morality of self-denial and commitment to the common good, here associates are joined in devotion to the common purpose. In such a state the office of government is the proper management of the pursuit of this common good, but included in this is the task of engendering and maintaining enthusiasm and devotion to the end of the state, that is, an educative function to initiate ensuing generations into the 'mystery' of the common purpose. Unlike *despotism*, this is a genuine mode of human association because it acknowledges men's intelligence, but as a way of life it is difficult to maintain, it is seriously restrictive and the conduct of the associates is constantly to be scrutinized and judged by the authorities. Obviously the model of this state is Sparta or Rome. For Montesquieu modern examples of this mode of association could be found in the New World colonies but in Europe one can find only states which vaguely approximate to it.

Oakeshott tells us that Montesquieu uses the expression *la monarchie* to refer to a mode of association characterized 'as a many joined solely in terms of rules of conduct: *la loi*' (OHC 249). Unlike the republican association the law does not promote the pursuit of a common purpose but is, rather, 'a system of conditions, indifferent to the satisfaction of wants'. The associates are related only in recognition of the authority of a system of law expressing conditions to be subscribed to and used in making their own choices of what to do or to say in contingent situations. In place of a common interest they have a concern that the obligations prescribed in law should be respected and that civil association should not be disrupted or destroyed. The disposition in this mode of association is characterized by *l'honneur*, that is, to be and to find virtue in being a distinct person. And the office of government is the 'custody, care, interpretation and administration of the conditions imposed upon conduct by law'.

> Of this mode of association Montesquieu says that it is preeminently human: intelligent relationship in terms of understood norms of conduct. It is less onerous and more relaxed than relationship in terms of an inexorable common substantive purpose, be it *la vertu* or any other. It requires no elaborate 'education' in a way of life, and it may be enjoyed between relative strangers .... This mode of association corresponds to and accommodates the dominant moral disposition of the inhabitant of modern Europe: the historic disposition to be 'distinct'.
>
> (OHO 251)

Thus Oakeshott discloses in Montesquieu an account which illustrates what he has referred to as *societas*, the union of free men.

Oakeshott finds beneath the misleading vocabulary of Montesquieu an understanding of the modern European state in terms of the proper engagement of government. He argues that the confusion of 'institutional structure' with 'mode of engagement' has been one of the more bewildering errors of political thought. For a government can be an 'democracy' and be oppressive and a government can be an 'aristocracy' and be benign. These matters might become more clear if we move on to Oakeshott's interpretation of the other great intellectual harbinger of *societas* Jean Bodin.

For Bodin's major concern, Oakeshott argues, is to investigate the type relationship which composes this emergent form of association. As with Montesquieu's *monarchie*, Bodin's *republique* is an association composed of people who understand themselves to be free agents, as distinct intelligent beings whose actions are choices to procure imagined and wished-for satisfactions. Bodin recognizes two modes of association, the first, corporate associations for the promotion of common interests, agents related in the performance of substantive actions to procure agreed satisfactions – 'prosperity', 'happiness', 'truth', etc. In such substantive associations the 'free' agency of those concerned is not denied because it is a relationship voluntarily entered into and freely sustained. However there is another type of association, the state, which is not voluntary and which we are not free to leave.

> [A] relationship in terms of puissance (authority) and obligation ... relationship not in terms of substantive action but of obligations to subscribe to conditions in choosing actions, communion ... in terms of *la justice* of *la vertu* and of obligation.
>
> (OHC 253)

In such a state civil authority is the attribute of an office, the right to make, to amend, repel, and to administer laws. Such office is exercised by those who are, for the time being, the rightful occupants, such a right being a matter of provenance, an institution inherits respect by sustaining its identity as the rightful holder of power, it is the beneficiary of the continuous recognition of those who are obligated to it (OHC 154).

* * *

The true genius of the modern European state as identified in the ideal form *societas* lies in the linked elements of law and authority. Our notion of civil freedom is inseparable from the specific type of law that has evolved here and its related notion of authority. In attempting to understand this phenomenon we need to appreciate a distinct mode of association, one which despite being compulsory sustains the autonomy of the individual.

> And if it be asked how such compulsory subjection to civil authority spares the imprescriptible autonomy of a human being, the answer is that it obliges, not to substantive action but only to conditions to be subscribed to in choosing actions, and that it does not require approval of these conditions but only the recognition of their authority.
>
> (OHC 255)

This is the root of Oakeshott's theory of the modern state, it is an association of free men, by which he means 'intelligent' beings, compulsorily associated not in an enterprise or a common purpose but in obligation to recognize the authoritatively and properly constituted laws. Oakeshott argues that the validity of the law does not rest upon approval but upon legitimacy, that is to say, to it being properly constituted. Moreover our recognition and subscription to the law does not entail approval only respect for its authority. Our 'freedom' lies the conditionality of such obligation. For law does not specify what should be done but, rather, prescribes conditions we are obliged to recognize in our own pursuit of life. Understanding this conditionality is the vital clue to what Oakeshott believes to be the genius of modern political life.

> To have an obligation is not to be relieved of the necessity, or to be denied the opportunity, of choosing what to do or to say, and to fulfil an obligation is always a choice. This choice is neither choosing the rule to be subscribed to, nor is it choosing to fulfil an obligation; it is always a choice to perform an action which subscribes to the conditions specified in a rule.
>
> (OHC 155)

Hence civil freedom is characterized by the unobtrusiveness of authority, by the lack of substantive direction. The task before us is to investigate how association in terms of laws can leave men free, and here we must investigate, firstly, the nature of 'law' and, secondly, the nature of rule governed practice.

* * *

Oakeshott's considerable achievement is to distil from the confused character we casually designate as 'political life' a mode of association that is a distinct, specific and unique achievement of our civilization; the 'civil condition' a mode of association constructed upon law. Oakeshott, we have already gathered, makes a primary distinction between an association of individuals joined in the pursuit of a common enterprise and the *societas* which is a formal relationship. Now we must specify what is meant by this 'formal' relationship. We ought begin this task by tracing the two ideal forms of the state back to two modes of associations the *universitas* to 'enterprise association' and the *societas* to, something more obscure and rare, association in terms of the acknowledgement of authoritative conditions.

We are told that the most common form of human relation is transactional we are buyers and sellers, bargainers one related to another in an attempt to secure the satisfaction of a want (OHC 123). It is a purposive relationship designed to secure for those so engaged an imagined and wished for satisfaction. It is an 'intrinsically terminable relationship' belonging to a particular place and time and composed of identifiable, named, individuals. This relationship is 'instrumental' or directed purposefully towards an end.

Of greater complexity is the instrumental association, that is, an enterprise association. Here we are associated both in terms of an end and of rules or practices some prudential, that is, useful for the purpose and others merely procedural. In transactional relationships and in enterprise associations we seek substantive satisfactions, in the former these are immediate and manifest but in the latter they are pre-established and institutionalized. Oakeshott claims that in all such end driven relationships there are considerations other than those which are useful for the end, such considerations are merely procedural and concern the performance of the participants but do not aid or enhance the actual achievement of the end. These practices are what Oakeshott calls non-instrumental or 'moral' practice. It is the genius of the civil condition to be composed entirely of such practices, of having no substantive purpose, goal or end. Oakeshott's thesis depends upon the single claim that moral observance is not reducible to prudential designs, they refer to the way things are done not to what is to be accomplished.

It is the argument of *On Human Conduct* that civil association is not a substantive endeavour. Oakeshott insists that the erroneous identification of the state with an enterprise association is responsible for much that is wrong with political theory. This characterization has been so widespread that many 'find it impossible to imagine association except in terms of a common purpose'. The task of *On Human Conduct* is to bring into focus an alternative view of the state, that which is manifest in the ideal character *societas*. Oakeshott seeks to isolate the relationship which is unique, specific and essential to that type of association. And we are told that the essence of this relationship is the acknowledgement of rules.

Rules exist in enterprise relationships; rules which specify methods of organization, arrangements, practices and routines, hierarchies of responsibility and management, they are, by and large, prudential considerations instrumental to the pursuit of the engagement and aimed at expediting the purpose in hand. But Oakeshott insists that no practice, not even the most mundane is totally artless, that is, they all possess procedures which are without specific or identifiable purpose, considerations which are non-instrumental. What is unique about moral and civil relationship is that here association is solely in terms of non-instrumental terms, what might be ancillary to an enterprise relationship is the very stuff of the civil relationship.

We are informed that the recognition of rules is one of our most familiar experiences and that while we might have difficulty in the abstract identification of its distinctive quality we actually have little difficulty in distinguishing a rule from a piece of advice, a request, a plea or a warning; that is, from argumentative or persuasive utterances. Or indeed from orders, commands, injunctions and prohibitions as these are imperatives. For both acts of persuasion and command are specific deeds enacted in particular concrete occasions, that is, in a specific transaction between ascertainable agents seeking substantive satisfactions. A rule, however, is characterized as an authoritative assertion which 'does not invoke approval or disapproval …. It calls only for assent in any performance to which it may relate'. A rule, in short, asserts a norm of conduct. Oakeshott summarizes the idea of a rule.

[Rules] do not enjoin, prohibit, or warrant substantive actions or utterances; they cannot tell the agents what to do or to say. They prescribe norms of conduct; that is, abstract considerations proper to be subscribed to in choosing performances but which cannot themselves be either 'obeyed' or performed.

(OHC 126)

Civil association begins and ends in the recognition of rules. In the context of the state these rules are usually referred to as 'law' but, once again, Oakeshott gives the ideal form a technical title, speaking of them as 'lex' in order to distinguish them from the actual laws, statutes and provisions belonging to existing European states. These rules are *sui generis* because the laws of civil association unlike any other rules:

> Are not imposed upon an already shaped and articulated engagement; they relate to the miscellaneous, unforeseeable choices and transactions of agents each concerned to live the life of 'a man like me', who are joined in no common purpose or engagement, who may be strangers to one another, the objects of whose loves are as various as themselves, and who may lack any but this moral allegiance to one another.
>
> (OHC 129)

This is perhaps the most important passage in the work for it binds together the central themes of Oakeshott's view of the achievement of political order. The essential structure of the libertarian state, that which has no substantive purpose but is merely association in terms of law, rests upon the formulation that law is a set of conditions to be subscribed to in the self-chosen transactions of free agents. Its members are free because their performance is never actually directed; the state imposes nothing but conditional requirements upon its members. Hence individuals are free, firstly, because they can enter and leave transactional and substantive engagements as they choose and, secondly, because the association which is compulsory commits them to no substantive endeavour.

In order to understand how law prescribes but permits our integrity as intelligent beings we must consider more deeply than we have done thus far the conditionality of rules. We are told association in terms of *lex* is a relationship in terms of rules which:

> [Prescribe] conditions to be subscribed to by *cives* in their chosen transaction with one another, conditions which may impose obligations or disabilities or specify protected practices. And in this respect *lex* is to be recognized as a vernacular language in which *cives* understand themselves and their mutual relations.
>
> (OHC 141)

What I think Oakeshott has in mind may be expressed by an imaginary example. Say the law specifies that a householder, on finding an intruder in his house may use reasonable means to defend himself should he be attacked and may use the minimum necessary force to restrain and confine him until the proper authorities arrive. Then, in a concrete instant, a householder, on finding an intruder in his house in the middle of the night, searching through drawers, etc. creeps up behind the burglar and hits him with a candle stick, thereby being able to hand him over to the police but injuring him to the extent that the intruder is required to spend the next two days in hospital. Now, presuming that in our example, the police press charges against the householder, as well as against the intruder, and that the householder pleads 'not guilty' to the charge of using excessive force, what a court would have to decide is, Was this minimal force in these specific circumstances? And a jury, judge, etc. would have to use their judgement as to whether 'reasonable force' was indeed used, i.e. were the conditions adhered to in this exchange.

Now the existence of the law did not tell the householder what to do, it told him the considerations he must subscribe to in doing. He had a considerable number of options open to him but he chose to strike the man from behind without challenge, without requesting his identity, etc. etc. And the jury, being people of the same culture, will have to judge whether it is reasonable for this man; frail, elderly, in these circumstances; alone in the middle of the night, to behave in this way. What they judge ultimately is not the deed but the judgement of the man, his plea demonstrates he believes himself to have acted reasonably and what the jury actually judge is his exercise of judgement. Their decision being of civil importance because it is only the shared recognition of rules which makes civil association possible and permits people of diverse ambitions to live together in the first place. The trial condemns or affirms the judgements made taking as their measure the quality of judgement that the society requires of a citizen.

Here we have an example, I believe, of 'conditions to be subscribed to in self-chosen transactional deeds'. And we see that the law does not compel or manipulate but may, by requiring matters to be taken into account at the point of our acting, effect the quality of our considerations, these being the subject of any formal adjudication. Such a scheme upholds Oakeshott's demand that law, the courts and the force available to the rulers must not deny our nature as intelligent agents.

A performance, e.g. striking an intruder, is open to interpretation, and a jury is obliged to examine the performance in the light of the civil rules authoritatively constituted, i.e. the law. The jury, then, judge the performance in the light of the rule. This is the most important and most difficult part of Oakeshott's theory. As actions are phenomenal and performances are not, 'subscription' will always be a matter of the finest judgement. The jury must work from the appearance to the performance to attempt to compare the performance, as reconstructed in their minds, with the considerations which were mandatory upon it. And what they judge is the performance, as an employment of the considerations, the exercise of intelligence which must always be a matter of the most elaborate imaginative reconstruction.

* * *

For Oakeshott law or *lex* is the essential feature of civil association, of the relationship between free men. His view of government, its office, its legitimacy and authority are all understood in terms of the exercise of *lex*. Law is the phenomenon which units the various offices of the state and their respective functions can be best characterized by explaining their relation to law. Indeed it is the fact that each office; the courts, the executive or 'rulers' and the legislative relate to law and not to individuals which sustains the unique character of the political relationship. The courts determine 'how a prescribed norm of conduct stands in relation to a contingent situation' (OHC 133). The question considered in adjudication is: What meaning may this rule of law justifiably and appropriately be made to tolerate here? And what is authoritatively declared by a court is whether the specific deed under consideration demonstrated adequate or inadequate subscription to the law.

The task of the executive or 'ruling' office is to command, to require substantive responses from assignable individuals. But Oakeshott insists that, even though it has the responsibility to require or forbid, as the concern of rulers is to maintain the reputation of the law and the civil order, it has no end or purpose other than the proper functioning of law as a system of conditions to be subscribed to in the self-chosen transactions of its citizens. Rulers do not maintain the laws with the motivation of managers of an enterprise association, their substantive activity is done to maintain the legal system and is, hence, part of our liberty. As for the legislative office, it is responsible for establishing or 'enacting' norms of conduct which 'describe conditions to be subscribed to by *cives* in making their own unforecastable substantive choices in unforeseeable contingent situations' (OHC 139). Because there must be more than one opinion about what constitutes a desirable condition of a system of *lex* the office of legislation will always be contentious.

As this office alters the conditions of the association it is undoubtedly a substantive engagement. However, it is not an engagement to gain a substantive satisfaction, that is, personal advantage, rather, the satisfaction is the alteration of the conditions. Its concern is the conditions which should be required to be acknowledged and subscribed to under threat of civil penalty. It is this activity that Oakeshott wishes us to take as politics in its truest form, one unique to civil association, having 'none but a distant analogue anywhere else' (OHC 161). The political debate determines what is to be considered 'civilly desirable' and which conditional responses should be prescribed to this end, and the term 'politics' may be used to refer to all the activities of persuasion and debate related to this consideration.

Ultimately, what is being attended to in politics is 'a vernacular language of civil intercourse' and 'every proposal for deliberate innovation in the conditions of conduct specified in a *respublica* is both an appeal to current achievements in civility and an exploration in the intimations of these achievements' (OHC 180). Here we see that the idea of politics found in the earlier essays, most notably *Political Education* and *On Being Conservative* remains largely intact. Oakeshott completes his treatment of politics proper by saying.

> Although this engagement of caring for the conditions of a civil association may seem less demanding, as it is certainly less exciting, than that of deliberating the policy and conducting the affairs of an enterprise association, it calls for so exact a focus of attention and so uncommon a self-restraint that one is not astonished to find this mode of human relationship to be as rare as it is excellent.
>
> (OHC 180)

However, the conditionality of laws or rules cannot of itself maintain the character of the free individual or limit the power of the state. For while we might find many examples of authoritarian regimes using *categorical* commands, e.g. 'By the age of 28 all citizens must have served two years of military service', we find most rules, even the most intrusive, to be *conditional*. For a government that wishes to 'manage' its population may do so quite adequately by expressing its commands in conditional terms. Such directions as: 'If you wish to consume drugs and stimulants they must be on prescription from a registered doctor', or 'If you wish to employ staff it must be from an approved trade union' are both conditional and manipulative. Such restrictive commands are still 'conditions to be subscribed to in choosing ...' hence it is obvious that the practice of law making in the libertarian state entails something other than 'conditionality'. To isolate what this might be will require a closer examination of the distinction Oakeshott wants to make between moral and prudential practice.

* * *

A 'practice' is defined as a set of conditions which qualify performances.

> These conditions may be somewhat indefinite uses or customs, they may even be no more than general maxims of conduct, or they may have the marginally less indeterminate character of rules or regulations; but I have called them 'considerations' because they qualify but do not determine performances ... they are understood conditions, subscribed to by agents choosing and acting.
>
> (OHC 120)

They are:

> A set of considerations, manners, uses, observations, customs, standards, canons, maxims, principles, rules, and offices specifying useful procedures or denoting obligations or duties which relate to human actions and utterances. It is a prudential or an authoritative adverbial qualification of choices and performances, more or less complicated, in which conduct is understood in terms of a procedure .... They postulate performances and specify procedural conditions to be taken into account when choosing and acting.
>
> (OHC 56)

Most performances are 'governed' by a variety of practices, overlapping and competing with or elaborating each other. Most are the by-product of performances related to the satisfaction of substantive wants acquiring authority or acknowledged utility.

And an action is an identity in which substantive performance and procedural considerations may be distinguished but are inseparably joined. And the considerations, be they customs, principles, rules have no force of their own, they cannot tell a performer what to do, they only announce conditions to be subscribed to in making choices, they must be used or put to an application to have a meaning.

> Practices, or the considerations they are composed of, are never 'applied', they are used; and they can be used only in virtue of being learned and understood.
>
> (OHC 120)

Of all the ways a practice may be characterized Oakeshott most prefers the image of language. For like a language it seems dormant until used, its rules do not specify what should be said and it is learned and used well or badly, stylishly or awkwardly and one may be impressed or troubled by the way it is used apart from what it is used to communicate and, of course, one may be deceived or misled by any such impressions.

> The requirements of a practice are not obeyed or disobeyed; they are subscribed to or not subscribed to .... Further, a practice cannot itself be 'performed'. Purely regularian conduct is impossible: to make a grammatically faultless utterance is always to say *something*, to use an implement 'properly' is always to make something, to follow a routine is always to do something .... A practitioner is always a performer.
>
> (OHC 58)

Indeed we are told that the two most important practices in terms of which agents are durably related are a common tongue and 'a language of moral converse'.

Most frequently individuals are related in terms of the prudential practices which promote the fulfilment of such engagements. These have been spoken of as 'instrumental' these 'epitomize experience in respect of the achievement of some particular wished-for satisfaction' (OHC 60). However, moral practice is not prudential, it is not instrumental to the achievement of any substantive purpose or to the satisfaction of any substantive want. Advantages may accrue from a particular performance but this would be incidental, indeed, compliance is often at considerable cost. Its concern is solely with the quality of the act, with the impact agents make upon one another and themselves in doing.

Now there is some difficulty here for in the first instance we are impressed by the similarity of the two species of practice; according to Oakeshott they are both conditions to be subscribed to in doing, that is both are 'adverbial', no practice is able to dictate or dominate the agency of the individual. The distinction between the two is not then that one directs in a way that the other does not, neither can do this. The distinction between them is that the prudential relationship is a relation in terms of the usefulness of the considerations for an end, that is, an instrumental relationship, and moral relationship is simply in terms of the authority of the conditions and nothing more. What I think Oakeshott means by this is that in an enterprise association 'satisfactions rule', they govern or specify the procedural considerations of those involved, the practices or considerations are chosen by the associated agents with a view to achieving a substantive end, they are therefore 'prudential' and are judged in terms of their usefulness. In moral relationships agents are governed by the propriety or conventionality of performance this having no objective, end or purpose save that it be acknowledged as being proper; it is handsome or agreeable, it is 'our way'. It has no use beyond itself.

The fact that all practices are adverbial has caused confusion, some of Oakeshott's commentators have thought the adverbiality of practice to be the key to understanding the distinction between civil and moral rules on one hand and prudential rules on the other. This view is mistaken, adverbiality merely confirms that the agent, being an adept in practice, must always choose. The issue of adverbiality is actually a contribution to the primary issue of agency, that is, the relationship between practices and understanding. This is a matter which will be pursued in the next chapter.

A moral practice is not a prudential act or skill, it is not instrumental its sole concern is with the performance of agents as agents, as adepts of practices and as associates. It is concerned with agents as doers making an impact upon one another. And this is the key, these are conditional rules concerned with our impact upon one another and while no engagement, relationship or association, not even the simply transactional, lacks these conditions moral and civil relations are composed entirely of them.

What must be accepted for Oakeshott's argument to be valid is not only that there are rules or practices which are 'non-instrumental', I think we have to accept that some are, but the much more extensive claim that morality is composed solely of non-instrumental rules and that civility, because it is a non-prudential relationship is also composed of a version of these 'moral' rules. As has already been pointed out 'civility' is a development of morality, the two are closely related but are not the same for the ideal subject of morality is the 'man', the ideal subject of civility is the 'citizen'. The agent manifests himself in a performance constrained by 'propriety', the citizen manifests himself in performances constrained by 'civility'. Both are non-prudential and non-instrumental.

Instrumental and non-instrumental practices are learned simultaneously.

> Like any other language, it is an instrument of self-disclosure used by agents in diagnosing their situations and in choosing their responses; and it is a language of self-enactment which permits those who can use it to understand themselves and one another, to disclose to one another their complex individualities.
>
> (OHC 63)

Oakeshott continues, reminding us of much that has been developed in the earlier essays.

> Every such vernacular of moral converse is a historic achievement of human being. Each is a continuously accumulating residue of conditional relationships learned in an experience of intercourse between optative agents. It emerges as a ritual of utterance and response, a continuously extemporized dance whose participants are alive to one another's movements and to the ground upon which they tread. Its abstract nouns (right and wrong, proper and improper, obligation, dueness, fairness respect, justice, etc.) when they appear, are faded metaphors, and it is only the uneducated who insist that each must have a single unequivocal meaning indifferent to context.
>
> (OHC 63)

We find ourselves in a world which is saturated with moral considerations. They are joined to everything we learn to do and think, and it is only with the greatest of difficulties that we can separate the moral from the prudential, the element of pure agency from the substantive endeavours of life. Moreover the insistence upon abstract ideals, 'rights', 'freedom', etc. is a vulgarization of a language which when well learned and skilfully applied is an effortless and seamless art of propriety, a cultured performance. In this aspect of his thought Oakeshott remains faithful to the ideas expressed in the essays. For the demand of the moralist, his insistence upon rules, discloses an impoverished appreciation of moral practice.

However, even the most articulate user of moral practice is likely to resort to what Oakeshott calls 'a basic vocabulary and some elementary constructions familiar to all whose native language it is', that is, to a body of rules of conduct .... What moral practice intimates as, in general, proper to be said or done, a moral rule makes more explicit in declaring what it is right to do' (OHC 66). In being reduced to rules the relationships of moral practice lose some of their dexterity and fluidity, but in the created expectation such relationships as duty and obligation develop as 'passages of stringency', and should be pictured as 'densities obtruded by the tensions of spoken language of moral intercourse', these may help to keep a moral practice in shape but they are not the source of its patterns. They are, rather, 'abstractions which derive their authority from the practice itself as a spoken language in which they appear as passages of somewhat exaggerated emphasis' (OHC 68). It is a key to Oakeshott's moral philosophy that 'rightness is never more than an aspect of moral response' it is merely a 'relatively precise' consideration to be subscribed to in conduct, which on its own cannot designate choices.

It should be pointed out that an area where the abbreviated form of practice is useful is in justification of a performance as subscription to rules. That is, as part of a substantive endeavour to rebut a charge of delinquency. Indeed Oakeshott insists that rule-orientated indictment of actions rests upon a foreshortened understanding of the character of moral practice. To justify an action, that is, to invoke rules and rule-like principles as reasons for having chosen actions, is to embark upon a 'casuistical enterprise of distinctions, exceptions, and obliquities related to rules in which the vitality of a spoken language of moral intercourse is impaired and its integrity compromised' (OHC 70). It is obvious from this that Oakeshott maintains the 'judgmental' character, the social moralist, to be vulgar and ill-educated and the calculated observance of specified rules to be a less desirable way of living than the 'singleness and spontaneity of morally educated conduct' (ibid.). However, in stipulating general conditions for choosing 'less incidental than the choices themselves, in establishing relationships more durable than those which emerge and melt away in transactions ... and in articulating rules and duties which are indifferent to the outcome of the actions they govern, it may be said to endow human conduct with a formality in which its contingency is somewhat abated' (OHC 74).

So for Oakeshott moral practice is a set of conditions which reflect our self-understanding as persons concerned with the quality of our deeds and with relationships other than the transactional associations in which we seek satisfaction of our wants. This language, like spoken languages, may be well or poorly learned, applied with dedication or with disinterest and is sometimes impressive and sometimes inadequate. As with a spoken language, humanity presents a considerable range of variation of these with some appearance of similarities and divergence. This plurality 'cannot be resolved by being understood as so many contingent and regrettable divergences from a fancied perfect and universal language of moral intercourse' (OHC 80). But while we are encouraged to accept this diversity we are warned that some will seek an imagined master pattern 'reason', or whatever it may be called, and that some will resist the artificiality of these creations being 'disconcerted unless they feel themselves to be upheld by something more substantial than the emanations of their own contingent imaginations' and the plurality will 'tease the monistic yearnings of the muddled theorist and disconcert an unfortunate who, having 'lost' his morality (as others have been known to 'lose' their faith) must set about constructing one for himself' (ibid.).

So morality is not concerned with substantive ends, that it is not instrumental and has no extrinsic purpose. This 'language', vulgarized by abridgement and dogmatism, 'emerges as a ritual of utterance and response' and a 'continuously extemporized dance whose participants are alive to one another's movements'. It is not additional to our prudential practices but inseparably associated with them such that 'there is no practice which is totally artless', that is, free from stylistic display. The key, indeed, comes in the opening paragraph of this section where we are told that morality is the 'practice of agency without further specification' (OHC 60), in moral conduct we disclose ourselves, our artistry of being our skilfulness, attentiveness and inventiveness.

In summary morality as a practice appears to be the stylishness or elegance of our doing what we chose to do, it is the compliance with a practice which is more like the movements of a dance than any productive enterprise. The freedom of civil association rests upon this type of practice, but here it is not the stylishness of doing *per se*, i.e. morality, which is pursued, it is the stylishness of being a *cive*. We are free because this ideal character is constructed of a medley of practices which are non-instrumental, developed by a culture which views itself as having no collective substantive end and having, as an ideal member, a being occupied in his own adventure qualified only by the requirement that whatever he does he does in a way that does not disturb the rest of the community. Law, or *lex*, is the measure of that sense of security, the courts are its place of imposition.

But this account is not without its difficulties. While it is important to recall that this ideal is only one aspect of our tradition, that of *societas*, there is no doubt that Oakeshott's aim is to promote those aspects and tendencies of political order which permit us to pursue our own lives in our own ways. There is, of course, a circularity to his case, for even if we accept that morality is a non-instrumental practice it does not follow that the civil order should also be unless one first assumes that civil association is the type of order which is not a joint enterprise. The real weight of Oakeshott's argument is, then, that because *cives* do not have the choice whether or not to belong to a civil association, i.e. it is not a voluntary order, if its members are to determine their own ends in life then it must be composed of non-instrumental rules. The presupposition of Oakeshott's civil association is, then, self-determination, our cultural disposition to pursue personal distinctiveness and this is the strain within our tradition of association he wishes us to cherish and nurture. His readers are, confronted by the question, whether this is the type of society they would like to live in. A civil community with no collective endeavour. So it is proper that we should think of the problems that such a state would encounter.

Oakeshott's account raises two fundamental questions; (1) Is there such a thing as non-instrumental 'activity'? and if there is, (2) Is it the substance of our moral and civil relationships? I think that the answer to the first is almost certainly affirmative, but as regards the second there must be much more doubt.

What Oakeshott's account seems to require is a boundless field of opportunity, where competition and mutually exclusive enterprises are either of minimal consequence or easily overlooked or ignored. But the common law, the rules and morality of a people, is surely not something we can treat with casual disdain as though we can pursue our lives regardless of its developing form or character.

We have an interest in its nature and it is this common interest which is the ground of competitive politics and the passion of social debate, it is very hard to be disinterested in the destiny of the common resource because it is the common resource, the ground of our being who we are.

The world, in both the sense of 'nature' and the Hegel 'second nature', as the resource of our manifestation and the resource of our comprehension, i.e. as a physical resource and as a set of discourses, is vulnerable, and delicate. The actions or endeavours of others may by innocence, perversity, indulgence, abuse, or excess spoil, ruin or destroy the patterns natural or social we treasure. The scarcity of land and the stuff of property, the fragility of the 'environment' which sustains the diversity of life gives us an interest in others' exploits. As does the significance of the cultural resource, its role in our life, being both the origin of the patterns we know as reason and justice and the structure which permits us to pursue our daily adventures amidst the throng of unknown others without the terror of absolute unpredictability.

What troubles us is the fate of the common resource, the language we use for self-disclosure, not because we are authoritarian, though some are, but because we know we are actually dependent upon these structures.

We are troubled because our ability to live as we have become accustomed and even our ability to remain sane rests on the continuity of respect for a given way of life. We are composed of shared activities and can never be concerned merely with our own project. People are unnerved by 'bad language', and are angered by crude public displays not because they are personally offended, though they might be, but because they fear the repercussions for the whole of which they and all they love are a part. All they enjoy is sustained by a totality which is there to be ruined or saved. We are concerned for the whole because no matter how liberal or how tolerant we might be we have to make our way amidst a set of structures which we jointly inherited and of which we are joint custodians.

In the first instance Oakeshott seems to doubt whether this 'common resource', the 'second nature' of Hegel, actually has real substance. He seems to believe that the subject is the ground of the real. This issue will have to be dealt with in the next chapter. But at a more mundane level Oakeshott's liberalism is very Jacksonian, it treats man as though he is a frontiersman, taming the wild world. This is a most shallow delusion, for the world is full; wilderness, where it is not a 'park', has vanished, we dwell in a world which is crassly synthesized, where we must hold our own by gaining the compliance of others. The ways of our world matter immediately and profoundly to us because we cannot even begin to be ourselves with confidence or expansiveness without some grasp upon the common recourse. We cannot sustain our adventure if the world around us has taken to some fashionable madness, a new religion, a new asceticism. Our liberal society, as Oakeshott so brilliantly saw in his essays, is a joint inheritance which we must husband both for the sake of ourselves, that we may continue to perform the habits we have acquired, and in order that this way of life should be sustained for the generations to come.

We might conclude this part by saying that while the idea of non-instrumental practices is interesting and original, and while there seems some reason to hold that morality exists, at least in part, in this form, there are a great number of reasons for believing that the civil law is not of this form, that it not only does deal in substantive goods but it must do so. And while it may or may not be right for it to be distributive in the socialist sense, by arbitrating between the competing demands of the 'communities' in its charge it must, by necessity, distribute the 'expressive space' which has value and is a resource which colours the lives of its inhabitants.

Oakeshott in *On Human Conduct* is asking us to be less aggressive in our demands of the whole, less attentive to the plight of the totality, this is a much more optimistic outlook than we surely have a right to hope for. Like Locke and Mill before him he seeks to school our legislators into a sense of respect for an open way of life. For, like them, Oakeshott has started with an abstraction, man as self-governing and then proceeded to find laws which permit this abstraction to thrive. Thus, by default, he appears to have rejected the other argument used to support the legitimacy law – the Hegelian view that law is a vital constituent of who we are, a component of our psychology – the argument of the *Sittlichkeit*. It seems he felt that, while this might be philosophically or psychologically true, it is not a sufficient regulating principle. The 'reason' spawned by our social and political order is too diverse too open to interpretation for us to entrust to it alone the reasonableness of law. Why this should be is revealed with the element at the centre of Oakeshott's intellectual scheme – the idea of the atomic individual, the agent – which we must now proceed to investigate.

9

The User of Practices

The sceptical tradition of British Idealism is often characterized by Bradley's remark that 'the deed comes first and later reflection', and a pervasive theme of Oakeshott's philosophy is its attempt to comprehend the distinction between doing and reflecting. One of the clear ambitions of *On Human Conduct* is to sustain and clarify this distinction. The task that Oakeshott sets himself is to disclose the character of the type of thinking or judgement we use in doing and explain how it differs from the species of thought which seeks to understand in the sense of 'make intelligible' or 'explain'.

As theorists of human conduct we have a particular interest in the nature of theorizing as well as the theoretical abstraction 'human conduct' and its essential element the 'human agent'. We should therefore preface our remarks on Oakeshott's concept of the agent with an account of his understanding of the office of the theorist.

The activity and scope of theorizing is the main interest of the first essay of *On Human Conduct*. It argues that an explanation of events, no matter how exacting, universal or sophisticated, can never advise of its own accord. Oakeshott suggests we think of theorizing as the activity of a specialist; a 'theorist', creating something; 'a theorem', in the course of a particular activity; 'theorizing'. This is a skilful activity but its products are instruments which, of themselves, have no power or authority, like any tool they do not specify the performance of those who employ them. A theory, like any practice or 'language', is portrayed as a neutral structure, there to be used or employed.

The distinction between such structures as a theory, a maxim, a practice, a language, etc. and the 'performance', the substantive engagement of the person who uses such structures, serves as the ground for a renewed assault upon the intellectual and an emboldened defence of the rigour and the originality of ordinary life. His arguments are designed to convict the theorist who advocates anything more than a theorem, i.e. one who seeks to advocate a policy or a way of life, of a category error. And it therefore continues the pervasive quest of Oakeshott's work: the deliverance of mankind from 'experts'.

As a work of philosophy *On Human Conduct* is an attempt to explain the limits of the office of the theorist through a brief and rather difficult reiteration of Oakeshott's theory of knowledge. The opening argument of the work is extremely involved and very dense. This results from the fact that we are simultaneously being introduced to the nature of the understanding and the character of the theorist.

The argument we are offered is reminiscent of the opening pages of *Experience and its Modes* 'To be human and to be aware is to encounter only what is in some manner understood' (OHC 1). We inhabit a world of understandings in which distinctions are at once discoveries and achievements.

> It may be said that understanding is an unsought condition; we inexorably inhabit a world of intelligibles. But understanding as an engagement is an exertion; it is the resolve to inhabit a more intelligible, or an ever less mysterious word.
>
> (ibid.)

While many, if not most, of the basic patterns we use are acquired in the course of everyday life, that is, they are identities or 'facts', the more complex are created by deliberate intellectual exertion, Oakeshott calls these more elaborate identities 'theorems'.

'Theorist' is the name given to both, the person who composes these instruments and the person who uses them in order to identify and understand. Hence we are attempting to understand the process of the creation, the use and the criticism of this tool of the intellect with the ultimate objective of recognizing that substantive deeds, human action, will necessarily lie beyond the province of the theorist.

A sketch of Oakeshott's argument might be presented as: all engagements are undertaken because of a perceived deficiency, but there are two utterly distinct types of lack:

1. A lack in the world, a defect which demands a response, an action, this is what he shall refer to as a substantive engagement.
2. A lack of comprehension which may trouble us just as deeply, if we are so inclined, but which of itself requires no outward show of effort, no substantive engagement.

While action is a unique and specific self-declaration to theorize is to explore the conditionality of a given phenomenon, that is, to attempt to make a universal statement which is either true or false, it exhibits a resolve to inhabit a more intelligible world. Whereas doing is a speculative enterprise, an adventure, theorizing involves a suspension of the actual adventure of life.

Oakeshott's argument is involved but it is necessary to follow some of the text because it prefigures much that is important in the account of agency which is to follow. The theory of knowledge we are offered is based on an emerging and developing clarity, sometimes casually acquired sometimes achieved by design.

> Intelligibles emerge out of misty intimations of ineligibility when noticing becomes thoughts and when, in virtue of distinguishing and remembering likenesses and unlikenesses in what is going on, we come to inhabit a world of recognizables. These recognitions may often be vague, obscure, and tentative, and often mistaken; that is, unlikes mistaken for likes and likes for unlikes. But continually gone over, rehearsed, revised, and refined they endow what is going on with the intelligibility of familiar characteristics.
>
> (OHC 3)

These resources are extended by constant exercise and repetition. Greater exactness is achieved when recollection assists remembering, when thought attains more definite shape in ideas. Learned mental skills of abstraction and inference are developed into an educated imagination which is better prepared for the recognition and ultimately identification of new experiences.

The theory of knowledge we are offered is centred around 'platforms of conditional understanding'. The platforms mark degrees of critical awareness. The most basic type of understanding is recognition; the distinction of two things on the basis of an immediate difference in characteristics. What is distinguished is an unknown X from an unknown Y on the basis of some characteristic, e.g. 'faster', 'slower'.

The real advance in the capacity of the intellect comes with the ability to detach characteristics from their contingent circumstances and combine them into abstract 'ideal characters', to identify them in terms of universals, e.g. horse, car, plane. These are the basis of an understanding of the world developed by relating them in terms of their features or the circumstances of their occurrence. This is the level at which diagnosis, choice and activity take place where we encounter the world as ready to hand, as equal to our 'practical' needs where doing takes the place of questioning. It is a world of opportunity and satisfaction and, Oakeshott declares, it is an oddity that anyone should want to pass up the opportunities presented and further problemize the identities encountered.

But for the 'theorist' this absorbing level of understanding is 'a prison from which he seeks release'. What distinguishes a theorist is his undistracted concern with the unconditional, critical engagement of understanding in which every understanding – be it 'fact' or 'theorem' – is recognized as a not-yet-understood and therefore and invitation understand. The conceptual identities which, for the greater part of mankind, form the structure of their lives are viewed by the theorist as matters to be subjected to interrogation. He sees his task to lie in specifying them more exactly so they can be further investigated and made more intelligible 'by seeking to understand them in terms of their postulates; that is, in terms of their conditions' (OHC 9).

The theorist requires that identities are more rigorously specified hence everyday identities are interrogated. What is abstracted is a relation of greater generality and a more stringent specification, a theorem, itself an instrument of conditional understanding. Theorems are complex systems of relations, recognized as laws, or rules of occurrence, a 'science'.

To occupy and explore this level or 'platform', is to attempt a sophisticated understanding of events in terms of rules, laws, theorems, practices, etc. where actual identities are merely contingent examples, illustrations of such rules, laws practices.

> Thus a command of the theorems of mechanics will enable a theorist to abstract a mechanical identity from a balancing act in a circus and to display it as a parallelogram of forces; but he will have to think in different terms if he is to understand an identity abstracted and specified in the programme as 'Stello and Stella in their world-famous act ... the act of the equilibrist', for this is certainly not a mechanical identity.
>
> (OHC 19)

The theorist may be said 'to be seeking to understand a familiar identity in terms different from those in which it is already understood'. Oakeshott's point is that the theorist's desire to interrogate identities sufficient to the needs of everyday life is an eccentricity, one which he illustrates by a retelling of the allegory of the cave in Plato's Republic. The theorist turns his back on the ordinary interest of analysis, to attain the satisfaction of rather cerebral wants.

Understanding based upon the application of theorems is more vulnerable to error than is identification because the theorem used must be a deliberate choice of the theorist and its adoption might be inappropriate to the matter in hand. Oakeshott insists that erroneous selection of the theorem is the origin of a great deal of misunderstanding and misinterpretation. For instance if we say that a trapeze act is an example of the laws of mechanics we must be specific as to exactly where and how these laws apply and not pretend that they govern the whole performance. For the validity of any understanding attained by the use of such theorems rests on their applicability to the identities they claim to comprehend. One might explain a man waiting for a bus by reference to the laws of inertia, but the understanding achieved would be quite tangential to the identity 'a man waiting for a bus'.

Thus different identities predicate different sorts of inquiry. But while what is actually appropriate is always debatable and the history of thought is full of eccentric interpretations rooted in tenuous theorems or idiosyncratic use of solid theorems, Oakeshott insists that there is a primary distinction which must be observed if the theorist is not to become involved in nonsense. One might say that he is offering us a theory of theorizing. This 'categorical' distinction is composed of, on one side, those which must be understood as exhibitions of intelligence and, on the other, those which predicate and understanding in terms of being themselves not the exercise of intelligence. These two categories or 'orders' of identities can be found mixed together, as in the example of the trapeze act, but the identity to be explained must be categorically unambiguous, if we are not to be led badly astray.

The first 'order' is composed of a going-on identified as a human action, agents responding to an understood situation meaning to achieve an imagined and wished-for outcome. If they are to be intelligently understood and the mystery of their character be abated, Oakeshott tells us, it is necessary that the postulates of such identities must be theorems concerned with the understandings which constitute them. The second categorically distinct order is composed of those goings-on recognized, in virtue of their characteristics, as not themselves exhibitions of intelligence. A conditionality which determines what is going on but which does not have to be learned in order to be operative, that is, what we normally refer to as causal conditions. These two 'orders' are expressed as the ideal characters 'procedure' and 'process'.

This may be clarified by the example of a categorically ambiguous event, the movement of a human eyelid. This may be a wink or a blink, an exhibition of intelligence or of a causal process. At the level of everyday life we may make the wrong judgement and hence the wrong response. But when we reflect upon this event, that is, accept the engagement to understand, what matters is that we recognize that whatever our verdict we must acknowledge that our understanding of the problem, of distinguishing the options, rests upon two categorically distinct fields of inquiry.

Theorems do not explain the structure of the world they are the structures we use to understand the world, they are criteria of selection which narrows down the plethora of all that is going on to recognizable patterns. For Oakeshott this is as true of the theorems of non-intelligent events, the physical sciences, as it is of the 'human sciences'. The theorist concerned with physics actually has no more predictive power than the theorist concerned with ethics. The 'orders' do not predicate a difference in the authority of the theorist. Theorists explain, i.e. offer an understanding on the basis of theorems.

Obviously the degree of specification of, say electro-magnetism, is so exact that a theorist, of a creative disposition, is able to apply his understanding to imagined and invented applications, e.g. invent the motor. The theorems of human conduct, however, can never achieve the same level of specification because intelligent identities are inherently ambiguous. Patterns of behaviour do exist but only in so far as individuals adopt and subscribe to them, and such subscription may be well or ill applied and more or less diligently implemented. Agents choose, they are not outcomes, they are involved in performances not processes.

At this point our interest lies in the distinction between doing and theorizing, and our specific concern is the 'competence' of the theorist with regard to human conduct. What limits the competence of the theorist is his platform of understanding, the fact that it is not at the level of identities but at the level of theorems. His job is 'to investigate the conditions of their enterprises not to engage in them' and he will be simply ridiculous if he attempt to act as a teacher to those who do not share his abstract level of concern.

This deplorable character has no respectable occupation, in virtue of being a theorist he purports to be concerned with the postulates of conduct, but he mistakes these postulates for principles from which 'correct' performances may be deduced or somehow elicited. He understands it to be his business to umpire conduct, certifying performances to be 'correct' or condemning them as 'incorrect' inferences from the theorems of an alleged understanding of conduct in terms of its conditions.

(OHC 26)

The 'order' of the inquiry predicates what kind of theorem may be used but it does not indicate the kind of activity undertaken by the theorist. It is the level of abstraction at which he operates which prevents him from being a cultural arbiter. Thus it is not the type of 'order' which prevents the sociologist from advising but the fact that he is a theorist. The additional fact that he is postulating identities and concrete events which are intelligently performed only serves to exaggerate the distance between his activity and that of the agent.

Our concern as theorists of the identity 'human conduct' is to discern its postulates. So we must turn away from the issue of the abstract character of the theorist and attempt to pursue the theorems which belong to the complex identity 'human conduct', or more accurately to Oakeshott's theorems on this matter.

The attempt to specify the office of the theorist is intimately associated with the theory of human conduct. From the previous chapter it will be recalled that the work turns upon a the characterization of practice as 'conditions to be subscribed to in doing', we must now pursue the nature of the agent, the actual human being whose nature is to subscribe to such practices. In doing so we will find ourselves compelled to recall that we too are theorists rooted in abstraction. This self-doubt marks the real distinction between Oakeshott early and late thought.

* * *

Oakeshott's later thought is distinguished from the earlier essays by its understanding of the way in which learning is acquired, retained and applied. Structures and practices appear to have lost their character as the pattern of the intellect and become something more analogous to an instrument. As a corollary the human individual becomes a determinate centre, the bearer of a natural, innate and *a priori* self-possession. What we have to clarify is whether this shift in thought is as radical as it appears, or whether it is an outcome of the fact that we are dealing in the stuff of the theorist rather than the substance of life.

The identity 'human conduct' like all identities has emerged through generations and remains provisional and rather 'rough and ragged'. Its actual form is an historical accomplishment of a particular group of people. We might say that this, like all identities, is composed conversationally in the course of everyday life. But this is a unique character in that it concerns our own identity. Oakeshott remarks that the real historical achievement lay, not in acknowledging the importance of this character but in establishing its limits, 'in the discrimination which returned the idea from whence it came, namely, to "goings-on" exclusively characteristic of human beings' (OHC 31). But what was achieved Oakeshott claims, was a relatively unambiguous identity.

> A human being responding to his contingent situation by doing or saying this rather than that in relation to an imagined and wished-for outcome and in relation, also, to some understood conditions.

> The more important marks of this identity are: beliefs distinguished from organic conditions, a world of pragmata (things and occasions related to wants), situations recognized to predicate action, imagined future conditions of things, agency, deliberations, choices, decisions, intelligible utterances, performances, satisfactions, procedures, practices, motives, and here they are no more than characteristics (each itself an identity recognized in terms of its features) held together so as to delineate a recognizable character.
>
> (OHC 32)

His claim is that the elements listed are the constituent features of our recognizing something as action rather than occurrence, as 'an exhibition of intelligence'. When we deny agency to a falling apple it is because we refuse to recognize this as an act of intelligence. And we are told that 'our recognition of a cat sitting mute before a door waiting for it to be opened as a performance is an attribution (correct or incorrect) of intelligence'. This can be re-expressed by saying that in claiming that a 'going-on' is 'conduct' we assert that it is a demonstration of something which has had to be learned.

Effectively Oakeshott is doing little more than defining human conduct as intelligent activity, directing the theorist of 'human conduct' to his unique field, by saying 'attend to what is intelligently done not to what is causal'. If the theorist should attempt to theorize 'human conduct' as a mixture of volition and causal process the character he theorized would, according to Oakeshott, not be conduct. Of course, in actual life, in the everyday encounter of identities, as has already been made plain, our identifications are necessarily more speculative. However, the ideal character, the subject of interest to the theorist, can be further clarified:

> An agent is one who is recognized to have an understanding of himself in terms of his wants and his powers and an understanding of the components of the world he inhabits; and action is recognized as an illustrative exhibition of this understanding. The attribution of agency and the recognition of action is already the attribution and the recognition of reflective consciousness.
>
> (OHC 32)

Thus the abstract character 'conduct' is further refined by the qualification that it necessarily implies reflective consciousness. Any attempt to theorize human activity must, by definition, assume that man directs himself knowingly, were the theorist to assume otherwise the character he would be theorizing would not be human conduct. This point might become clearer when we follow some more of the text.

> Doing identified as a response to a contingent situation related to an imagined and wished-for outcome, postulates reflective consciousness; that is, an agent who inhabits a world of intelligible pragmata, who is composed entirely of understandings, and who is what he understands (or misunderstands) himself to be. Further it postulates an agent whose situation is what he understands (or misunderstands) it to be ... and when alternatives present themselves to his imagination, he must be able to choose between them and decide upon a performance. In short, conduct postulates what I shall call a 'free agent'.
>
> (OHC 36)

We should note the conditionality of the first remark, 'doing identified as a response', it is this identification which entails the assumptions 'reflective consciousness' and a being who 'is what he understands himself to be'. Thus Oakeshott is not claiming that man is categorically free, that is, actually divorced from all conditionality, but that 'doing' identified as a response entails the assumption of freedom hence that 'man' as the object of theorizing is either free or he is not 'doing', he is in some form of trance or captivity.

In actual life, operating diagnostically at the level of identities any such identification may or may not be correct, just as with the cat 'mute before the door' we can never be certain that the act is an exhibition of intelligence, that is, 'conduct' in this restricted sense. Oakeshott's claim is that the attribution 'conduct' assumes freedom, and this entails only that when our behaviour is part of a process, when we are acted upon and are outcomes then our action is not 'conduct'. For instance, returning to our example; the blink of an eyelid is a potential doing, i.e. a wink, but also perhaps not a 'doing', but part of a causal system, that is, at least some of the things done by men are process rather than procedure. This is an issue we actually confront everyday in our efforts to interpret the activities of others, e.g. did he jump or did he fall?

The point is amplified still further by the apparent dual usage of the term 'agent' in his discussion of freedom: Oakeshott tells us that he uses the word 'free' because he is concerned with 'the formal detachment from certain conditions which is intrinsic to agency', I presume he means by 'agency' the ideal character. He then says he is not concerned with the 'quality of being substantively "self-directed" which an agent may or may not achieve'; here I presume he means by 'agent' a concrete person, or named individual, that one may encounter. This double usage of the word is worrying because we must distinguish putative ideal characters, used to interpret and understand our world, and the ambiguous and miscellaneous identities we find confronting us. Just as there is no European nation which is a *societas* or *universitas* and no system of law which is a system of *lex* we ought to hold that there is no person who is an agent and no human existence which is conduct. We are dealing with the abstractions that theorizing requires.

Having given this warning we ought now to pursue the character of this freedom based upon 'formal detachment'. Oakeshott's case is that the independence of the agent rests upon his situation being what he understands it to be, a verdict predicating action or inaction. The condition of freedom is a reflective consciousness: the agent's own understanding of his situation, 'what it means to him'.

It is in respect of this starting-place in an understood contingent situation that the agent in conduct may be said to be 'free'; all other considerations which point in this direction are subsidiary and derivative.

(OHC 37)

Each engagement is constituted by an agent who must consider and decide which action or utterance responds to what he understands his situation to be. All the alternatives he presents to himself rest only upon his interest. Oakeshott justifies this remark by saying:

Understanding his situation as that of being in debt and finding it unacceptable, Z recognizes himself to be invited to respond in an action or utterance; he discloses in himself the character of an agent and acquires an employment. His situation is specific; he is not merely 'unhappy' or 'in pain', he is unacceptably in debt .... Recognizing himself an agent, Z recognizes himself as having to choose what course of action he shall embark upon as a rejoinder to his situation. But choosing is an engagement in thinking, and consequently this reflection in the service of acting may be said to be a postulate of conduct, it is to be identified as deliberation.

(OHC 42)

The ideal abstraction is now fully characterized, conduct is reflective, free and deliberative. These give us a single identity, the agent. These ideal characters stand together mutually defining each other; to say that something is 'done' postulates all of them. To deny any one of them would be to assert that it occurred rather than was done. And whilst in everyday life, e.g. in a court of law, this issue features very largely, as in: 'Was the defendant responsible for his actions?', the theorist of human conduct has to proceed on the assumption that human conduct is 'human conduct'; reflective, deliberative and free.

No doubt many actions are performed off the cuff without any considerable engagement of choosing, and a choice of what to do or to say is often made without any significant deliberative engagement .... But, of course, none of these considerations impugns the status of deliberation and choice as postulates of conduct. A postulate is not an engagement, it is a condition in terms of which an engagement may be understood.

(OHC 42)

That man is capable of 'doing', in its proper sense now defined, assumes that he has the capacity to be free. If this capacity is denied then the everyday use of the term 'done', the diagnostic identity which we specify tentatively and provisionally, is ruled out *a priori* and becomes absurd.

In life the mystery we have to confront is whether the attribution of authorship to a named individual is substantiated to our satisfaction. Here the normal test is: 'Could he have done otherwise?' it is always a perplexity, each answer being a provisional contribution to the character 'human intelligent action'. The concrete problem is to distinguish 'behaviour' from 'done deliberately as a response' and defining 'done' as done intelligently obscures the point that we are looking at human actions and asking ourselves what is intelligently done, only gradually are we able to distinguish these two characters not by applying the test of intelligence but by learning what it is to be intelligent. The actual concrete doings of human being are a mixture of characters; that is, all the things that have been done by human beings have not been 'done' in the stringent sense of the term, for some were hypnotized and some were damaged by disease or by injury, some were attacked or were at the point of violence. Oakeshott wants us to distinguish between real doing and what has been done, some of what has been done was not 'human conduct', the question becomes how much of conduct is this non-human human conduct, that is, non-intelligent action.

But we have already come to the conclusion that this is not the business of the theorist. He is dealing in the conditionality of identities not the nature of identities themselves. For Oakeshott, he is, by definition, not part of the conversation of everyday life, he deals with its assumptions. The issue, therefore, arises whether the theorist, in theorizing human conduct, defined in this way, is dealing with anything other than an abstraction, his conclusions being contained in the presuppositions. This is an important point for it may well qualify the value of *On Human Conduct* as a theory of human conduct; concrete and actual. Has Oakeshott achieved anything other than the marginalization of the theorist as one who explores sterile assumptions instead of joining the real adventure of life.

The Oakeshottian self, the 'agent' is not our everyday sense of self but one constructed from abstracted features. The most important of which rest upon the fact that there is a sphere of calculation which is free, not determined, but intelligent. To be intelligent means to be able to set one's own rules.

He is 'free' not because his situation is alterable by an act of un-
constrained 'will' but because it is an understood situation and
doing is an intelligent engagement .... He can have come by [this
understanding] only in learning, and in learning he acquires
only what he accepts and makes his own in an understanding.
In short, the starting-place of doing is the agent himself as a
'historic' self-enacted reflective consciousness.

(OHC 37)

This remark contains the germ of a substantive characterization,
not just an abstraction, but a description of man that is to be the
base for the rest of *On Human Conduct*. For not only is intelligence
acquired, as it was indeed in the earlier essays, but it is acquired by
choice, the key remark is 'in learning he acquires only what he
accepts and makes his own in an understanding', this assertion is
the true assumption of *On Human Conduct*. Here it is not being used
to marginalize the theorist but to construct the positive thesis of *On
Human Conduct* as a work of political theory.

The question of the character of the agents remains, What part
does he play in selecting or obtaining these acquisitions? The
radical alternative presents itself to us as whether choice precedes
practice or practice precedes choice. That is, whether the agent as-
sembles his abilities to taste upon an innate power of opting or
whether practices are acquired ad hoc and 'choice' is some abstract
character itself a product of the assembly.

This, indeed, seems to characterize the distinction between *On
Human Conduct* and the arguments found in the essays. For it goes
beyond the claim that we learn the behaviour we display to claim
that we chose to learn it. We dwell in a relation to ourselves that
possesses absolute self-control. We pursue our lives intelligently,
'He is "free" because his response to his situation, like his situation
itself, is the outcome of an intelligent engagement' (OHC 39). It is
not just that we are the starting point of doing but we are a particular type of starting point, one that does deliberately. This is reductive in a way the essays were not, for not only are we what in
learning we become, but we are the point in control of that learning. This is distinctly different from the thesis of the essays where
human intelligence was seen as a collection of a miscellany of
practices not necessarily reducible to one 'governing' practice. To
put this important point another way, it seems that all the skills we
learn feed our self-mastery, whereas, in the earlier essays one

was led to believe that the self was never more than a gathering of practices each of which controlled a certain sphere of life. This having been said it is important to make clear that this still does not amount to the simple substance of Descartes, the noumenon of Kant or even the *Néant* of Sartre. It seems to be closer to the substantive individual found in Schopenhauer or Nietzsche, a spirit or innate character which is the ground of all shapes, of all appearance, a germ of individuality which is natural, unique and particular, the personal demiurge or soul which colours all reality.

The agent as the adept of practice is the central pillar of the positive thesis of *On Human Conduct*, it is the key to understanding how man can be said to have an existence separate from the moral and practical practices of his country. Practices do not command, once learned, that is absorbed, copied or acquired they are passive to the judgement of the person. It is the faculty of judgement which decides which practice should be employed on any specific occasion rather than the practice itself determining our judgement. The courageous notion of the essays that there are any number of orders, structures and patterns each of which had their own charge upon our activity and each of which has its own legislative scope has been set aside, and with it the themeless choreographies described in *Rational Conduct* or *The Tower of Babel* which offered us the suggestive thesis of men acting out a series of acquired dance-like manoeuvres, skills and talents circumstantially acquired by emulation. A thesis which entailed that we feel our way through various encounters without necessarily being able to 'give a reasoned account' of what we were doing, talents which were themselves simply historical products, the accumulation of a series of accommodations and unspecified adjustments to our predicament, our nature and our world. *On Human Conduct* replaces this blind tactility with a uniform language based structure which pictures the agent as one giving himself a spoken 'running commentary' on what he is in the act of doing.

The theorist's assumption has become the criterion for man, the human essence. Oakeshott's advice to the theorist, that he should identify the 'order' of an inquiry; intelligent or non-intelligent before theorizing, is transformed into the substantive ontological claim that human conduct is itself categorically distinct from the causal world. The working assumption of the theorist has become the working assumption of ourselves as political theorists. An assumption upon which we are to construct a liberal theory of government. But in actual political life we deal not with the abstract man of the theorist, but with the concrete, sensuous man and the question which hovers over Oakeshott's political theory is, 'Do these political structures, i.e. *societas, civitas, lex*, address the needs of the actual man?'

Oakeshott actually wants the political theorist to construct his theories upon the postulates of the abstract character 'human conduct', rather than the ambiguous identity found in actual affairs. The problem for us, however, is that this abstraction is much more than a working assumption, it is the basis for the 'agent' who in turn defines moral practice and *lex* and the whole thesis of non-instrumental considerations. That is, this agent is the assumption for the thesis of *On Human Conduct* and if we find this abstraction difficult to accept then the whole body of the work falls.

The theorist of human conduct has the right to ask if, or more accurately, when, such a phenomenon as 'the agent' is actually manifest in the world. And we, Oakeshott's readers, have the right to ask whether *On Human Conduct* offers a political theory for 'agents' or for humanity. That is, is it really anything more than a defence of the achievement of the modern European state, the man whose life is a quest for self-disclosure of his distinctness. This does, in fact, capture the central thrust of *On Human Conduct* for it attempts to secure the products of this civilization, the 'agent' and the 'cives'; these Oakeshott appears to hold are safe in the ordinary ambitions of men in everyday life but need to be protected from theorists and from politicians who would reduce them to mere aspects of their own personal schemes. Hence, men should be encouraged to live by the rule that they produce themselves, that only those forces, processes and practices, which are internalized and animated by them can have dominion over them. And as a counter manoeuvre it is an attempt to disarm the theorist who seeks to incarcerate men in 'circumstances' which are, of course, never more than an aspect of the theorist's imagination. Oakeshott seeks to remind the theorist of his limitations, that his office is essentially parasitic.

Surely, as theorists we delude ourselves if we think that we can find the character of conduct through its postulates, we can find postulates only through an identity. Freedom, intelligence, deliberation, choice, agency freedom have no meaning apart from the concrete concept 'human conduct'. They do not, themselves, specify a concrete identity but are specified by what we have come to accept as a concrete identity, the 'sensuous content' of the 'postulates' is taken from actual conduct and actual conduct is not discovered by reference to the ideal but is worked out in experience. What we seek in conduct is the actualization of our substantive designs, Oakeshott knows that the theorist can address this performance only as something already completed. In short, the theorist deals with dead things, institutions, customs, procedures and the like, the theorist deals with man as a disclosed rather than a disclosing being, as though he were dead. But the agent must live, must deal with the challenge of change, others and himself.

Oakeshott holds that no language, structure or practice can hold power over us, we must first 'subscribe', we are users not products. In terms of the vocabulary I have used in this work this is a 'pathetic' as opposed to a 'mimetic' thesis. However, it is worth repeating that for Oakeshott in *On Human Conduct* the ability of the agent to command himself rests upon the ability to organize recognitions, dispositions and considerations. That is, we dwell in an utterly positive world, a world totally composed of acquired skills, one without the dialectical conflict caused by an intrusive negation. For in Oakeshott's world unlike that of Hegel or of Sartre there is no detached other state, a state of being above or beyond the world, no abstract ability to become nothing, to transcend all content. The situation of the Oakeshottian agent is always concrete. Phrases such as; 'his situation is an understanding' and 'he can have come by this only in learning and in learning he acquires only what he accepts and makes his own', designates an individual who is the outcome of a personal past not one that is capable of abstraction from all content and total self-invention, we are prey to the skills we have. Hence the power of self-determination is certainly more modest than that offered to us in *Being and Nothingness*.

Again with regard to Oakeshott's earlier work the difference is not that understanding is acquired but that it is personally acquired. Each individual is made the fulcrum of determination as to what he learns and does not learn whereas before the emphasis was upon the resource that the community had to offer. In terms of Oakeshott's work, then, the point is that personal history takes the place of collective, cultural forces. The practices and skills spoken of in the essays are now merely an offering which may be adopted or ignored. They are still to be thought of as a resource but not one that directs or intimates future events. Indeed, the enigma of *On Human Conduct* is that the 'objective', historical achievement of intelligence is paid so little regard. Oakeshott, it seems, feels that the structures themselves are not a matter of genuine concern, that they will be sustained and renewed so long as we do not lose sight of the fact that we must adopt them in order to make them live. He seems to have reached the conclusion that either enough attention has been paid to the abstract idea of practices already, i.e. in his essays, or else that it is the vitality and vigour of the person who must learn and who must choose and make an effort to learn that must be the writer's first concern. What is of significance is the vulnerability of our willingness to make our own life.

Perhaps the ideal character of the free agent has been adopted in order to defend the achievement of the personal adventure against the morbidity of thought encouraged by sociology and psychology, by the domination of science. *On Human Conduct* may be counted just one more attempt by a philosopher to limit the imperiousness of scientists, to contain the kingdom built upon causality. In one sense he appears more optimistic, more ready to let the individual judge for himself to leave on one side the fate of the traditions, customs and habits which are the actual collective resource which individuals must employ to live well. But from another point of view he seems more pessimistic, fearful that the capacity of our culture to produce renewal and the necessary skills and dexterity to live in this world and cope with ourselves is vulnerable to deterioration. Moreover, that the success of physics and the appeal of the 'human sciences', would continue to lure intelligent men to adopt reified notions of self. Perhaps he fears that the dominance of science, the regimentation of thinking it has entailed, has corrupted and impoverished our vital practices of decorous self-disclosure and that a bulwark must be set against it. Hence in Oakeshott's work the scientist is categorically excluded from speaking of intelligent activity and the theorist is bound to the exploration of conditions and the analysis of identities, both are removed from the conversation of mankind.

That five centuries of evolution of modern man, the free man, devoted to personal distinctiveness should need protection from academics might seem odd. In this book the project of the modern European state to create practices which enabled men to disclose themselves to the world appears curiously vulnerable. Of course, Oakeshott lived through a very disturbed period of history, revolution and its associated iconoclasm, Communism, Fascism, world war, and the sterility of commercial mass culture. He felt that he ought to remind men that human civilization is sustained only by a willingness to be civilized, that the resources of our civilization are there to be employed but can be preserved only in so far as we sustain the enthusiasm of our civilization; to live our lives in our own way.

* * *

The thesis of *On Human Conduct* seeks to quell the ambitions of the theorist, to limit the scope and intrusiveness of the political engagement and to curb the state's tendency towards regimentation of its citizens. It thereby offers ordinary people the space to find their own way. As creatures composed of personally acquired understandings the more lively, brilliant and gifted among them could rejoin the adventure of this civilization 'to be distinct' and to live a life legislated by their own judgement. As an assault upon the morbidity of conformity *On Human Conduct* belongs to the tradition of *The Sickness Unto Death* and *Being and Nothingness*. But it lacks the otherworldliness of both; either the neurotic strenuousness of Kierkegaard or the intellectualism of Sartre. This is a very down to earth earnestness.

Any critique of *On Human Conduct* must as a priority acknowledge the fact that this is an account of how to theorize; it is not an account of how to live. It advises how to think about human life not how to make the everyday diagnostic decisions which disclose our individuality. It would therefore be wrong to accuse Oakeshott of replacing the experiment of life with abstract principles, these abstract principles, are, of course, abstracted from what man has created. Freedom, intelligence, deliberation and choice have no meaning apart from the concrete identity 'human conduct'. Human endeavour re-identifies humanity and through this alters the 'postulates of conduct'. The actual man is an experiment in conduct, such concepts as freedom and intelligence, are the residual by-products of this endeavour. As far as the day to day identities are concerned Oakeshott's 'conversational' theory still stands and is merely remodelled to give the initiative of innovation to the person rather than the practice. And it is to this substantive matter, the character of the agent which we ought to attend.

Criticism of *On Human Conduct* should centre upon the capacity of the agent to be the ultimate determinate of his own understanding, to be the unquestioned master of his learned capacity. The issue of this agent is the issue of the homogeneity of choice. That is, are we actually able to give a universal character to 'the act of choosing' which would enable us to give it unchallenged priority as Oakeshott does in *On Human Conduct*?

The active conception of learning lies at the heart of the thesis. It accounts for the agent being an 'adept' of practices, for the non-instrumentality of moral practices, for the subscriptive or adverbial character of *lex*. And while we can argue that the concrete features of this agent; 'conduct', 'reflective consciousness', 'choice' and 'freedom' each evolve with the unfolding adventure of mankind, in the manner of Hegel's 'concept', what does not evolve 'conversationally' is the relationship between this agent and the structures, practices and procedures which it uses to understand its world, this is governed by 'choice'. It is the issue of this stable relationship, between the self and its acquired understanding which must be questioned. And the mimetic model we encountered in Hegel's *Sittlichkeit* can be used to criticize Oakeshott's stable notion of choice.

The question has already been expressed as: 'Does choice precede practice or do practices precede choice?' The emblem of the character of the 'agent' is found in the expression 'to do this rather than that', to opt between alternatives that one presents to oneself upon the basis of one's own understanding of the situation. But while the options presented are a product of one's learned capacities the act of opting itself is universal and innate. What we need to know is, is there actually a universal act of 'choosing' which applies in all the varying situations, is there some ubiquitous quality which stands behind them all?

We use the word 'choice' to designate the acts and words we acknowledge ourselves to have originated where we believe ourselves to have had the power to offer an alternative. We feel that we could have done or said something else and it is this feeling which lies behind our sense of responsibility and our admission of authorship. But it is at least plausible that the feeling rests not upon some innate 'power', i.e. 'choosing', but upon the fact that we recognize ourselves as operating, in this regard, in a field of gratifying self-control, possessing an adequate skill in this respect, designating no more than we are operating within a practice. Such a feeling of power, of being able to choose would itself be an outcome of the practices we have acquired. Choice would always be related to a specific practice and not to an abstract self.

Hence to say of a performance; 'it was learned', only expresses the idea that the practice, of which it is an illustration, was itself acquired. To say that some deed or expression discloses a learned capacity is not to say that each manifestation of it is itself chosen, or that in each concrete circumstance that particular person could have done otherwise.

So there are two reasons for questioning the primacy of the idea of choice, the first is that the qualification; 'practices are acquired' does not, of itself, tell us it was voluntarily adopted we may well absorb a great deal without expressly desiring to do so. Secondly, that in choosing what to do we are always embroiled within the confines of a practice, 'choice' being simply part of the operation of the practice. 'Choosing', in the sense of deciding, agonizing over, deliberating is, in fact, merely an integral part of a practice. In which case while troubling over alternatives may well be an attribute of intelligence, 'choice' and 'intelligence' as they actually manifest themselves would be a part of a practice. The generalized sense of the terms would, then, be a composite of the medley of practices current in a society. They could not be part of a universal essence of mankind but, rather, faculties abstracted from practices, learned by each in inadvertence through the miscellany of skills they are fortunate enough to acquire. This would then be a diverse character varying from culture to culture and from language to language, even within a culture the quality of the act of choice varies from practice to practice. Choice is an aspect of human sophistication; that we act or speak, that we declare ourselves does not mean we are free from practice, freedom is always locked within practice, always an aspect of what has been learned.

It was the burden of Oakeshott's essays that practices are a richer resource than the deliberative notion abstracted from them can ever be. Indeed what is deliberately done is an impoverished aspect of what we simply know how to do. What is deliberately chosen is, in one sense, a secondary deceptive type of action for it pretends to be what it is not. Sartre remarked[1] that by the time the options for choice come to light in consciousness the real choice has already been made, for such options are 'loaded', the 'act' of choice has been completed in the characterization of the choice at our disposal; that is a phenomenological account of choice, Oakeshott's is strangely naturalistic, indeed, it is in the classical sense 'rationalistic'.

But I have said more than once that Oakeshott's concern is not metaphysical, to describe the world, but to describe the way we structure our understanding. And the point he is reiterating is that the way we designate the natural condition, natural causality, cannot be used to characterize ourselves, as it is we who must make that designation, i.e. causality is one achievement of human intelligence. His work wishes to save man from thinking of himself in terms that he uses to understand things. But this raises another point; 'choice' simply designates man as not-being natural, and thereby condemns the non-human world to a rigid and, rather one dimensional structure, something *Experience and its Modes* expressly sought to discourage. Room is made for man at the expense of degrading nature. It is in this regard that Heidegger's 'being' has brought man more profoundly into question.

An example which may clarify the change in Oakeshott's view of practices is found in the controversy relating to the so-called 'multi-cultural' society. Truly 'mimetic' philosophers hold practices to be the paradigm of thought, our way of thinking, existing not just to be used by a calculating detached agent but the pattern of reasoning itself, an attitude given classical expression in Hegel's *Sittlichkeit*. To such thinkers a synthetic association would be deleterious to the well-being of all involved. The way of being would have to be deliberately cobbled together, it would be the merest product of whatever crib happened to be fashionable at the time, the capital resource of the cultures involved set aside, replaced by a mishmash composed of modish settlements between competing interests founded upon calculations of immediate need. The product would be impoverished and debased, the population vulnerable to civil breakdown, ill-equipped to meet the challenges of natural disasters and inadequate to the task of mutual accommodation and hence liable to civil disorder. The individuals involved would be impoverished in character and prone to mental illness.

This position I infer to be that argued in Oakeshott's essays. But the 'practice user' theory of Oakeshott's latter period is equivocal on this matter. For while it certainly holds that a society where vulgar rules have replaced the subtlety and grace of a moral language would be awkward and less well equipped to manage its various enterprises, it does not seem to hold that such individuals are themselves impoverished and vulnerable to confusion, bewilderment and mental illness. For the 'agent' a multi-cultural nation might well be more frustrating, but it might well be more invigorating offering a greater range of choice, more practices in which to become involved and more styles with which to become acquainted. The agent's power to choose is not dependent upon the symmetry of the practices which surround him, it is natural, residual and immune to all degradation. Such a theory I hold to be abstract, rationalistic, intellectualistic and empirically inaccurate.

A second critique of Oakeshott's concept of agency can be constructed from the key argument that our understanding is rooted in learning and in learning we acquire only what we 'accept and make our own in an understanding' (OHC 37). Even if we accept that we learn what we choose to learn we are obliged to acknowledge that such choosing rests upon an already acquired understanding itself the outcome of a previously acquired understanding. This offers us a regression which presumably must be traced back to our infancy and ultimately to some form of 'original self', or 'original understanding'. Since we are what we understand ourselves to be and have acquired this understanding in learning the infant must trace his self understanding back to his pre-lingual days. Surely 'choice' in such a youthful condition is not the same sort of thing as 'deliberation' the employment of an adult reflective consciousness. Sartre had confronted this problem head on as, for him, our frame of reference, the project which gave shape to each situation, was traced back to an 'original project', a way of being in the world. Oakeshott seems to find this question uninteresting but his thought seems to suggest that the smallest child is choosing what he should learn from the first moment. Thus Oakeshott's concept of freedom – the voluntary acquisition of our understanding – requires that we accept that the agent has come into the capacity of deliberation with no 'habits' of being or style of relating to the world.

Such a conclusion is implausible, for in everyday life we hold the child to be a product, an outcome of its dispositions and of the events of its life, the term 'responsibility' is applied to the child only to the degree it has been acknowledged to have learned some designated practice. Similarly 'responsibility' is applied to adults by degrees, for as it is inappropriate to categorically designate the child as responsible so it is wrong to categorically designate the adult, the estimation of the 'degree' itself being part of the education of mankind.

We must now turn to the issue of personal freedom – the matter at the heart of the identity of the agent – the 'adept of practice' and, therefore, at the centre of the characterization of morality as non-instrumental. The argument for autonomy – substantive self-direction – rests upon the presupposition that we possess a certain form of intelligence, one which permits us the power to acquire only those skills and capacities we find suitable for 'a man like me' and to resist the impact of practices we do not feel suit us. Moreover, with regard to those practices we do adopt and employ, the concept requires that we are able to determine just how the acquisition of any adopted practice influences our lives. That is, each practice must be from first to last as a dead tool in our hands. Each act must belong to the agent and not the craft. Such a specification belongs to that alienated man which has haunted European thought since Descartes – the being who is in a world of his own. The character Sartre sought to bury.

We might note Oakeshott's own formula:

> The race of men is recognized to be saddled with an unsought and inescapable 'freedom' which in some respects he is ill equipped to exercise …. This condition [has become recognized] as the emblem of human dignity and as a condition for each individual to explore, to cultivate, to make the most of, and to enjoy as an opportunity rather than suffer as a burden. What has to be reckoned with is a historic disposition to transform this unsought 'freedom' of conduct from a postulate into an experience and to make it yield a satisfaction of its own.
>
> (OHC 236)

Although Oakeshott's argument is complex and ambiguous, there can be no doubt that conduct, agency, reflective consciousness and freedom are attributes of an identity which is not itself a social or cultural achievement, it is our nature. It might be a type of Nietzschean demiurge, but it is a naturally particular and autonomous self, which our culture has amplified from a small voice of dissent into an affection for distinctness. However, we ought not overlook the fact that the ambition of *On Human Conduct* is to protect this vital force from the ossification of the theorist, for while there may be general agreement that authoritarian government is a violation of our way of life there has been less acknowledgement of the corrosive impact theories of human conduct have had upon the tradition we have inherited.

The 'freedom' thesis of *On Human Conduct* is an attempt to preserve the vigour of the quest for life, also an attempt to blunt those who inadvertently dull it, the theorists. But it achieves this at the price of having to introduce as a polemical instrument, a naturalistic structure. This thesis seeks to assist the defence of the brave and the bold, and to quell all the forces of regimentation, setting aside the role of philosophy and placing its trust in the practical person and the man of affairs. Philosophers are deprived of their historic place in our cultivation as a people, a nation and a civilization. The education of mankind is to be left to the people on the ground. Each according to his own disposition and talent to make his own way.

Compared with the pugnacious political thought of Sartre and the suggestive philosophy of Heidegger this might seem a bland philosophy. But Oakeshott's life's work was to limit the scope and 'authority' of those who sought to direct other peoples' lives, be they scheming politicians or audacious academics. At the heart of his thought is his affection for the opulence of the human creation and a liberal respect for the vitality of human life. He is impressed by this vitality's reliance upon our inheritance; the habits of organization and recognition, but also by the fragility of this vigour; its tendency to decadence, and the vulnerability of this inheritance to desuetude and neglect.

And when one compares his life and work with Heidegger one is impressed by his unwillingness to be downcast by the ordinariness of most of life, his natural disposition to avoid the grandiose notion that it might be otherwise. And when one compares his work with Sartre one is struck by its accomplished understatement and its eagerness to permit rather than to command. To accept the diversity of mankind as it presents itself and not to be drawn into anticipating what it might become.

Conclusion: Reconstructing the Self

Freedom is our not being bound, beyond this it can have no meaning without further specification. Freedom in its most general sense has mankind as its subject and poses the question; to what is man bound? It seeks to comprehend how man, as a species, has command over his life and how the individual fits into this scheme of self-creation.

The problem of freedom is part of man's attempt to picture his place in Creation. We find ourselves unsure as to how our way of being relates to the ways of the world, the things around us and our fellow creatures. This perplexity itself distinguishes us from the things we live amongst, things which appear to occupy their place without the degree of bewilderment we find in ourselves. Man is a creative being whose creativity is cumulative and has changed the earth, the issue of freedom explores the nature of this creativity.

The metaphysical idea of freedom – the view that man is a unique phenomenon amidst nature – represents one of our most profound beliefs about ourselves. This idea, like all primary concepts, is both a product of the way we live and an instrument which alters our ambitions and aspirations. For this reason an understanding of freedom must include not only putative facts about the character of mind and nature but also some account of those beliefs about ourselves and our world which have altered our interpretation of experience. While such influences and relationship are, by their very nature, ethereal and vague, there are a number which are salient factors in the development of our view of freedom.

First among these is the belief that there is one God, omnipotent and omniscient, for associated with the rise of monotheistic religion is an idea of creativity; God was seen as the source of himself and the cosmos. This notion deeply impressed the thinking of our civilization. Man, who considered himself uniquely close to God, saw himself as a source of change, an original moment in the events of nature, as a being who carried responsibility and would be called to account.

Monotheism promoted respect for that which is unchanging, for 'ideas' in the Platonic sense, and a correlate of this was an ascetic

231

ideal, a distrust of 'feelings' and intuition and an exaggerated trust in the disciplined and rigorous exercise of mind. It encouraged a style of attentiveness dominated by regularities, by geometry and mathematics, which has shaped our way of thinking and helped to glorify our sense of detachment – of contemplation and the sense of other-worldliness. A significant product of this was a belief that experience was a species of intellect rather than intellect being a species of experience.

However, the negative side of this sense of being 'outside nature' was the feeling of alienation – an awareness that we possess attributes which are lawless and excessive – a distrust of very considerable aspects of ourselves, our drives, affection and desires. It was a body of belief which required a refined *self*-discipline. Our sense of self owes much to notions of sin and final judgement.

This was heightened by the Christian view that each individual person has unique and particular value in the sight of God his Father, and each individually has an eternal destiny. It has promoted the view that each person will be held to account, examined by his Creator, that we shall be known as we know ourselves. The exaggeration of this theme in Protestantism served to increase the importance of immediate self-possession, that aspect of one's experience which was uniquely and peculiarly one's own.

The advent of systematic quantitative science can be seen both as an aspect of the evolution of the monotheistic tradition and as a moment of real transformation, for the image of nature as a system composed of universal and comprehensive laws confronted man with a dichotomy; either he was embroiled in these laws or he was beyond them. The rubric of causality engendered an image of the world where man understood his performance as a type of cause. Thinkers saw man placed within a causal system but also as a cause of himself, a type of cause distinct from that found in nature. This was and has remained a focus of our understanding of ourselves.

Within this world-view a concept of the self as isolated and particular attained the status of being natural and innate – a view which still dominates 'liberal' thought. Thought seems private, discrete and self-initiated and a consequence of this was that each of us found ourselves being at a distance from one another. Much of the controversy regarding freedom rests upon the extent to which this sense of isolation is natural or acquired and, if acquired, how it is acquired. This has taken up much of the discussion of this work.

* * *

The views we have followed accept that man, the species, has had some role in constructing his 'nature', that is, some part of him is 'artificial', he has in some way made himself. But such a thesis itself entails questions as to the nature and extent of this self-creation.

1. To what degree is personal individuality, the *self* as we know it, part of this artifice?
2. Which practices, activities or behaviour are responsible for our being as we are – this species possessing this form of individuality?
3. To what extent can we take command of this power of making ourselves; does man have the ability to control his self-making so that his being will be 'synthesized' by his own determination, that is, reformed by deliberate attention?

This latter point is, I realize, rather convoluted but it is essential to an appreciation of the significance of the idea of freedom to political philosophy. If our being human, including our being individuals, has been made by us why, then, should it not be within our power to make ourselves in a different way.

Understanding the exact nature of the intellect, its relation to experience, has been the key to the development of this issue. In the work of Kant, as we have seen, the epistemological phase of philosophy was brought to its culmination by the recognition that our experience of the world is dependent upon the mind's abilities – reality is composed of judgements. The reality grasped by our understanding was a product of the intellectual tools at our disposal. More profoundly, for Kant, there was a sphere governed solely by inner determination, shaped totally by the individual, an area of unqualified freedom.

Hegel's more thoroughgoing Idealism deprived such a divorced 'inner sphere' of any real meaning. For Hegel, the comprehension of experience rests on concepts formed, reformed and changed through our encounter with the world. Hegel saw the intellect as a product of the way we order and arrange our world, a 'way' inherited and acquired from our culture. Even the most vital concepts as, 'cause', 'reality' and 'self' are products altered in their active deployment.

The view that the understanding is constructed of dynamically evolving concepts we have called 'phenomenology'. In short, for Hegel, ideas are always mediated through our engagement with the world, and this is as true for the concepts of 'self' and 'freedom' as of any other idea.

The distinction between Kant and Hegel on the issue of freedom can ultimately be reduced to the fact that for Hegel freedom is phenomenal and for Kant it is real. By phenomenal is meant it is a concept which we have attained through organization and reflection upon that organization, accumulated from our sense of command over the world, a recognition of human power, assembled, accumulated and abstracted from experience. This is to be sharply contrasted with Kant's view. For Kant, freedom is a stable part of our experience known without mediation – it is innate and universal, that is, it is 'real'. The distinction that these terms – 'real' and 'phenomenal' – represent accounts for a momentous divide in the understanding and use of the concept of freedom which has spanned this work. We must now examine it further.

In pursuit of this distinction, it might be helpful to return to the primary awareness of freedom, the sense of 'otherness', of being beyond the world, as Kant and Hegel differ in their view of the efficacy of this sense. For both Kant and for Hegel, all human beings regardless of their civilization and culture, have immediate and personal contact with their sense of otherness, with a contemplative abstention from ratiocination. However, whereas for Hegel this otherness is 'indeterminate' and without shape and hence literally meaningless, for Kant it represents a real insight into our humanity.

For Hegel, it is exactly because this vacuousness is innate and universal that it is without meaning; it is the very icon of indeterminacy. This complete abstraction indicates man's primal status as being distinct from the stuff of the world and is positively understood as the power of negation; the source of the confrontation from which all meaning issues. For Hegel, the truth of our sort of vitality lies in our active re-ordering of that stuff of the world to accommodate our sort of being. Meaning issues from this 're-ordering'. The freedom that matters is the actual power we have over the world, the product of the accumulated skills, techniques and crafts of our being here. Such freedom is the craft of being human. It varies between generations, between nations and between individuals within nations and generations. It is a phenomenon, an achievement.

Both Hegel and Kant hold that man is free in the metaphysical sense, but for Kant this freedom is an operative element within our experience, that is, it is real. Freedom is a part of our experience as members of this species. All, regardless of time or place, have resort to this experience, it is a universal reference, unvarying and invulnerable. It is a moment of experience which is, quite literally, essential. But of greatest significance, for Kant, this aspect of experience is of vital, practical importance, being the ground of the peculiarly human power of self-determination. For Kant, man is essentially other than the phenomenal world, he has the power of self-legislation to set his own rules of conduct to determine the intention of his action in a way that he can determine nothing else.

This is to be contrasted with the phenomenal view of freedom, namely, that our power of self-control is learned and that the 'self' is a correlate of this education. Our sense of self is mediated through the crafts, skills and abilities acquired from the community in which we are brought up. Hence, while it can be said that man is categorically free in the sense of not being bound to nature, his practical separation is a cumulative achievement of his culture, available to the particular individual via the institutions, skills etc. which each individual must master. Experience of freedom is then mediated through the phenomenal world. To determine oneself is to operate a skill and 'self-determination' is a concept the meaning of which lies within the structure of phenomenal understanding. Freedom is the power to achieve a concrete end.

In short, between Kant and Hegel there was a schism which has been of enormous significance in the history of the idea of freedom. On one side we find those who hold man's separation from nature to be of merely notional value, e.g. an element of some form of Hegelian 'logic'. On the other side we find those who, with Kant, hold freedom to be a 'real' possession, an actual universal characteristic of man and essential to an understanding of humanity. This, very basically, marks the distinction between 'freedom' viewed as the essential concrete quality of man and 'freedom' understood as an accumulation of various skills, abilities and habits which provide and sustain an enjoyable life-style, a way of life attained through education and artistry.

The ramifications of the distinction between 'real' and 'phenomenal' freedom will dominate this conclusion, it will require further qualification. For while it is my argument that Sartre belongs to one school and Oakeshott the other and that 'shifts' or 'turns' in their thought occur within these schools, there is no doubt that changes do occur. It will be necessary to clarify the nature of these changes in order to maintain the thesis that Oakeshott's idea of freedom is always 'phenomenal' and Sartre's is always 'real'.

* * *

Before we begin to compare the work of Sartre and of Oakeshott, we need to make another distinction one that is more manifestly political than those dealt with so far. It is a distinction which falls within the theory that humanity is 'artificial', one specified by the qualification that this artificiality is 'synthetic'.

The problem here centres upon the origin of order, specifically, whether or not we have command – determinate control – over the phenomenalization of the world. This really refers to that aspect of phenomenological thought characterized by Hegel's 'owl of Minerva' passage[1] – most succinctly stated in Bradley's remark that 'the deed comes first and later reflection'.[2] Those who hold a radically phenomenal position believe that reflective calculation cannot be used to transform the state of man. Thought is a product of our encounter with the world and cannot be used to pre-empt the toil of experiment, adventure and mishap. The structures produced as we organize and develop our world become the structures of thought and we must be patient with our misadventures. For Hegel, history was a nasty business, cruel, bloody and merciless. Man as a species wandered blithely into a world complex beyond his ability. Knowing this might give us fortitude but nothing can lessen the tragedy. The process of education is haphazard and is acquired through courage and foolhardiness at a terrible price in human happiness and life. Hegel believed this, Oakeshott believed it and it seems Kant believed it, but Sartre did not. Understanding why Sartre gave mind such an extensive degree of self-command was the major task of the first part of this work.

Sartre, taking as his first principle, a 'real' notion of freedom believes that man has an unconditioned hold on his plight. In his early work this is expressed in terms of the interaction of 'being' and 'nothingness' a technical structure which gives the individual a real grasp upon being, unmediated by the order the world. Sartre sees mind as founded upon a universal and unvarying paradigm, a principle at work in each individual at all times, regardless of circumstance, culture or condition. The paradox of Sartre's view is that the 'fact' that the primal ground of consciousness is utterly atomic also means it is radically ubiquitous. Man at root is the same. The structure of self-determination offered by Sartre invites the sobriquet 'rationalistic' because all meaning and significance is dependent upon and secondary to the pattern of the intellect. No experience has independent existence.

This is modified in the *Critique* where consciousness is viewed as being separated from its self-creation by a perverse social order. But even in this altered form consciousness is the principle of truth and experience. There is no force which ever robs the primal force of consciousness of its sovereignty, it is merely distorted by an elaborate form of self-deception – toil and tragedy is a product of human determination, a consequence of mystification.

Thus both Sartre's phenomenologies are utterly anthropomorphic. There is no shape in human experience which is not under the command of the intellect. We are truly self-limiting or self-finitizing. The distinction between the two lies in the fact that in the first, that is, in *Being and Nothingness*, the clouding of self-possession is a product of individual indolence and indiscipline – clarity being attained by self-determination. In the second, in the *Critique*, the clouding is caused by objective distortion of awareness and the achievement of clarity requires a joint effort. Sartre's phenomenologies are 'synthetic', first as individual and later as species – experience is a pure construct of human design.

I take Oakeshott's understanding of the intellect to be that it is 'artificial'. He follows Hegel and Bradley in holding that we discover the nature of life only as our endeavour gives it reality. The changes that we find in Oakeshott's thought do not trouble this element, in neither the essays nor *On Human Conduct* is man presented as possessing immediate self-command. Man's experience is comprehended within an intellect constructed by man, but his being is always further into the darkness than his knowing.

To understand the changes which occur within the work of Sartre and of Oakeshott, we need to introduce another distinction one that distinguishes the two modes of the acquisition of understanding. That distinction is between the 'mimetic' and 'pathetic' basis of learning. If we learn mimetically we acquire the pattern of comprehension from the social practices in which we are immersed. If we learn pathetically, then it is rooted in an inner motivation. This distinction we take from Kierkegaard who held that Hegel's phenomenology was *mimetic*; each individual took their goals, their ultimate values, from the disciplines and structures into which they were educated. Kierkegaard, wrongly I believe, thought that this mimicry left no room for true individuality and reduced mankind to a hive of clones. He offered a view which interjected a purely subjective moment into the structures which were acquired, a 'pathetic' or inward moment. Thus we have the distinction between objective structures as ultimately determinate of meaning and value – a 'mimetic' determination – and subjective feeling as the final arbiter of value or worth – a 'pathetic' determination.

I have argued that Oakeshott holds a *mimetic* view of man in his essays and a *pathetic* view in *On Human Conduct*. Sartre, on the other hand, discloses a *pathetic* view in his early work and a *mimetic* view in his *Critique*.

My task now is to conflate the distinctions I have made: real and phenomenal freedom, the synthetic and non-synthetic views of human artifice and the *pathetic* and *mimetic* modes of learning. I shall begin by comparing the various concepts of self which we are offered by Sartre and by Oakeshott.

Sartre views the concrete individual to be a construction. His early work largely rests upon the principle that the self is not innate and immediate, but is a secondary structure gathered from the world – a product of an innate, atomic but characterless determination. The key concept of 'nothingness', elaborated in *Being and Nothingness*, is used by Sartre to develop the idea of an individual with immediate and sovereign self-possession which, in its ultimate vacuity, is at the same time a universal being. However, this ubiquitousness is deeply compromised by our encounter with others, which Sartre sees as necessarily confrontational: self-awareness and self-hood arise in consciousness only as a product of the negating power of the other. This relationship is the focus of a project of entrapment which is inevitably manipulative.

Yet Sartre holds out the hope that conflict could be minimized by an open acknowledgement of the fact of our mutual dependence. He demands a frankness and an immediacy which would be faithful to our 'nature', a levity which would be true to our ultimate lack of identity. He seeks an open-ness which permits us to live in full acknowledgement of our project and its ramifications and breaks the spiral of guilt and bitterness borne of self-deceit. Understanding the plight of the *Néant* is viewed as the first stage in coming to realize the ways men come to undermine each other's existence and trample each other's freedom. But this is always a rather distant hope. He is not able to overcome the vampiric dependence of each upon the other and, hence, of our lack of mutual care, until he found a scheme which explained other-ness as itself a product of human invention. If the alienation of each from the other could be viewed as a product of human contrivance – part of the phenomenal world – then mankind would have a key to the radical transformation of his condition. Such a scheme is presented in the *Critique* and its introduction the *Problem of Method*.

In Sartre's later thought, the self is isolated as a consequence of the *Néant's* acquiring self-hood amid corrupting ideas of possessiveness which pervert its practice of self-finitization. The otherness of the other is itself seen as a product of organization, not as an unavoidable element of the logic of being. The point here for our purpose is that this 'self', like that of the earlier thought, is phenomenal. The distinction is that Sartre allowed objective forces precedence over particular determination.

Not only does Sartre hold the sense of personhood to be a construct, he also holds that the way the self is constructed falls within our sphere of attention, it is available to being done differently, to being altered by our deliberate intervention. This sort of attention I have called synthetic, distinguishing it from the Hegelian view of the 'owl of Minerva' which precludes us having an idea of our well-being in advance of the realization of the patterns in the world. That is to say, while Sartre altered his view of our self-determination – from a *pathetic* to a *mimetic* inspiration – he consistently believed we had unlimited command of this determination. Activity and skill are never permitted the secret brilliance allowed to them by Hegel. The mind has clear self-possession and as such is always within reach of a real universality. Sartre steadfastly argues that we should take possession of this universal and innate pre-personality and make it actually universal so as to realize the radical community or brotherhood of all human beings.

When we turn to Oakeshott, the picture is rather different. In his essays – *Rationalism in Politics* – Oakeshott saw the human person as a skill acquiring being, composed of the practices, traditions and habits to which he is exposed. It is a classic *mimetic* thesis. The self we know appears to be an almost random gathering of practices, a miscellany recognized as 'our way of life' and introspectively acknowledged as a 'personality'.

In *On Human Conduct* there can be little doubt that we are offered a *pathetic* view of the self. Determination is radically particular, and this insular determination commands meaning – the world is what one understands it to be. The human individual gathers his skills according to his inner sense of what he feels is his – he is a user of practices not a product. So, while the self as a concrete personality, that is, as expressed, is learned – composed of acquired practices – it is rooted in a deeper particularity which is presented as the natural and inevitable fulcrum of character. I take the *self* of this account to be real, not phenomenal.

The real question about Sartre and Oakeshott at this level, i.e. the level of the concept of self is; 'Is the self of *Being and Nothingness* and the self of *On Human Conduct* of the same form?' That is we must compare to two *pathetic* selfs.

I take Sartre's self to be phenomenal, to the degree that it is constructed from 'nothing' and is available to thematic and deliberate reconstruction, whereas Oakeshott's self is the 'real' ground of individual character, it is a soul, a demiurge which uses practices to give itself expression. It is actually just what Sartre was struggling to avoid; a dense, inner opacity which discovers within itself a set of problems to be managed and predilections to be mastered. Self-understanding is the exploration of an unchartered territory.

Whereas for Sartre the inner principle of the manifest self is simply nothingness, a universal *Néant*, for Oakeshott an 'inner principle' is known only as it manifests itself in the world and is certainly not 'nothing'. Our understanding the 'inner self' is, like every other understanding, phenomenal – it issues from what we have done, or what we have made of ourselves – it is always specific, concrete and particular. There is no universal principle lurking beneath what is manifest. He says 'we are what we understand ourselves to be', where the understanding is structured by practices. When it comes to explanation, or even introspective analysis, we are all historians of performance whose only recourse is to employ practices as tools of understanding, where practices are taken to be the established theorems we inherit or accept.

There are many similarities between Sartre's and Oakeshott's *pathetic* individuals, between *Being and Nothingness* and *On Human Conduct*. The real distinction, however, lies in the significance of the artificially created structures. For Sartre, the structure created by the *Néant's* attempt to be is consciousness, meaning and ambition; for Oakeshott the self uses and creates structures but retains a sense of self independent of and separate to such objective forms. Sartre can make a general, universal statement about mankind's individuality because it is built of one thing, the *Néant*. Oakeshott's individuality is built upon our natural diversity, which is an actual concrete content, a mystery to be revealed, known only in actualization. I have expressed this distinction by saying that for Sartre man has translucent insight, or, which is to say the same thing, he has immediate self-possession which grants him a synthetic grasp upon his self-making, Oakeshott's man does not. For Oakeshott individuality is real; mankind is naturally diverse; for Sartre individuality is made to be and mankind is naturally homogenous.

* * *

I now want to move on to compare the theses offered by Oakeshott in his essays and by Sartre in the *Critique*. Here we reach more obviously political issues as well as the more general problem of the relevance for political thought of the philosophical or metaphysical notion of freedom. It is not unreasonable to hope that Sartre and Oakeshott, as consummate political thinkers, would be able to offer some insight to this issue. Indeed, they may be taken to be the senior representative of the Left and the Right interpretations of the phenomenological perspective originated by Hegel. The distinctions we have made – between synthetic and non-synthetic artifice and between real and phenomenal freedom – underpin their political differences and serve to illustrate the significance of philosophical freedom for political theory.

The political significance of the philosophical idea of freedom originates from the man to whom both Kant and Hegel are indebted – Jean-Jacques Rousseau. Rousseau revived the classical idea that the society or community was a type of organism, that its structure and order gave its members a facility they could not attain in isolation. The state created a 'new individual' which, in turn, was dependent upon the collective for its sense of completeness. Rousseau outlined an understanding of the actual order of a nation, its laws and institutions, as the ground of each individual's powers of self command. This view, as we have seen, came to fruition in the work of Hegel who acknowledged Rousseau's influence.[3]

However, Rousseau's view of the matter was much more ambivalent than Hegel's. Rousseau argued that social order had the capacity to be perverting as well as propitiatory. For Rousseau, man had an inner light, a natural sense of life and humanity – the individual solitary person could by introspection cast off the clutter of acquired manners and glimpse an inner humanity. For Rousseau, in this mood, the conventional manners of society were not constitutive of our moral being but, quite the contrary, were 'mannerisms' destructive of his natural sense of propriety. A political order rooted in decadence and exploitation created social habits and customs which robbed all its members of the sense of the real inner being and created a brutal, callous and aggressive monster.

Rousseau gave to the history of political thought the view that the laws, customs and learned ways of being may make *or* break our spirit of humanity. Rousseau's work veers maniacally from denunciation to exaltation of the objective order, but his influence on both the political Left and Right has been enormous. This extends to both Sartre and Oakeshott – to Sartre via the notion of the perversity of social structures as developed by Marx, and to Oakeshott directly through Hegel's *Sittlichkeit*. The view that our way of thinking, the structure of mind, is acquired from objective structures I have referred to as 'mimetic' and it is now my task to compare the *mimetic* political theories of Oakeshott and Sartre.

The cue the Left – those who seek radical reform of society by collective action – have taken from the work of Rousseau reveals the reasoning behind the way they have employed the concept of freedom. For Rousseau man was naturally peaceful, accommodating and equitable. These characteristics could be realized if the social order was harmonized with our inner sensibilities. This remains the doctrine of the Left to this day. The inherited institutions – organizations, laws and conventions – distort our humanity and turn us to hatred and violence. For the Left re-organization is the key to the emancipation of this innate and natural 'humanity'. The romantic notion that the lone individual has communion with an inner truth spills into modern political thought in the image of the human being ruined by social forces. In short, the radical is fired by the belief that there is a true being separate and apart from the existing order which may be rescued by determined endeavour. I have characterized this as the 'synthetic' view.

In the *Philosophy of Right*, the institutions, habits and skills of man actually compose his reason. The Rousseauean 'critical' attitude is lost because, for Hegel, we do not possess any notion of ourselves other than that which is produced by the 'reason' of contemporary order. This I have laboured to characterize as the 'artificial' as distinct from the 'synthetic' view. For Hegel and the Right we understand 'too late' to avoid the fumbling necessity of bloody experimentation. Understanding is the reflective deployment of practical achievements. We come to understand the world and ourselves only through the actual practices and order we create in the world. We do not possess nor do we have access to an abiding truth, nature or insight which practices 'pervert'. There is no order which is reasonable before it jells in the actual world.

From the *mimetic* view, objective or social structures are the basis upon which we understand ourselves. Another way of expressing this is to say that our power of comprehension is acquired, learned or absorbed from the structures, practices, rules and 'games' in which we are immersed. What has to be explained with reference to Sartre and Oakeshott is the distinction between the critical view of this acquisition offered by Sartre and the appreciative view offered by Oakeshott, that is, between political radicalism and political conservatism. This, I think, returns us to the distinction already sketched between the synthetic and the artificial self-determination.

For Oakeshott, in the essays, man's capacities – practical and intellectual – are the product of the 'objective' structures – which he refers to as 'traditions'. We are viewed as apprentices to crafts and skills of engaging the world and each other. We have no other resource save that which we draw from this source. Our self-knowledge, our ambitions, our plans all rely upon the patterns we absorb from the world – mind is made in the real world. The two great aphorisms of idealism; of Hegel ('the real is the rational and the rational is the real'[4]) and of Bradley (the deed precedes reflection) both apply to Oakeshott's world view. It is a classic 'artificial' view of the world for all comprehension is borne of structures of man's creation and yet we only comprehend the significance of these structures when they are 'old', when their task is complete. The speculative capacity of mind, its fluency in abstraction, can never bring us to practical well-being before we have stumbled upon it in the actual world.

Oakeshott's conservatism extends from the fact that the skills, habits and 'traditions' are the instruments of our way of life. If they are destroyed, damaged or 'reformed' then we put our well-being in peril. Abstract thought can not, of itself, elaborate a way of life. Thought, as a resource, is parasitic and is too frail to secure our well-being. The inherited order needs to be preserved in all its manifold richness if we are to retain our existing capacities. General and inclusive 'social reform' based upon speculative judgement will impoverish life. It degrades our ability to experiment in our own individual way, it reduces the possibility of diversity and personal liberty. It is for these reasons that Oakeshott is a conservative.

I take Sartre's *Critique* to be *mimetic* and synthetic. It is *mimetic* because objective structures determine our view of the self, the shape of all concepts and values. A nation's legal and political structure is the primary base upon which we understand the world and ourselves. However, for Sartre, this objective structure is constructed upon a subjective base which remains an abiding resource, for consciousness is ultimately a *Néant*, it gives itself to itself, all external influence upon the *Néant* is permitted by the *Néant*. I have argued that this element of Sartre's thought remains intact from the earliest essays to his final interviews. The primal translucidity of consciousness is the source of his radicalism throughout his work. For Sartre the first truth of man is that his world is made and sustained by him. The distinction between his two periods, as we have already remarked, lies in the nature of the otherness of the other as the ground of experience. For in the early work the destabilizing impact of the other is insurmountable, whereas in the later period this type of otherness is seen as a product of social practices.

In the *Critique*, this social order is available to our contrived intervention. It is capable of synthetic re-organization such that the practices associated with the alienation of the other can be dispensed with. We can engineer a different order, where self-finitization of the *Néant* is actively empowered and its universal nature can be given real being. For Sartre, at root, we are all the same – we are all *nothing*. In the new order consciousness would no longer be structured by practices of exclusivity and the subjective project would be de-mystified. The true freedom and 'clarity' of the *Néant* would be liberated and the project of isolation would be replaced by the inclusive project.

Sartre, therefore, stands in the Rousseauean tradition, holding many institutions and social habits to be artifice in the negative sense, they are a perversity, they blind us to the clarity of our basic condition – the universality of having to act in order to exist. It is for this reason that Sartre is quite properly placed in the Romantic tradition; he sees us as lost to our true selves but dedication, determination and revolutionary zeal can wipe away the layers of distortion. The superficial contentment of established society masks an abiding inner truth which always lies within our grasp. Take away the smug order of conformity and a bright, vital and spontaneous life awaits all mankind.

* * *

I said earlier that the issue of freedom turns upon the idea of artifice; 'To what extent and in what manner does man make man?' In this question the philosophical issue of the nature of man meets the political question of the legitimacy of organization. The nature of human order stands at the centre of our concern because it has been presented as the source of freedom and as the enemy of freedom. We should now attempt to isolate the presuppositions which underlie this dispute.

I think it is useful to distinguish three forms or levels of order. There is an order of mind – the pattern of the intellect – we might call it 'reason'. This 'primary order' has been described as, in turn, natural, innate and universal or derivative and dependent upon other structures – it may be stable or dynamic. Secondly, there is an order of society inherited and often perceived as 'natural', an 'ethos', which belongs to the community, the tribe or nation; a *Volksgeist* manifest as a common law or moral code. This 'code' may be enforced by various forms of penalty: formal and informal. There is a tertiary form of order, one deliberately contrived and managed. This is manifest as positive or statute law and is enforced by specific agencies in express ways. What we seek is the relation between order and freedom at each level, and a comparison between the view of the Left and that of the Right.

Normally, it is at the level of statute that we take care of our liberty. We lobby and campaign for legislation to favour our interests. In this sphere we recognize freedom to be the absence of onerous regulation of our affairs. But lawlessness is a burden and if 'freedom' entails disorder it instigates an unfreedom, we find ourselves in bondage to unpredictability. It is in this sense that law, paradoxically, permits men to be free. At the level of statute law it will always be a matter of the finest distinction whether the restriction of law is more onerous than the restriction of chaos.

It is this level of debate which is the concern of 'liberal' thought, for here freedom is viewed simply and coherently as the successful attainment of one's desired projects. Government is viewed as an agency which may facilitate the accomplishment of these projects, by providing resources, e.g. education, the redistribution of wealth, etc. Alternatively, government may be an obstacle, a barrier to realization by authoritarian and disciplinarian attitudes, by 'over-regulation', taxation and censorship. Most political debate centres upon whether government aids or hinders our immediate set of projects, and one's view depends upon one's circumstances, fortuity and personal disposition. There is no reason to hold one view rather than another and there is no real reason why one should not hold differing positions on differing days depending on one's sense of well-being.

In truth, Sartre has little to say about this tertiary level of order. His early, *pathetic*, thesis views legal restriction as simply an aspect of the other. Perhaps dwelling in Nazi occupied France did not lend itself to thinking about the nature of fairness in administrative order. The point was to emphasize that whatever the circumstances, man finds his world only as mediated by his projects. In the *Critique* the law, i.e. bourgeois law, is viewed as sustaining patterns of alienation suitable for the maintenance of bourgeois property.

For the Oakeshott of the essays, statute law represents the skill of the political class in their attempt to maintain order in a world of competing pressures and interests. Liberalism is merely the political manifestation of the English 'tradition' of fairness. In *On Human Conduct*, he reverts to a more doctrinaire form of liberalism holding that the statute law being compulsory and involuntary must make only marginal impact upon the adventure of the agent. He offers us a view of law which is a variation on contractarianism, each rule is conditional upon the adoption of a specific enterprise. They are 'conditions to be taken into consideration in doing', conditions which ideally should not determine the individual's adventure and which should guide rather than command. I have tried to show that there is an element of law which does operate in this fashion but that all actual states are substantive projects and that this is both unavoidable and desirable. Oakeshott's view of non-instrumental practice as the root of law is a rhetorical device sustaining his view that most room ought to be given to self-direction, that is, to the manifestation of inwardness, to the distinctiveness which we have come to hold as a cultural value.

The secondary level of order, the 'propriety' of our culture or community – the order that is inherited and the values into which we are educated – serves to highlight the divisions between the radical and the conservative. Here 'freedom' is used to designate a collective liberty – it means being able to live as is felt to be right, honourable and according to the propriety of the land. 'Being bound' means being a nation subjugated and enslaved to the ways of others. At this level we recognize the wars of independence of the nation states, the national, ethnic or racial separatist movements found amongst various 'minorities' within established states. Freedom means self-government in the sense that the contrived and enforced 'positive' order conforms with the ordinary and common sense of right.

The *Philosophy of Right* brilliantly demonstrates the place of this customary order in human life. For Hegel, custom was the root of truth – ordinary morality was the foundation upon which both statute law and good judgement could be firmly established. However, while it was a necessary element in judgement, it was not, in itself, adequate as the sole source of law. It was simply too rigid and conventional to permit the human spirit its individuality. It could educate but it could not govern a nation.

Hegel saw that the modern state needs the liberty of the market place for individuals to make their own way, to develop their own skills and use the rewards gained from such enterprise to fund their own indulgences according to their whim and fancy. The order of the *ethnos* or 'Family'[5] needs to be supplemented by civil society, by positive law and by the state because only in a open market of self-determining individuals could man express his vitality. The paradox of inherited morality is that it is the essential but inadequate ground of modern life and positive law must respect and sustain the propriety of the people while operating to lessen its tendency to suffocate innovation.

The views of the Right and the Left differ as to the importance of this customary law and Sartre and Oakeshott follow what might be called the 'party line'. For Sartre such propriety is essentially inauthentic and compliance with it is a denial or our essential self-legislative capacity – by following convention we delude ourselves to the nature of our being, we languish in bad faith. In order to understand Sartre's hostility to customary ways we have to move on to his view of the primary order, that of reason itself.

For Oakeshott the opposite is true. Like Hegel, he holds the established order to be the principle resource of our understanding of the world, the substance which forms the context of our self-awareness. It is important to repeat that this is just as much the case with *On Human Conduct* as it is with the essays. The burden of the change rests on what I have referred to as the fulcrum of comprehension. In the essays, it seems that the practices or traditions themselves direct or 'intimate' what should be done. In the second, or *pathetic*, thesis it is the inner sense which appears as the final judge of action. The distinction is ultimately very fine.

When we move on to look at order at what I have called the 'primary level', the level of mind, we find the issues which have occupied this work. Here the question of freedom becomes philo-sophical in the fullest sense of the term; What is the source of our power of understanding? 'Do we have real command over the con-dition of the psyche?'

I have remarked that reason is itself a form of order, a pattern or *logos*. The nature of this *logos* is crucial to the idea of freedom, for the political Right have sided with Hegel in holding that our comprehension is a practical attainment, while the Left, Marx and the Left Hegelians, hold with Rousseau that the social order is as likely to pervert man's self-possession as to sustain it. This returns us to the distinction we have made between 'artificial' and 'synthetic' self-determination. Freedom for the Right rests upon the skilful employment of available resources, practical and intellect-ual. Freedom for the Left rests upon the liberation of an 'inner nature' of man.

The Left scorn the link between the practice and reason and seek to overthrow it in the interest of a universal principle, 'nature', the *cogito*, etc. This marks the most profound distinction in the idea of freedom, for the Right hold freedom to be a skill of living well, the accumulated, historic achievement of the culture, while the Left hold living well to be living in harmony with the universal princi-ple, with humanity. This entails that freedom requires the overcom-ing of difference; both in the form of particularity and in the form of cultural diversity.

Both Oakeshott and Sartre accept that the legitimacy of law rests upon its propensity to free. That the right of authority rests upon its ability to permit humanity a greater degree of self-control. Both have to confront the issue of how it can be that authority, the specification of conduct, can be a good for those who are con-trolled. Sartre's answer is very Kantian in that he believes that beneath the diverse manifestation of life there is a single state common and accessible to all men. It is a possibility which rests upon his principle of 'nothingness', that flight from emptiness he holds to be the primordial life force, and root of all meaning. Nothingness provides the opportunity for holding out for a common destiny of mankind – it justifies the authority of the revo-lutionary. We need to remove the layers of mystification, reification and alienation so that men can find themselves together in this playful mood of immediate self-control, where the self is utterly and spontaneously situated. This is the situation of operative translucidity, that age where man will be fully human.

Sartre lies in the Left tradition because he believes that restriction, oppression and constraint are artificial, unnecessary and open to remedy. It is an audacious philosophy which takes Kant at his word. It is a view of life which strives for opulence but which, in its critical zeal, is always on the verge of austerity and asceticism.

Oakeshott's essays are one of the clearest doctrines of the Right view that there is no order beyond the structures which we inherit. If these are destroyed then order is destroyed. If order is destroyed then there is no power over life and men can achieve nothing. As freedom is our capacity to attain what we seek, to skilfully manage our affairs, such chaos would be the negation of freedom.

We are returned to the basic observation that, for the Left, freedom and order are real, man creates disorder and discomfort which is his bondage whereas the Right views both order and freedom to be artifice, made by man in the face of natural, real and pervasive chaos.

* * *

Since Kant, European thought has held that the dignity of man rested in his choosing his way. The idea that he might choose not to choose, hand his life over to some other agency or offer some authority unquestioning obedience has been an abomination violating both man's intelligence and his moral capacity. In post Hegelian thought, this notion of 'authenticity' of the determinate moment is of particular significance. Kierkegaard and, later, Nietzsche condemned the abuse of humanity represented by Hegel's vision objectification of consciousness. They sought to rouse the 'individual' to a heightened sense of determination. For them, history was an aspect of personal awareness not the structure of consciousness. Man was viewed as the decisive being, the one who must choose in order to be. To simply comply with one's society – to fall into a mimicry or a mechanical conformity – was tantamount to death. Being authentic was presented as a sort of wakefulness, an alertness to one's self-command. We can all choose to be dull and ordinary but should not feel proud to do so. This is the 'earnest inwardness' I have called, in line with Kierkegaard, the *pathetic* point of view.

Sartre's *pathetic* thesis made him justly famous for its impressive and remorseless insistence on the individual as the origin and source of the experience of life. As has been explained, for Sartre, freedom is 'real'. It is one way of expressing or describing the condition or nature of mankind. We are 'not free not to be free'. Freedom, or the *Néant*, or translucidity is the key to knowing how the understand consciousness, determination and the individual project come into existence. The *Néant* seeks to give actual substance to its innate freedom, but the attempt to be someone requires that another person gives recognition to our decisions. To become a 'self' we need the voluntary acquiescence of another. This is a complete contradiction and impossibility, for in acquiescence they cease to be an 'other'. Sartre's *pathetic* theory detailed the poignant tragedy of the 'nothing' which wants to *be*. He could offer no hope – but gave a vivid and stirring account to steel his readers to face with equanimity an exertion which would never lead to anything other than more drudgery. He used all his literary and philosophical powers to give a sense of nobility to the futile and romantic quest to overcome our not being. The point of his writing was to loosen the hold of those idols to which 'we are wont to go cringingly', to make us confront the fact that only we are the source of ourselves, to make us accept the unpalatable truth that the self we are is the self we have made. Yet, the paradox of this being which must make itself be is that the 'self' it creates is 'artificial'. The choosing agent as we know it – isolated and unique – is seen as a product and in Sartre's view it is a product of deception. Whether writing as an existentialist or as a Marxist, Sartre always held the isolation of the person to be something made to be – a phenomenal attribute which could be abolished.

It is, however, impossible to deal with Sartre's work without saying something of the contradiction represented by the 'shift' in his outlook. For the argument offered in the *Critique* would have been dismissed by the author of *Being and Nothingness* as another form of self-delusion. While conversely the radically atomic notion of being presented in *Being and Nothingness* – the freedom which can be attained only by the denial of the autonomy of the other – would have been viewed by the author of the *Critique* as a product of mystification.

I have tried to argue that, while there was a 'shift' to the objective origin of meaning, this represents an alternative reading, by Sartre, of his own basic assumptions, not in the abandonment of these assumptions. Sartre's primary allegiance was to the translucidity of consciousness. Sartre altered his view on the origin and structure of the 'delusion of the self' but he never altered his view of what was the 'true' state of mankind. All human beings are, in 'reality', nothing. At bottom we are all the same. For behind consciousness is the *Néant*, a yearning to be which is essentially universal. It is the 'universality' which excites Sartre. In truth, humanity is homogeneous.

The existential interpretation is one reading of the *Néant* – the dialectical interpretation is another. Which of these is more true to the principle of translucidity is, I think, impossible to say. Sartre's dilemma merely illustrates the difficulties inherent in the Hegelian view that meaning is made. In terms of philosophy, it is merely a matter of emphasis whether one stresses the objective or the subjective 'moment' of this *artifice*, but the rhetorical significance of this emphasis is vast. The shift from the *pathetic* to the *mimetic* thesis permitted Sartre a programme which he could recommend, a path or way to the practical possession of 'real' freedom. More importantly, it offered Sartre a role he found attractive.

This remark leads us directly into Oakeshott's work. For while his work sought to dignify personal freedom and to prize political order, neither of these represents his primary concern. For Oakeshott the primary issue is the protection of our achievement from the critical attention of a certain breed of intellectual, to serve the cause of the richness and abundance of life. In a sense much of his work is negative, in that it seeks to limit the impact and damage that the 'priesthood' of the academics may do to European culture.

Oakeshott believed that the technique of the 'rationalist', the abstraction and reduction of concepts appropriate to intellectual exercise, had, through the arrogance and excess of these intellectuals, been inappropriately applied to practical life. The reflective abstractions of academic life had become the language of ordinary reasoning. Every skill and every arrangement were to be subjected to the stringencies of this inquisition. The impoverishment that resulted from this intrusion was the cause of an ignorance of appreciation and an awkwardness in execution of many of the most essential skills of ordinary life.

In this sense 'freedom' has been as much a tool of deceit and delusion as 'progress' or 'social justice', if by freedom one means some abstraction isolated from actual practice. Indeed, it would be difficult to find a more extreme example of such an intellectual construction than Sartre's notion of freedom drawn as it is from the most tortuous metaphysical speculations. For Oakeshott's individual, both life and the world are an unfolding challenge, even a mystery, which can be met only by an agility of body and mind, a competence acquired in life. Freedom is a proficiency of life. It is, in

the language we have been forced to employ in this work, phenomenal. Freedom is a miscellany of skills, talents and abilities which
match attainment with ambition.

For Oakeshott freedom is never 'real' and the immediate moment
of being (*nothing*) so central to Sartre's interpretation of the world,
and the principles of clarity and translucency, have no significance
outside the rhetorical system of their author. If we seek to explain
their appeal we must look not to their usefulness in bringing order
and peace but to the odd pleasure we find in increasing the strangeness of life. The inner universality of humanity which Sartre attempts to present is a true emptiness, a postulation which is just as
likely to create new conflicts as resolve old ones.

Even in his 'liberal' work, *On Human Conduct* – a work which
places great emphasis upon the abstract notion of personal autonomy – Oakeshott does not offer us a 'real' view of freedom.
Freedom is a postulate for intellectuals, it is 'real' in the sense that
they must assume an *a priori* distinction between will and causality
if they are to avoid the error of measuring man by the same models
as they measure things. Paradoxically, it is because we are a self-in-
venting and self-developing creature that we need to be weary of
the sort of metaphors which 'social scientists' have used to explain
behaviour.

It is in this regard that Oakeshott's thought comes closest to
Sartre's. *On Human Conduct* like *Being and Nothingness* seeks to
deprive us of the indolence of 'bad faith'. However, Oakeshott's instruction to the theorist to assume man is not caused does not mean
that Oakeshott thought man was categorically free, only that each
person was categorically beyond any theory. For in action and in
understanding we are the users of practices not the products of
practices. The agent that employs a practice is, for Oakeshott, a
unique mystery whose life's task is to realize his potential.

Such a view implies that man has access to an inspiration that is
not entirely drawn from this world, from experience. Oakeshott
avoids dwelling upon the nature of this 'noumenal' stuff, firstly,
because as pure potential it can support no characterization before
it is manifest, and secondly, because, as Wittgenstein has made
clear, that which is essentially individual can have no meaning. The
most that can be said is that mankind has a capacity for heterogeny.

The individuality we actually treasure is phenomenal. It is constructed from the resources, natural and artificial, we find at our
disposal. The truth is that we value our distinctiveness – this is our

way – it is not essentially so, or necessarily so but we should not assume that life would be better if it were not so.

The *pathetic* individual of *On Human Conduct* is, then, quite distinct from that of *Being and Nothingness*. It is a self involved in self-discovery rather than in self-invention or self-production. This distinction has significant ramifications for political thought, for if Sartre's thesis is true, we each have access to, not only a universal nature, but a nature that we can actually contrive, whereas, if the atomization of man is due to his being the product of a unique inspiration, then freedom can never be more than the realization of a particular design. We are denied the transparent access to a pre-phenomenal ground which is the root of Sartre's radicalism, of his belief that we, as a species, hold within us the potential to annul the vicissitudes of individuality. Rather, we are forced to accept that the best we can hope for in life is an awkward and fragile accommodation of competing personalities. Such innate diversity is, of course, precisely what Sartre sought to avoid.

For Oakeshott man is always caught up in designation – he finds himself within his world. The 'opaque' self of *On Human Conduct* learns the game of life like he learns any other game; to varying degrees of accomplishment according to interest, disposition and skill. As adepts of practice we exist within practices. Our understanding of ourselves, no less than of the world, is acquired – we can never discern amongst the torrent of experience a moment of immediate self-possession. For Oakeshott 'freedom' means that the person is always more than simply an assembly of practices, but this 'more than' is not transparent self-possession but some substance, a disposition or soul which it is his 'task' to master.

There can be little doubt that the arguments of *On Human Conduct* are of a different nature to those of the essays – there is a 'shift' is Oakeshott's thinking. This shift to a *pathetic* thesis represents a manoeuvre designed to buttress the idea of 'distinctiveness', the notion which Oakeshott holds to be the key to the evolution of the modern European state. The need to defend the achievements of civilization from the degradation of social science and the popular Socialism of his day led Oakeshott, paradoxically, towards the employment of abstractions.

There is a tendency in his later work to give ideas a cogency – an autonomy and an independence of context – which his earlier thought had derided. This has led some to say Oakeshott ultimately employs a form of rationalism. There are certainly trends in *On*

Human Conduct which appear 'rationalistic' but I have tried hard to show that, for Oakeshott, theories are merely one of the structures we use to live. So, while it may be true that the later work of Oakeshott gives theorists a control over their work which is timeless and free from context, the theory – their creation – is still only one species of the structures we use to make our lives. They are structures of interpretation, of justification and of explanation, but they are not central to the true calling of mankind; to live well. There are other skills which evolve under their own rules and are not dependent upon nor subject to the discourse of comprehension.

Rationalism, in the true sense, holds that all structures have a merely dependent significance on the one true structure – thought – which is true because it is self-governing. Oakeshott never believed this. We may need theories to justify or explain but we do not need theories to succeed.

Such a statement could not be further from Sartre's position. Sartre believed that an analysis of the nature of consciousness provided the pattern of all truth and reality. This view was both a product of and a cause of Sartre's belief in the leadership of intellectuals.

When we come to compare the views of Sartre and Oakeshott on the issue of freedom we have an array of permutations which I have tried to list. There is, however, an ultimate and unvarying distinction which accounts for their way of writing, for the didactic force of their works and for their politics – conservatism and radicalism.

Sartre sees man's diversity as a product of inattention. Mankind, in his true being, is homogeneous and, therefore, possesses a natural unity. All that divides us is made by us, and we can by discipline, by commitment or by revolutionary social reform begin again.

He belongs to the romantic tradition in holding that there is, available to us all, an experience that is original, universal and 'natural' – an aspect of man free from artifice. Sartre remains the most forthright spokesman of this century for that element of romantic thought which sees the inherited order as a confusion to be removed. He thus, continues that tradition of European thought which views the philosopher as the guardian of the purity of man. It is most strange that Sartre, who is supposed to have learned so much from Nietzsche, never understood that to take the struggle from a man's life might be to remove the one thing for which he lives.

On these matters Oakeshott's view is entirely opposite. He holds we are as we find ourselves. He offers no vision beyond the veil of appearance. Our diversity is a fact of life. Man is necessarily diverse or naturally heterogeneous. Social and political order represents a body of skills, a collective resource, which we may learn and use to make and know ourselves amidst the company of others and the predicaments of the world. Oakeshott is a conservative because he holds this order and, therefore, the sense of self which it has come to sustain, to be vulnerable. The rise of the authority of intellectuals – particularly social scientists – and the impoverished way of thinking they have made fashionable is seen by Oakeshott as the most pressing cause of corruption of our ability to live well. For Oakeshott an understanding of life should be poetic, it must serve to enrich, not 'reduce', the fund of eloquence.

* * *

Contrary to the generally held prejudice, Sartre's work is an attempt to comprehend the position of the individual in order to overcome isolation and atomic being. It is his principle belief that only self-deception or social mis-organization actually accounts for the distinctiveness of human individuals. For Sartre, the oneness of humanity is a natural fact and its realization is within our grasp. What altered in Sartre's work was the original attempt at achieving human community through authenticity was replaced by the project of achieving authenticity through common endeavour.

While Sartre is impressed by the superficiality of human division and the perversity of human institutions, Oakeshott is impressed by the frailty of order and the artistry contained in what has been created. They, therefore, represent two views of freedom, one natural and innate the other phenomenal and artificial, and two views of political order, one corrupting and deluding the other the sole key to our self-awareness.

The idea that we are free in the sense that we are distinct from the world has deified man's rational function and legitimized the idea that we are masters of our own destiny, that we create ourselves, and are without like on this planet. It is the genius of Heidegger to have reminded us that such a prejudiced view of the world sets man above all that dwells around him and beyond all that he must dwell amongst. The cost of this contempt is an ever increasing bewilderment, a mis-identification, which in turn makes our situation more perilous and precarious. Our lack of care is embodied in our love of freedom. We dwell in a world created by those who believed man to have infinite worth and the world to be an instrument. The price for this indulgence has been the degradation of the earth and the demoralization of our humanity and our vitality.

Freedom as 'not caused' has been deleterious for the world and for ourselves. It is part of the austerity of vision which we take from the Hebrews and the Stoics, a view that childishly fears the fragile, the partial and the incomplete and replaces it with notions of the unchanging, certain, complete, that is, with self-deception. This abstract idea of freedom has driven man into a manic arrogance. The sadness that colours the preceding pages results from the fact that both the individualism and the collectivism borne of this idea have played their part in the excessiveness of mankind.

Sartre, for all his humanity, his 'humanism', is a disciplinarian. In its contempt for habit and for the unexamined life, his work echos the Puritanism of Kant. It vigorously affirms the radical homogeneity of mankind. The lesson of the twentieth century is that the spirit of fraternity, a universal brotherhood of mankind, leads directly to the Gulags and there is no doubt in my mind that Sartre's *mimetic* thesis has implications as imperious and desultory as the solutions of Rousseau and Marx.

As for Oakeshott, his *mimetic* thesis is one of the most engaging and compelling of conservative theories, its affection for the spirit of human expression cannot be doubted. However, for all the reasons laboriously entered into, I fear Oakeshott, in his latter work, in attempting to defend the audacious individual has given legislative right to that creature which has laid waste the world.

Notes

1 Nature and Mind

1. For some of these observations regarding Kant's two conceptions of freedom I am indebted to Lewis White Beck's Commentary on Kant's *Critique of Practical Reason* 176–208.

2 The Past and the Self

1. Johann Gottfried von Herder 1744–1803 – *Outline of a Philosophy of the History of Mankind* 1791.
2. George Wilhelm Frederick Hegel; born Stuttgart 1770, died Berlin 1831.
3. *Naturrecht und Staatswissenschaft im Grundrisse* 1821.
4. Hegel's acknowledgement of the contribution of Rousseau is particularly generous (PR 156). He credits Rousseau with the realization that the State was the manifestation of Will, this, for Hegel displays the recognition that the true comprehension of the existence and right of the State must be in thought. Here Will is the form, and State is the substance. Each without the other is an empty abstraction.
5. Søren Aabye Kierkegaard born Jutland 1813 died Bredgade 1855.
6. *Afsluttende Uvidenskabelig Efterskrift* 1846.
7. Gotthold Ephraim Lessing 1729–81.

3 The Condition of Consciousness

1. Jean-Paul Sartre, born Paris 21 June 1905 died Paris 15 April 1980.
2. *La Nausée* 1939.
3. Husserl, Edmund Gustav Albert 1859–1938.
4. 'Phenomenology' the name given to the philosophy of Husserl is designated in this work by a capital 'P' so it can be distinguished from the general use of the term which originated with Kant's thinking.
5. *The Imaginary* [*L'Imagination*] 1936 p. 2.
6. *L'Être et le Néant* 1943.
7. *La Transcendence de l'Ego* 1936.

4 The Playful Project

1. *L'Etre et le Néant* 1943 all quotation in this work are from *Being and Nothingness* trans Hazel Barnes 1958.
2. Sein und Zeit 1928 translated *Being and Time* 1974.

3. Dasein, literally there-being is the *cogito* of Heidegger, it is the initial point of going out into the world or projecting into being. Unlike Sartre's *Néant*, it has no immediate relation to itself, its being is being and its relations are those of being.

5 The Sources of Fragmentation

1. *Questions de Méthod* 1960, originally published as *Between Existentialism and Marxism* 1957 then edited as the introductory essay to the *Critique of Dialectical Reason*.
2. *Critique de la raison dialectic* 1960.
3. The Singular Universal, p. 150.
4. The Singular Universal, p. 158.

6 Understanding Experience

1. Michael Joseph Oakeshott, born Kent 11 December 1901, died, Acton, Dorset 19 December 1990.
2. *The Importance of the Historical Element in Christianity* p. 365.
3. Francis Herbert Bradley 1846–1924.
4. The reference to Boethius I owe to R. McKeon, *Selections from Medieval Philosophy* Vol. 1 p. 67.
5. F. H. Bradley, 1893.
6. Michael Oakeshott, 1933.
7. *The Presuppositions of Critical History*, p. 81.

7 The Vigour of Inheritance

1. Michael Oakeshott, 1962.
2. Collective Dream of Civilization, *The Listener* Vol. 37, 1947 p. 966.
3. Ibid., p. 966.

8 The Achievement of Legal Order

1. Published as a note in Political Studies XIII 1965 responding to the article of D. D. Raphael.
2. Michael Oakeshott, 1975.
3. Social and Political Doctrines of Contemporary Europe, p. xxii fn.

9 The User of Practices

1. Sartre *Being and Nothingness* p. 451; see also ibid., Chapter Four.

Conclusion: Reconstructing the Self

1. The Preface to the *Philosophy of Right* p. 13.
2. Bradley says: 'Alike in the life of mankind and in the development of the individual, the deed comes first and later reflection; and it is with the question, 'What have I done?' that we awake to the facts accomplish and never intended, and to existences we do not recognize, while we own them as creations of ourselves'. *The Presuppositions of Critical History* p. 81.
3. For Hegel's view of Rousseau see *Philosophy of Right* p. 156.
4. Hegel's identification of the real and the rational; The *Logic* §6.
5. Hegel's notion of 'The Family'; *Philosophy of Right* p. 110, 'It is ... ethical mind in its natural or immediate phase – the Family'.

Bibliography

Note: I have limited this bibliography to works which have been mentioned in the text.

Simone de Beauvoir, *Adieux: A Farewell to Sartre*. Trans. Patrick O'Brian. Penguin Books. 1985.
——, *The Prime of Life*. Trans. Peter Green, Penguin Books.
Lewis White Beck, *A Commentary on Kant's Critique of Practical Reason*. The University of Chicago Press, 1960.
F. H. Bradley, *Ethical Studies*. Clarendon Press, Oxford. 1927.
——, *Appearance and Reality*. George Allen & Unwin Ltd, London. 1897.
——, *The Presuppositions of Critical History*. Ed. L. Rubinoff. Quadrangle Books, Chicago. 1968.
R. G. Collingwood, *The Idea of History*. Oxford University Press. 1946.
——, *The Idea of Nature*. Oxford University Press. 1945.
René Descartes, *Meditations on First Philosophy*. Trans. John Cottingham. Cambridge University Press. 1986.
Joseph P. Fell, *Heidegger and Sartre: An essay on Being and Place*. Columbia Press, New York. 1979.
G. W. F. Hegel, *Introduction to the Lectures on the History of Philosophy*. Trans. T. M. Knox and A. V. Miller. Oxford University Press. 1985.
——, *Phenomenology of Spirit*. Trans. A. V. Miller. Oxford University Press. 1977.
——, *Logic*. Vol. I. *The Encyclopaedia of the Philosophical Sciences*. Trans. William Wallace. Oxford University Press. 1975.
——, *The Philosophy of History*. Trans. J. Sibree. Dover Publications Inc., New York. 1956.
——, *Philosophy of Right*. Trans. T. M. Knox. Oxford University Press. 1952.
Martin Heidegger, *Being and Time*. Trans. John Macquarrie and Edward Robinson. Basil Blackwell, 1962.
——, *Basic Writings* 1927–1964. Ed. David Farrell Krell. Harper, San Francisco. 1977.
——, [*Letter on Humanism*] Trans. Edgar Lohner in Philosophy in the Twentieth Century. Vol. 3.
——, *Contemporary European Thought*. Ed. William Barrett and Henry D. Alken. Harper and Row, New York. 1971.
——, [*What is Metaphysics*] – in *Being and Existence*. Trans. R. F. C. Hull and A. Crick. Vision Press, London. 1949.
Edmund Husserl, *Phenomenology and the Crisis of Philosophy*. Trans. Quintin Lauer. Harper & Row, Publishers, New York. 1965.
Emmanuel Kant, *Critique of Pure Reason*. Trans. J. M. D. Meicklejohn. Dent. London. 1934.
——, *Critique of Practical Reason*. Trans. Lewis White Beck. Macmillan. 1956.

——, *Prolegomena to Any Future Metaphysics*. Trans. Lewis White Beck. Bobbs-Merrill, Indianapolis. 1950.

——, *Perpetual Peace*. Trans. Lewis White Beck. Bobbs-Merrill, Indianapolis. 1957.

——, *Grounding for the Metaphysics of Morals*. Trans. J. W. Ellington. Hackett Publishing Company, Indianapolis. 1981.

Søren Kierkegaard, *The Sickness Unto Death*. Trans. Alastair Hannay. Penguin Books. 1989.

——, *Fear and Trembling/Repetition*. Trans. H. V. Hong and E. H. Hong. Princeton University Press, Princeton, New Jersey. 1983.

——, *Philosophical Fragments/Johannes Climacus*. Trans. H. Hong and E. H. Hong. Princeton University Press, Princeton, New Jersey. 1985.

——, *The Concept of Anxiety*. Trans. R. Thomte and A. B. Anderson. Princeton University Press, Princeton, New Jersey. 1980.

——, *Concluding Unscientific Postscript*. Trans. D. F. Swenson and W. Lowrie. Princeton University Press, Princeton, New Jersey. 1968.

Karl Marx, *Economic and Philosophical Manuscripts of 1844*. Trans. Anon. Lawrence & Wishart, London. 1977.

——, *Selected Writings*. Trans. David McLellan. Oxford University Press. 1977.

Friedrich Nietzsche, *Beyond Good and Evil* Trans. W. Kaufmann, Vintage Books, New York. 1966.

——, *On the Genealogy of Morals/Ecce Homo*. Trans. Walter Kaufmann. Vintage Books, New York. 1969.

Michael Oakeshott, *Experience and its Modes*. Cambridge University Press. 1933.

——, *Rationalism in Politics and Other Essays*. Methuen & Co. London. 1962.

——, *On Human Conduct*. Clarendon Press, Oxford. 1975.

——, *On History and Other Essays*. Basil Blackwell. 1983.

——, *Social and Political Doctrines of Contemporary Europe*. Cambridge University Press. 1939.

——, *Hobbes's Leviathan*. Basil Blackwell, Oxford. 1955.

——, [*The Masses and Representative Democracy*] American Conservative Thought in the Twentieth Century. Ed. W. F. Buckley in Bobbs Merrill, New York.

——, [*The Vocabulary of a Modern European State Political Studies*. pp. 319–41. 1975. Vol. 23.

——, [*On Misunderstanding Human Conduct*] Political Theory Vol. 4 No. 3 August 1976.

——, [*The Claims of Politics*] Scrutiny. Vol. 8 1939–40.

——, [*Rationalism in Politics: A reply to Professor Raphael*] Political Studies. XIII. 1965 89–92.

——, [*Religion in the Moral Life the 'D' Society* Pamphlets No. II Cambridge. 1927.

——, [The Importance of the Historical Element in Christianity] *The Modern Churchman*. XVIII 1928–29. pp. 360–71.

——, [The Authority of the State] *The Modern Churchman*. XIX. 1929–30. pp. 313–27.

——, [The Collective Dream of Civilization] *The Listener* 37. 1947. pp. 966–7.

Jean-Jacques Rousseau, *The Basic Political Writings*. Trans. D. A. Cress. Hackett Publishing Company, Indianapolis. 1987.
——, *Reveries of the Solitary Walker*. Trans. Peter France. Penguin Books. 1979.
Jean-Paul Sartre, [*Intentionality: A Fundamental Idea of Husserl's Phenomenology*] Trans. Joseph E. Fell. *Journal of the British Society of Phenomenology*. Vol. I No. 2. 1970.
——, *The Transcendence of the Ego*. Trans. Forrest Williams and Robert Kirkpatrick. Noonday Press, New York. 1957.
——, *Nausea*. Trans. Robert Baldirk. Penguin Books. 1963.
——, *The Emotions: Outline of a Theory*. Trans. Bernard Frechtman. Philosophical Library, New York. 1948.
——, *The Psychology of the Imagination*. Trans. Anon. The Citadel Press, Secaucus, New Jersey. Undated.
——, *War Diaries. Note Books from a Phoney War*, November 1939–March 1940. Trans. Quintin Hoare. Verso Editions, London. 1984.
——, *Being and Nothingness*. Trans. Hazel Barnes. Methuen & Co., London. 1958.
——, *Saint Genet, Actor and Martyr*. Trans. Bernard Frechtman. Heinemann, London. 1988.
——, Three Plays: 'The Respectable Prostitute', 'Lucifer' and 'The Lord, In Camera'. Trans. Kitty Black and Stuart Gilbert. Penguin Books. 1982.
——, *The Age of Reason*. Trans. Eric Sutton. Penguin Books. 1961.
——, *The Reprieve*. Trans. Eric Sutton. Penguin Books. 1963.
——, *Iron in the Soul*. Trans. Gerard Hopkins. Penguin Books. 1963.
——, *Search for a Method*. Trans. Hazel E. Barnes. Alfred A. Knopf Inc., New York. 1963.
——, *Critique of Dialectical Reason*. Volume One 'Theory of Practical Ensembles'. Trans. Alan Sheridan-Smith. Verso, London. 1976.
——, *Critique of Dialectical Reason*. Volume Two 'The Intelligibility of History' (unfinished). Trans. Quintin Hoare. Verso, London. 1991.
——, *Sartre in the Seventies: Interviews and Essays* [Situations X] (first published as Life/Situations) Trans. Paul Auster and Lydia Davis. Andre Deutsch, London. 1978.
——, [*Kierkegaard: The Singular Universal*] 'Between Existentialism and Marxism'. Trans. John Matthews. Verso, London. 1974.
F. W. S. Schelling, *Ideas for a Philosophy of Nature*. Cambridge University Press. 1988.
Arthur Schopenhauer, *The World as Will and Representation*. Vol. I. Trans, E. R. S. Payne. Dover Publications Inc., New York. 1966.

Index